PRAISE FOR THE REF(
BIBLE COMME~~~~~ ~~~~~~

The *Reformation Heritage Bible Commentary* is a unique series that promises to be a valuable resource for laity and preachers. The verse-by-verse commentary focuses on major topics, providing clear interpretation and devotional insight in keeping with how the Reformers approached Scripture, and emphasizing themes that were central in their teaching. This focused approach gives a clear reading of the text which engages one's mind and heart.

—The Rev. Dr. Rodney A. Whitacre
Professor of Biblical Studies
Trinity School for Ministry
Ambridge, Pennsylvania

Busy pastors and teachers of the Scriptures need commentaries that are biblical, theological, and practical. Fortunately, the Reformation Heritage Bible Commentary series fulfills those requirements. The scholarship is reverent, demonstrating that the truths of the Reformation are relevant today just as they were in the 16th century. The volumes are accessible to a wide variety of readers, for it is written in a wonderfully clear way. I commend this work gladly.

—Thomas R. Schreiner, PhD
James Buchanan Harrison Professor of New Testament
The Southern Baptist Theological Seminary
Louisville, Kentucky

The Reformation Heritage series is a "Heritage of Reformation theology" now put at the fingertips of every serious Bible student, young or old.

This commentary helps anyone to dive deeply into the Scriptures, verse by verse, even word by word. I was blessed with its academic rigor in straightforward language, the sidebar articles explaining overarching Biblical themes, and the voices of the Reformers demonstrating again that this Good News of Jesus is a message for all times. If one yearns to know the unique message of the Scripture and its meaning for life, now and forever, then join me in having the Reformation Heritage Series in your library today.

—Rev. Gregory P. Seltz
Speaker, The Lutheran Hour

Reformation Heritage Bible Commentary promises to be an asset to the library of serious Bible students, whether layman or clergy. This series exemplifies the reformers commitment to sola scriptura, that the revelation of God's saving purposes is in scripture alone, which is primarily about Christ alone. The blend of overviews and insights from our protestant forefathers with exegesis and application from contemporary reformed theologians makes for an interesting read. Contemporary readers will also appreciate the devotional notes in these commentaries. Because the study of God's word is not just an academic endeavor, it engages the mind, heart, and will of those who trust Christ for their salvation. While many modern commentaries seem to focus on the application of the scriptures, the intent here is gospel-centered interpretation, resulting in devotional application. This is a work of serious scholastic intent combined with theological scrutiny and integrity. I am grateful for such a work and confident that it will be profitable for years to come in aiding the church's effort to know Christ more fully as He is revealed in holy Scripture.

—Kenneth R. Jones
Pastor of Glendale Baptist Church, Miami, FL
Co-host of nationally syndicated talk show—White Horse Inn
Contributed to: "Experiencing the Truth", "Glory Road", and
"Keep Your Head Up"; all published by Crossway.
Contributed to Table Talk and Modern Reformation magazines
Frequent conference speaker

The Reformation of the church brought with it biblical insights that revitalized churches and radically changed the course of theological studies as giants like Luther, Melanchthon, Calvin, Chemnitz, and Wesley commented extensively on Holy Scripture. The new *Reformation Heritage Bible Commentary* is a one-stop resource where the observations of these and other distinguished Reformation leaders are brought together around specific books of the New Testament.

—The Rev. Dr. R. Reed Lessing
St. Michael's Lutheran Church
Fort Wayne, IN
Longtime Professor of Exegetical Theology at
Concordia Seminary, St. Louis, MO

HEBREWS

ALSO FROM CONCORDIA

Biblical Studies

The Reformation Heritage Bible
Commentary Series
  Colossians/Thessalonians,
    Edward A. Engelbrecht and
    Paul Deterding
  Revelation, Mark Brighton
  Galatians, Ephesians, Philippians,
    Jerald C. Joersz
  Luke, Robert A. Sorensen.
  Mark, Daniel Paavola
  General Epistles, Clinton J. Armstrong

The Lutheran Study Bible, Edward A.
  Engelbrecht, General Editor

*The Apocrypha: The Lutheran Edition
  with Notes,* Edward A. Engelbrecht,
  General Editor

Lutheran Bible Companion, Edward A.
  Engelbrecht, General Editor

Today's Light Devotional Bible, Jane L.
  Fryar

LifeLight In-Depth Bible Study Series
  More than 50 studies available on
  biblical books and topics

*Concordia's Complete Bible
  Handbook,* Jane L. Fryar, Edward A.
  Engelbrecht, et al.

Concordia Commentary Series: A
  Theological Exposition of Sacred
  Scripture
  Leviticus, John W. Kleinig
  Joshua, Adolph L. Harstad
  Ruth, John R. Wilch
  Ezra and Nehemiah, Andrew E.
    Steinmann
  Proverbs, Andrew E. Steinmann
  Ecclesiastes, James Bollhagen
  The Song of Songs, Christopher W.
    Mitchell

Isaiah 40–55, R. Reed Lessing
Isaiah 56–66, R. Reed Lessing
Ezekiel 1–20, Horace D. Hummel
Ezekiel 21–48, Horace D. Hummel
Daniel, Andrew E. Steinmann
Amos, R. Reed Lessing
Jonah, R. Reed Lessing
Matthew 1:1–11:1, Jeffrey A. Gibbs
Matthew 11:2–20:34, Jeffrey A.
  Gibbs
Mark 1:1–8:26, James W. Voelz
Luke 1:1–9:50, Arthur A. Just Jr.
Luke 9:51–24:53, Arthur A. Just Jr.
Romans 1–8, Michael P. Middendorf
1 Corinthians, Gregory J. Lockwood
Galatians, A. Andrew Das
Ephesians, Thomas M. Winger
Colossians, Paul E. Deterding
Philemon, John G. Nordling
2 Peter and Jude, Curtis P. Giese
1–3 John, Bruce G. Schuchard
Revelation, Louis A. Brighton

Historical Studies

*From Abraham to Paul: A Biblical
  Chronology,* Andrew E. Steinmann

*The Church from Age to Age: A History
  from Galilee to Global Christianity,*
  Edward A. Engelbrecht, General
  Editor

History of Theology, 4th Rev. Ed.,
  Bengt Hägglund

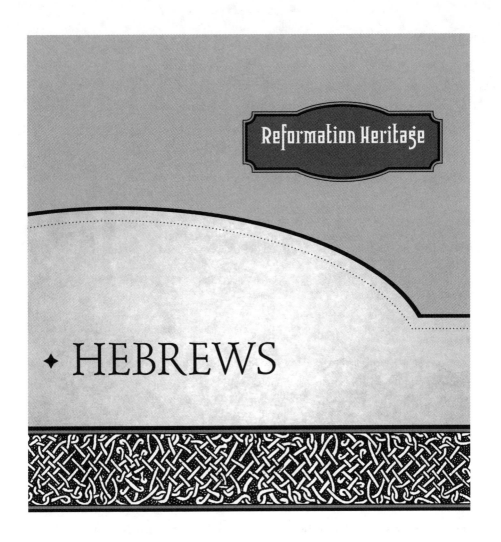

Reformation Heritage

HEBREWS

STEVEN P. MUELLER

CONCORDIA PUBLISHING HOUSE • SAINT LOUIS

Copyright © 2015 Concordia Publishing House
3558 S. Jefferson Ave., St. Louis, MO 63118-3968
1-800-325-3040 · www.cph.org

Library of Congress Cataloging-in-Publication Data

Mueller, Steven P.
    Hebrews / Steven P. Mueller.
        p.   cm. — (Reformation heritage Bible commentary)
    ISBN 978-0-7586-2763-6
    1. Bible. N.T. Hebrews. I. Mueller, Steven P. - II. Title. III. Title: Hebrews.
    BS2715.53.E54   2015
    227'.077--dc23   2011044778

1 2 3 4 5 6 7 8 9 10   24 23 22 21 20 19 18 17 16 15

CONTENTS

♦

✦
About This Series

The great reformers' influence upon the Bible's interpretation and application could not help but revitalize the Church. This is as true today as it was 500 years ago. This renewal happens in part because the reformers drew upon the insights of the Renaissance, which linked the medieval church back to her earlier roots in the classical world. There, the biblical texts sprang up. The reformers were among the earliest students to pursue classical studies, not only due to personal interest but especially due to the benefits such study brought to the study of the Bible. By reading the New Testament Scriptures in their ancient language and context, the reformers dispelled many misunderstandings.

Second, the fires of controversy, which followed Luther's proclamation of justification by grace through faith on account of Christ alone, served to refine the study of Sacred Scripture. So many ideas that medieval people took for granted or that were accepted based on human authority alone were tested and retested, leading to more careful study of God's Word.

Third, the reformers themselves taught with special insight due to their constant reading, study, translating, and preaching of the Sacred Scriptures. Their approach to the Scriptures and the insights they gained have continued to inform biblical studies even to the present day. For all of these reasons Concordia Publishing House wished to produce a readable commentary series that would serve the current generation by sharing with them (1) insights from the reformers and (2) commentary that stemmed from their heritage.

In preparing this commentary, we drew upon the insights of the following reformers and heirs to their evangelical approach to teaching the Scriptures:

John Hus (c. 1372–1415)
Martin Luther (1483–1546)
Thomas Cranmer (1489–1556)
Philip Melanchthon (1497–1560)
John Calvin (1509–64)

John Knox (c. 1513–72)
Martin Chemnitz (1522–86)
Johann Gerhard (1582–1637)
Johann Albrecht Bengel (1687–1752)
John Wesley (1703–91)

Not every commentary will include quotations from each of these authors since they did not all comment on Books of Scriptures with equal frequency. We have intentionally stayed away from more radical reformers such as Andreas Bodenstein von Karlstadt, Ulrich Zwingli, Thomas Münzer, etc.

Along with quotations from the reformers and their heirs, readers will also find quotations from some early and medieval Church Fathers. This is because the reformers did not wish to overthrow the earlier generations of teachers but to profit from them where they were faithful in teaching the Word.

Some readers will note that the writers listed above represent different branches in the Protestant family of churches and they may wonder how compatible these writers will be alongside one another. It is certainly the case that the reformers held different views, especially concerning the Sacraments, biblical authority, and other matters. Some authors for the series may at times describe differences between the various reformers.

However, while it is true that these differences affect the fellowship and work of the churches of the Reformation, it is also true that the reformers shared significant agreement. For example, early Reformation works like Melanchthon's *Commonplaces* and the Augsburg Confession served as models for the various traditions of Protestant confession and doctrine. What is more, as the writers focused on a particular biblical text for interpretation, they often reached very similar conclusions regarding that text. The text of Scripture tends to lead them toward a more unified expression of the faith. This is something I have described as "the text effect,"[1] which illustrates for us a way in which the Bible brings us together despite differences and always remains the most important guide for Christian teaching and practice. In view of the 500th anniversary of the Reformation in 1517, I believe it is fitting for us to draw anew upon the time honored insights of these great servants of God.

The Bible Translations

Among the translations for our commentary we have chosen, on the one hand, what many regard as the finest English translation ever produced: the King James Version. The KJV is a product of the Reformation Era and, although it is now more than 400 years old, remains a most valuable tool for study. Along with the KJV we are pleased to

---

[1] *Friends of the Law* (St. Louis: Concordia, 2011), 136.

present the English Standard Version, which has rapidly become one of the most widely used modern English translations. The success of the ESV is due in part to the translators' efforts to follow sound, classical principals of translation very like those used by the KJV translators. The result is a very readable English translation that also allows readers to grasp the biblical expressions and terms that appear repeatedly in the Bible. Due to this approach, we find the ESV an especially helpful translation for Bible Study. Our notes are keyed to the ESV but we have placed the KJV in parallel with the ESV for easy comparison. Since the ESV text is based on the broad consensus of biblical scholars who have consulted the early Greek manuscripts, it differs at points from the KJV text, which was produced when fewer manuscripts were available for study. Where significant differences between the translations appear, the notes include comment.

Our Prayer for You

The following prayer embodies the sense of study and devotion we wish to convey to all who take up these commentaries:

Blessed Lord, You have caused all Holy Scripture to be written for our learning. Grant that we may so hear them, read, mark, learn, and inwardly digest them that, by patience and comfort from Your holy Word, we may embrace and ever hold fast the blessed hope of everlasting life; through Jesus Christ, our Lord. Amen.

Rev. Edward A. Engelbrecht, STM
Senior Editor for Bible Resources
Concordia Publishing House

PREFACE

The Epistle to the Hebrews is an unusual book. Written anonymously, it therefore finds a place among the antilegomena—books whose canonical status has been questioned. Some of its teachings seem hard to understand, particularly if they are not carefully read in context or if faulty presuppositions are imposed upon the text. The author's use of numerous words that do not appear elsewhere in Scripture adds to the challenges of interpreting this book.

But Hebrews is also a deeply rewarding book. It is focused on Jesus, the founder and perfecter of our faith. Jesus is the Great High Priest who sacrifices Himself for the sins of the world—once, for all. Jesus is superior to every creature and yet graciously gives Himself to be our Savior.

This Letter helps us see how the Old Testament finds its completion in Jesus. Our Lord fulfilled the Old Testament covenant and provides everything needed by His people. By His gracious work, He now calls us His brothers and sisters. Indeed, Hebrews is a rewarding book that offers us rich sustenance.

I am deeply grateful to the many people who supported and aided me in writing this volume and in editing this series: these include my wife, Nina, and my sons, Matthew, Christopher, and Jacob; my colleagues at Concordia University Irvine; the students who have studied Hebrews with me; and the members of the congregations I have been blessed to serve. I am likewise grateful to Rev. Edward Engelbrecht for allowing me this opportunity.

As you read Hebrews, fix your eyes upon "Jesus, the founder and perfecter of our faith, who for the joy that was set before Him endured the cross, despising the shame, and is seated at the right hand of the throne of God" (Heb 12:2).

Steven P. Mueller, Ph.D.
General Editor

ABBREVIATIONS

AD	*anno Domini* (in the year of [our] Lord)	NT	New Testament
		OT	Old Testament
BC	before Christ	p.	page
c.	circa	pp.	pages
cf.	confer	St.	Saint
ch.	chapter	v.	verse
chs.	chapters	vv.	verses

Canonical Scripture

Gn	Genesis	Ec	Ecclesiastes
Ex	Exodus	Sg	Song of Solomon
Lv	Leviticus	Is	Isaiah
Nu	Numbers	Jer	Jeremiah
Dt	Deuteronomy	Lm	Lamentations
Jsh	Joshua	Ezk	Ezekiel
Jgs	Judges	Dn	Daniel
Ru	Ruth	Hos	Hosea
1Sm	1 Samuel	Jl	Joel
2Sm	2 Samuel	Am	Amos
1Ki	1 Kings	Ob	Obadiah
2Ki	2 Kings	Jnh	Jonah
1Ch	1 Chronicles	Mi	Micah
2Ch	2 Chronicles	Na	Nahum
Ezr	Ezra	Hab	Habakkuk
Ne	Nehemiah	Zep	Zephaniah
Est	Esther	Hg	Haggai
Jb	Job	Zec	Zechariah
Ps	Psalms	Mal	Malachi
Pr	Proverbs		

Mt	Matthew	Rm	Romans
Mk	Mark	1Co	1 Corinthians
Lk	Luke	2Co	2 Corinthians
Jn	John	Gal	Galatians
Ac	Acts	Eph	Ephesians

Php	Philippians	Jas	James
Col	Colossians	1Pt	1 Peter
1Th	1 Thessalonians	2Pt	2 Peter
2Th	2 Thessalonians	1Jn	1 John
1Tm	1 Timothy	2Jn	2 John
2Tm	2 Timothy	3Jn	3 John
Ti	Titus	Jude	Jude
Phm	Philemon	Rv	Revelation
Heb	Hebrews		

The Apocrypha

Jth	Judith	2Macc	2 Maccabees
Wis	The Wisdom of Solomon	Old Grk Est	Old Greek Esther
Tob	Tobit	Sus	Susanna
Ecclus	Ecclesiasticus (Sirach)	Bel	Bel and the Dragon
Bar	Baruch	Pr Az	The Prayer of Azariah
Lt Jer	The Letter of Jeremiah	Sg Three	The Song of the Three Holy Children
1Macc	1 Maccabees		
		Pr Man	Prayer of Manasseh

Other Books

1Esd	1 Esdras	Ps 151	Psalm 151
2Esd	2 Esdras	1En	1 Enoch
3Macc	3 Maccabees (Ptolemaika)	2En	2 Enoch
4Macc	4 Maccabees	Jub	Jubilees

Abbreviations for Commonly Cited Books and Works

Ap   Apology of the Augsburg Confession. From *Concordia*.

Bengel   Bengel, John Albert. *Gnomon of the New Testament*. 5 Vols. Edinburgh: T. & T. Clark, 1877.

Calvin.   Calvin, John. *Commentaries on the Epistle of Paul the Apostle to the Hebrews*. John Owen, trans. Edinburgh: Calvin Translation Society, 1853.

Concordia   McCain, Paul Timothy, ed. *Concordia: The Lutheran Confessions*. 2nd ed. St. Louis: Concordia, 2006.

Ep   Epitome of the Formula of Concord. From *Concordia*.

ESV   English Standard Version.

FC   Formula of Concord. From *Concordia*.

Gerhard	Gerhard, Johann. *Theological Commonplaces*. Richard J. Dinda, trans. Benjamin T. G. Mayes, ed. St. Louis: Concordia, 2009–.
KJV	King James Version of Scripture.
Knox	Knox, John. *Writings of the Rev. John Knox*. London: The Religious Tract Society, 1900.
LC	Large Catechism of Martin Luther. From *Concordia*.
LSB	Commission on Worship of The Lutheran Church—Missouri Synod. *Lutheran Service Book*. St. Louis: Concordia, 2006.
LW	Luther, Martin. *Luther's Works*. American Edition. General editors Jaroslav Pelikan and Helmut T. Lehmann. 56 vols. St. Louis: Concordia, and Philadelphia: Muhlenberg and Fortress, 1955–1986. Vols. 56–75: Edited by Christopher Boyd Brown. St. Louis: Concordia, 2009–.
LXX	Septuagint. Koine Greek Old Testament.
NPNF1	Schaff, Philip, ed. *A Select Library of Nicene and Post-Nicene Fathers of the Christian Church*. Series 1, 14 vols. New York: The Christian Literature Series, 1886–89. Reprint, Grand Rapids, MI: Eerdmans, 1956.
NPNF2	Schaff, Philip, and Henry Wace, ed. *A Select Library of Nicene and Post-Nicene Fathers of the Christian Church*, Series 2, 14 vols. New York: The Christian Literature Series, 1890–99. Reprint, Grand Rapids, MI: Eerdmans, 1952, 1961.
SA	Smalcald Articles. From *Concordia*.
SC	Luther, Martin. *Luther's Small Catechism*. St. Louis: Concordia, 1986.
SD	Solid Declaration of the Formula of Concord. From *Concordia*.
SLSB	Eales, Samuel J., trans. and ed. *Some Letters of St. Bernard, Abbot of Clairvaux*. The Complete Works of S. Bernard, Abbot of Clairvaux 1. London: John Hodges, 1904.
Tr	Treatise on the Power and Primacy of the Pope. From *Concordia*.
Wesley	Wesley, John. *Explanatory Notes upon the New Testament*. 12 ed. New York: Carlton & Porter, 1754.

TIMELINE FOR THE NEW TESTAMENT

Anatolia, Greece, and Rome	Egypt and Africa	Dates	Syria, Canaan, and Israel	Mesopotamia and Persia
		4 BC	Angel appears to Zechariah (c. Nov 15; Lk 1:8–22)	
		3 BC	The Annunciation (inter Apr 17–May 16; Lk 1:26–38); John the Baptist born (Aug; Lk 1:57–66)	
	Holy family in Egypt	2 BC	Jesus born (mid Jan to early Feb; Mt 1:25; Lk 2:1–7); Magi visit; flight to Egypt (mid to late in the year; Mt 2)	
		1 BC	Death of Herod the Great (after Jan 10; Mt 2:19); return to Nazareth (Mt 2:19–23)	
		AD 6	Judas the Galilean leads revolt against Rome; Judea, Samaria, and Idumaea combined to form the Roman province of Judea	
		10	Jesus in temple before the elders (c. Apr 8–22; Lk 2:42)	
		c. 10	Rabbi Hillel dies	
Tiberius, Roman emperor		14–37		
Revolt in Gaul; grain shortages cause unrest in Rome		21		
		29	Baptism of Jesus (fall; Lk 3:1–2)	
		30	Jesus at Passover (c. Apr 8; Jn 2:20)	
		32	Jesus at Passover (c. Apr 15; Jn 6:4); Jesus arrives at Feast of Booths (c. Oct 14; Jn 7:14); Feast of Booths (Oct 17 or 18; Jn 7:37)	

Anatolia, Greece, and Rome	Egypt and Africa	Dates	Syria, Canaan, and Israel	Mesopotamia and Persia
Roman senators unable to pay debts; subsidized by Emperor Tiberius		33	Triumphal entry (Sun, Mar 29); Last Supper (Thurs eve, Apr 2); crucifixion (Fri, Apr 3); resurrection (Sun, Apr 5); ascension (May 14; Lk 24:51; Ac 1:9); Pentecost (May 24)	Jews of Parthia, Media, Elam and Mesopotamia travel to Jerusalem for Pentecost
	Ethiopian eunuch baptized, returns home (Ac 8:26–39)	c. 35		
		35–42		Revolt of Seleucia on the Tigris against Parthian rule
		36	Paul's conversion (Ac 9:1–31)	
Caligula (Gaius), Roman emperor		37–41	Josephus, Jewish historian, born	
	Philo of Alexandria leads Jewish delegation to Rome	c. 39	Caligula attempts to place statue of himself in Jerusalem temple	
		41	Martyrdom of James (late Mar; Ac 12:2); Peter in prison (Apr; Ac 12:3–4); Passover (May 4; Ac 12:4); Peter leaves Jerusalem (May; Gal 2:11)	
		41–44	Herod Agrippa I rules Judea	
Claudius, Roman emperor		41–54		
Peter on mission in Asia Minor (spr/sum; 1Pt 1:1–2); [in Corinth (fall); at Rome (mid Nov)]		42	Peter in Antioch (May 41–Apr 42; Gal 2:11)	
		44	Herod Agrippa at festival in Caesarea (Mar 5; Ac 12:19); death of Herod Agrippa (Mar 10; Ac 12:21–23)	

Anatolia, Greece, and Rome	Egypt and Africa	Dates	Syria, Canaan, and Israel	Mesopotamia and Persia
		47–48	Paul's 1st missionary journey (Ac 13:1–14:28)	
Paul goes to Macedonia; Barnabas and John Mark go to Cyprus (mid May; Ac 15:36–16:10)		49	Conference in Jerusalem (Ac 15:1–35); Peter goes to Antioch (Feb; Gal 2:11); Paul confronts Peter (Apr; Gal 2:11)	
		49–56	[Peter in Antioch (seven years)]	
Paul's 2nd missionary journey (Ac 15:39–18:22)	Philo of Alexandria leads second Jewish delegation to Rome	49–51		
Paul's 3rd missionary journey (Ac 18:23–21:17)		52–55		
Nero, Roman emperor		54–68		
		55–57	Paul imprisoned in Caesarea (Ac 23:23–26:32)	
Paul's journey to Rome (Ac 27:1–28:16)		57–58		
Paul in custody in Rome (Ac 28:17–31)		58–60		
		62	Martyrdom of James, the Lord's brother	
Paul assigns Titus at Crete (Ti 1:5)		64–65		
Paul in Ephesus, where he leaves Timothy (spr–sum; 1Tm 1:3)		65		

Anatolia, Greece, and Rome	Egypt and Africa	Dates	Syria, Canaan, and Israel	Mesopotamia and Persia
	Tiberius Julius Alexander, of Jewish descent, appointed Roman prefect of Egypt	66		
		66–70	Jewish revolt against Romans	
Peter and Paul martyred		68		
Emperor Vespasian		69–79		
		70	Titus destroys Jerusalem temple; Rabbon Yohanan ben Zakkai at Yavneh Academy	Jerusalem Jews settle in Babylonia, which becomes the new center of Judaism
		c. 73	Fall of Masada	
Emperor Titus		79–81		
Emperor Domitian		81–96		
		c. 90–115	Rabbon Gamaliel II at Yavneh Academy	
Jews revolt in Cyprus	Jews revolt in Egypt and Cyrene	115–17		Trajan captures Mesopotamia; Jews revolt
	Founding of Antinoöpolis by Emperor Hadrian	130		
		132–35	Bar Kokhba revolt; death of Rabbi Akiva, Yavneh Academy leader who hailed Bar Kokhba as the messiah	

THE ROMAN EMPIRE. The vast Roman Empire began to rule little Judea in 63 BC. Under Roman rule the Jews received fairer treatment than they had under Seleucid rule. However, Jewish extremists kept Judea in constant unrest. They provoked two major rebellions. In AD 66–70, the first Jewish revolt ended with Titus destroying the Jerusalem temple. During the second Jewish revolt in AD 132–135, Hadrian defeated

DANUBE R.

DANUBE R.

BLACK SEA

Trapezus

Philippi
Byzantium
Thessalonica
SEA
disium

Pergamum

AEGEAN SEA

Tarsus

EUPHRATES R.

Ephesus

egium
ACHAIA
Athens Cnidus
Myra
Antioch

use
Sparta

CYPRUS

CRETE
Sidon
Damascus

Fair Havens
Caesarea Maritima

EDITERRANEAN SEA
Jerusalem

Alexandria

ajor
Cyrene
Petra
Aelana

Memphis
NILE R.
RED
SEA

ar Kokhba's attempt to throw off Roman rule. Hadrian practically destroyed the remnants of the Jews in
Judea and placed heavy restrictions on Jews throughout the Roman Empire. Jerusalem became a Roman
colony, Aelia Capitolina, and the Romans renamed the region Syria Palaestina.

HEBREWS

INTRODUCTION TO HEBREWS

Author
Unknown; see "Anonymous" below

Date
Before AD 70

Places
The temple; Jerusalem (Salem); Italy

People
"Us" (writer and colleagues); brothers; leaders; martyrs; high priests; "those who serve the tent"; travelers from Italy; Timothy; numerous biblical figures

Purpose
To exhort the brothers, washed with pure water and partaking of the altar, that Christ is their High Priest and all-sufficient sacrifice for sin

Law Themes
Retribution for disobedience; slavery to death and the devil; an unbelieving heart; rebellion; obligation to sacrifice; repentance from dead works; crucifying Jesus again; the living God's vengeance; struggle against sin; discipline; obedience to leaders

Gospel Themes
God spoke through Jesus; purification for sins; inheriting salvation; our High Priest and Mediator; sanctification; God's promises; Melchizedek; sprinkled and washed; assurance of faith; the founder and perfecter of our faith; the great Shepherd

Memory Verses
God spoke through His Son (1:1–4); God's living Word (4:12–13); Christ's blood purifies us (9:13–14); faith defined (11:1–3); run with endurance (12:1–2)

Reading Hebrews

Frost glistens in the light as it melts from the backs of woolly lambs, gleaming and shimmering and dripping as the animals doze. The lambs rise to stretch. They shiver, steam wafting from their warm legs and bellies. They look up expectantly toward a man standing near their gate. He leans on the edge of the pen and looks the herd over carefully, wondering which lambs to feed and which to choose for the morning sacrifice. It is a great and festive day—most holy. And yet, tomorrow he will have to choose again, and so the next day, and the next.

The writer to the Hebrews describes the glories of the old covenant but also reminds his readers of how it is surpassed by the glories of the new covenant. The annual cycle of sacrifice reached its consummation in one most holy offering—the blood of Jesus Christ for the forgiveness of all our sins. Jesus now stands as our High Priest, watching over the sheepfold of all who look to Him, the founder and perfecter of our faith.

Luther on Hebrews

In Luther's preface to Hebrews, cited below, he reflects some of the historic concerns raised about the Book, which was not at first universally received as an apostolic Letter or as a Book of Holy Scripture (see "Anonymous" below). Though Luther notes the Book's "hard knots" and "straw" weaknesses (see notes on 6:4–6; 10:26–27; 12:17), he elsewhere cites Hebrews as authoritative teaching (e.g., LW 2:393; 4:405–9; 35:247; 37:293). He sees the Holy Spirit bearing witness through the Book (LW 2:387; 20:292) and refers to it as "Holy Scripture" (LW 41:19; see also SC, Table of Duties, pp. xlii–xliv, and LW 2:294). The Lutheran Confessions cite Hebrews as God's Word alongside other texts of Holy Scripture (e.g., FC Ep I 5). For more about the Book's canonicity, see Gerhard on pp. 7–9.

> The author of the Epistle to the Hebrews—whoever he is, whether Paul or, as I think, Apollos—quotes [the Old Testament] most learnedly. (LW 8:178)

> If you would interpret [the Books of Moses] well and confidently, set Christ before you, for he is the man to whom it all applies, every bit of it. Make the high priest Aaron, then, to be nobody but Christ alone, as does the Epistle to the Hebrews [5:4–5], which is sufficient, all by itself, to interpret all the figures of Moses. Likewise, as the same epistle announces [Hebrews 9–10], it is certain that Christ himself is the sacrifice—indeed even the altar [Heb. 13:10]—who sacrificed himself with his own blood. Now whereas the sacrifice performed by the Levitical high priest took away only the artificial sins, which in their nature were not sins, so our High Priest, Christ, by his own sacrifice and blood, has taken away the true sin, that which in its very nature is sin. He has gone in once for all through the curtain to God to make atonement for us [Heb. 9:12]. Thus you should apply to Christ personally, and to no one else, all that is written about the high priest. (LW 35:247–48)

Up to this point we have had [to do with] the true and certain chief books of the New Testament. The four which follow have from ancient times had a different reputation. In the first place, the fact that Hebrews is not an epistle of St. Paul, or of any other apostle, is proved by what it says in chapter 2[:3], that through those who had themselves heard it from the Lord this doctrine has come to us and remained among us. It is thereby made clear that he is speaking about the apostles, as a disciple to whom this doctrine has come from the apostles, perhaps long after them. For St. Paul, in Galatians 1[:1], testifies powerfully that he has his gospel from no man, neither through men, but from God himself.

Again, there is a hard knot in the fact that in chapters 6[:4–6] and 10[:26–27] it flatly denies and forbids to sinners any repentance after baptism; and in chapter 12[:17] it says that Esau sought repentance and did not find it. This [seems, as it stands, to be] contrary to all the gospels and to St. Paul's epistles; and although one might venture an interpretation of it, the words are so clear that I do not know whether that would be sufficient. My opinion is that this is an epistle put together of many pieces, which does not deal systematically with any one subject.

However that may be, it is still a marvelously fine epistle. It discusses Christ's priesthood masterfully and profoundly on the basis of the Scriptures and extensively interprets the Old Testament in a fine way. Thus it is plain that this is the work of an able and learned man; as a disciple of the apostles he had learned much from them and was greatly experienced in faith and practiced in the Scriptures. And although, as he himself testifies in chapter 6[:1], he does not lay the foundation of faith—that is the work of the apostles—nevertheless he does build well on it with gold, silver, precious stones, as St. Paul says in I Corinthians 3[:12]. Therefore we should not be deterred if wood, straw, or hay are perhaps mixed with them, but accept this fine teaching with all honor; though, to be sure, we cannot put it on the same level with the apostolic epistles.

Who wrote it is not known, and will probably not be known for a while; it makes no difference. We should be satisfied with the doctrine that he bases so constantly on the Scriptures. For he discloses a firm grasp of the reading of the Scriptures and of the proper way of dealing with them. (LW 35:394–95)

5

For more of Luther's insights on this Book, see *Lectures on Hebrews* (LW 29:107–241).

Calvin on Hebrews

Not only various opinions were formerly entertained as to the author of this Epistle, but it was only at a late period that it was received by the Latin Churches. They suspected that it favoured Novatus in denying pardon to the fallen; but that this was a groundless opinion will be shewn by various passages. I, indeed, without hesitation, class it among apostolical writings; nor do I doubt but that it has been through the craft of Satan that any have been led to dispute its authority. There is, indeed, no book in the Holy Scriptures which speaks so clearly of the priesthood of Christ, so highly exalts the virtue and dignity of that only true sacrifice which he offered by his death, so abundantly treats of the use of ceremonies as well as of their abrogation, and, in a word, so fully explains that Christ is the end of the Law. Let us not therefore suffer the Church of God nor ourselves to be deprived of so great a benefit, but firmly defend the possession of it.

Moreover, as to its author, we need not be very solicitous. Some think the author to have been Paul, others Luke, others Barnabas, and others Clement, as Jerome relates; yet Eusebius, in his sixth book of his Church History, mentions only Luke and Clement. I well know that in the time of Chrysostom it was everywhere classed by the Greeks among the Pauline Epistles; but the Latins thought otherwise, even those who were nearest to the times of the Apostles.

I, indeed, can adduce no reason to shew that Paul was its author; for they who say that he designedly suppressed his name because it was hateful to the Jews, bring nothing to the purpose; for why, then, did he mention the name of Timothy? as by this he betrayed himself. But the manner of teaching, and the style, sufficiently shew that Paul was not the author; and the writer himself confesses in the second chapter that he was one of the disciples of the Apostles, which is wholly different from the way in which Paul spoke of himself. Besides, what is said of the practice of catechising in the sixth chapter, does not well suit the time or age of Paul. There are other things which we shall notice in their proper places.

What excuse is usually made as to the style I well know, that is, that no opinion can be hence formed, because the Greek is a translation made from the Hebrew by Luke or some one else. But this conjecture can be easily refuted: to pass by other places quoted from Scripture, on the supposition that the Epistle was written in Hebrew, there would have been no allusion to the word Testament, on which the writer so much dwells; what he says of a Testament, in the ninth chapter, could not have been drawn from any other fountain than from the Greek word; for *diatheke* has two meanings in Greek, while *berith* in Hebrew means only a covenant. This reason alone is enough to convince men of sound judgment that the epistle was written in the Greek language. Now, what is objected on the other hand, that it is more probable that the Apostle wrote to the Jews in their own language, has no weight in it; for how few then understood their ancient language? Each had learned the language of the country where he dwelt. Besides, the Greek was then more widely known than all other languages. We shall proceed now to the Argument. The object at the beginning is not to shew to the Jews that Jesus, the son of Mary, was the Christ, the Redeemer promised to them, for he wrote to those who had already made a profession of Christ; that point, then, is taken as granted. But the design of the author was to prove what the office of Christ is. And it hence appears evident, that by his coming an end was put to ceremonies. It is necessary to draw this distinction; for as it would have been a superfluous labour for the Apostle to prove to those who were already convinced that he was the Christ who had appeared, so it was necessary for him to shew what he was, for they did not as yet clearly understand the end, the effect, and the advantages of his coming; but being taken up with a false view of the Law, they laid hold on the shadow instead of the substance. (*Commentaries*, pp. xxvi–xxvii)

Gerhard on Hebrews

To the canonical books of the New Testament of the second rank belong the following: *the Epistle to the Hebrews*. Some in the Church used to doubt and still doubt whether this Epistle should be numbered with Paul's Epistles. [Gerhard cites numerous Fathers, who gave different opinions on the epistle's authorship. For example:] . . . Origen, in a homily on that Epistle recorded by Eusebius in *Histor.*, bk. 6, c. 25: "The character of the diction of the Epistle entitled 'to the Hebrews' does not have in its words the style of the apostle . . . for he confessed that he was unskilled in his speech, that is, in his diction. The Epistle, however, is quite Greek in the composition of its diction. . . . Anyone skilled in differentiating among styles will admit this. Again, anyone who pays careful attention to reading the apostle will admit that the ideas of this Epistle are great ones and by no means inferior to those letters that are, without contradiction, apostolic, and that this is true." [Gerhard cites still more Fathers about the epistle's composition and authorship. He then provides his conclusions.]

We . . . claim that the Epistle to the Hebrews is (1) a letter of Paul himself; (2) canonical, but it is of the second rank because some people in the Church once had doubts about it; (3) written in Greek. Clement of Alexandria (*Stromat.*, bk. 4), Eusebius (*Hist. eccles.*, bk. 3, c. 32), Jerome (*Catal. script. illustr.*), and certain others of the ancients think that it was written in Hebrew and was translated into Greek by Luke or Barnabas. We think, however, that it is more likely that Paul himself wrote it in Greek: (1) Because the Greek language at that time was familiar to most Jews, especially to those who were living in Asia Minor. (2) Since Peter and James wrote their Epistles addressed to the scattered Jews in Greek, it is likely that Paul did the same thing. (3) Since Paul wrote all the rest of his Epistles in Greek, it is likely that in this Epistle, too, he used the same character of speech followed by the canonical books of the New Testament. (4) With this Epistle, the apostle wanted to advise not only the Hebrews but also other nations, among whom the Greek language was in use. (5) The style and diction of this Epistle have the flavor of Greek eloquence, not of Hebrew. (6) Had the Epistle been written in Hebrew, Hebraisms ought to appear here and there in the Greek translation. Hebraisms, however, are less frequent in this Epistle than in the rest. (7) There is no ancient writer who testifies that he saw a Hebrew copy of this Epistle. (8) The Old Testament Scriptures are quoted in it not according to the Hebrew sources but according to the Septuagint translation. (9) The Hebrew name Melchizedek is translated as "king of righteousness" and Salem as "peace." This, however, in no wise fits, if he wrote in Hebrew. (Cf. Franciscus Junius, *Paral.*, bk. 3, on c. 9 of this Epistle, p. 479.) The subscript shows that it was sent from Italy through Timothy. Chrysostom adds that it was written from prison in Rome. Athanasius explains the theme of this Epistle in his *Synopsis* in this way: "Because the Jews were devoting themselves to the Law and its shadows, for this reason the apostle Paul became the teacher of the Gentiles and was sent to the Gentiles to preach the Gospel to them. When he had written to all the Gentiles, now, finally, he writes also to all the Hebrews—those of the circumcision who had believed. He writes to them this Epistle that is filled with statements and proofs of the coming of Christ and the Law's shadow, which Christ's coming brought to an end." Thomas notes: "This Epistle was written against the errors of certain people who, after their conversion from Judaism to faith in Christ, wanted to observe the legal matters of the Old Testament along with the Gospel, as if the grace of Christ were not sufficient for salvation." The aim and sum of the entire Epistle consists in this: that Jesus Christ, true God and true man, was promised in the Old Testament and revealed in the New as the Messiah, the only prophet, priest, and king of the Church; that He was foreshadowed by the Levitical ceremonies; that by Him the entire Church of God must be illumined and sanctified; that embracing His Gospel by faith, we should produce fruits worthy of the Gospel. It consists of thirteen chapters in which are discussed (1) Christ and His person and office; (2) the duties of Christians by which they must show their gratitude to their Redeemer, to which pertains also patience, which must be shown in persecutions suffered because of Christ. (E 1.274–78)

Bengel on Hebrews

Many anonymous writers, though unknown, endeavour to be useful to their readers; but the writer of this Divine Epistle shows, that he was known to those to whom he writes: xiii. 19. And the Apostle Paul is said to be the writer of the epistle, with the general consent of antiquity. Above all, Peter, writing to the elect strangers scattered through Pontus, Galatia, Cappadocia, Asia, and Bithynia, praises the letters of Paul, which he wrote to them also. But the other epistles of Paul were sent to Gentile converts; this one alone to the Hebrews, although he himself does not call them Hebrews; and in the title, no doubt old, but not prefixed by the hand of Paul, they are with less propriety called Hebrews, instead of Judaico-Hellenistic Christians, to whom we have observed below that he wrote, ch. vi. 10. Moreover the method and style of Paul may be easily recognised: for he puts the proposition and division before the discussion, ch. ii. 17. He distinctly and separately subjoins the practical to the doctrinal part: he puts the practical part at greater length at the end of the epistle. He quotes the same words of the Old Testament which he does elsewhere, ch. ii. 8, X. 30, 38 ; also, i. 6: he uses the same ideas and expressions. . . . In former times, some thought that Barnabas, or Luke, or Clemens Romanus was the author: in fact, because every one of them had this epistle without the author's name in his hands, each of them was considered as the author himself. But why did not Paul prefix to this one epistle his name, which, from ch. xiii. 19, was evidently dear to those to whom he was writing? He did not prefix it, because he did not use an inscription; for men in former times did not always use it in accordance with primitive simplicity. Comp. 2 Kings v. 6, x. 2, 6, where the word ["read"]) placed before them, scarcely permits us to believe that excerpts are given rather than the epistles themselves. And also the ardour of spirit in this epistle, alike as in the First Epistle of John, bursting forth at once into the subject, the more effectively strikes the hearers: but he compensates at the conclusion of the epistle for the absence of salutation and thanksgiving, which were usually placed by Paul at the beginning of the other epistles. This epistle of Paul, and the two of Peter (to which may be added those of James and Jude, which are very similar), were written to the same believing Israelites, scattered abroad in Pontus, Galatia, Cappadocia, Asia, and Bithynia, and much about the same time. Three years before the destruction of Jerusalem, Paul and Peter were put to death at Rome; therefore this epistle was also written to them when the temple was standing, ch. viii. 5. Peter wrote both of his epistles a little before his martyrdom; and in the second, praises the epistles of Paul—this one by name (expressly), which was then new (recently sent), many of the first hearers of the Lord being by this time dead; Heb. ii. 3.

As Peter, James, Jude, wrote in Greek, not in Hebrew, so Paul did the same here; for he quotes the Greek translation of Moses and the Psalms, where the reading is different from that of the Hebrew, ch. i. 6, x. 5. . . .

The whole application of the discourse is, to confirm the faith of the brethren in Jesus Christ, ch. xiii. 8, 9. Moreover, he confirms it, by demonstrating His glory. He calls this the sum (the principal point), ch. viii. 1. Hence all the divisions of the epistle, abounding in the sharpest admonitions, and the most powerful incitements, are set forth in one and the same form of discourse; and doctrine and practice are everywhere connected by the word, therefore. (Bengel 4:333–35)

Wesley on Hebrews

It is agreed by the general tenor of antiquity that this epistle was written by St. Paul, whose other epistles were sent to the gentile converts; this only to the Hebrews. But this improper inscription was added by some later hand. It was sent to the Jewish Hellenist Christians, dispersed through various countries. St. Paul's method and style are easily observed therein. He places, as usual, the proposition and division before the treatise, Heb 2:17; he subjoins the exhortatory to the doctrinal part, quotes the same scriptures, Heb 1:6; 2:8; 10:30,38,6; and uses the same expressions as elsewhere. But why does he not prefix his name, which, it is plain from Heb 13:19 was dear to them to whom he wrote Because he prefixes no inscription, in which, if at all, the name would have been mentioned. The ardour of his spirit carries aim directly upon his subject, (just like St. John in his First Epistle,) and throws back his usual salutation and thanksgiving to the conclusion.

This epistle of St. Paul, and both those of St. Peter, (one may add, that of St. James and of St. Jude also,) were written both to the same persons, dispersed through Pontus, Galatia, and other countries, and nearly at the same time. St. Paul suffered at Rome, three years before the destruction of Jerusalem. Therefore this epistle likewise, was written while the temple was standing. St. Peter wrote a little before his martyrdom, and refers to the epistles of St. Paul; this in particular.

The scope of it is, to confirm their faith in Christ; and this he does by demonstrating his glory. All the parts of it are full of the most earnest and pointed admonitions and exhortations; and they go on in one tenor, the particle therefore everywhere connecting the doctrine and the use. (Wesley 563)

Challenges for Readers

Anonymous. The Epistle to the Hebrews is actually a sermon ("word of exhortation"; 13:22) with a brief letter attached (13:20–25). The writing describes the temple sacrifices as though they were still in use (cf. 9:6–10) and describes a persecution, which may be Emperor Nero's persecution of Christians at Rome (cf. ch. 12; 13:24). The sermon-writer's name was not provided, nor was his name recorded

11

by early Christian historians. Despite this, churches of the Eastern Roman Empire (Greek- and Syriac-speaking) have always welcomed the Book as part of the NT. However, the anonymity of the sermon and some challenging content (see examples from Luther above) limited its approval for public reading in churches of the Western Roman Empire. Yet, Hebrews was highly regarded (cited by Clement, bishop of Rome, c. AD 96), and by the fourth century, it became part of the Western canon of Scripture. The apostolic content of the sermon is attested in 2:3. Over the centuries, many different authors have been proposed (e.g., Paul, Luke, Barnabas, Apollos), but none of these proposals are fully convincing. The earliest known copy containing much of the Pauline Epistles, Papyrus 46 (c. AD 200), includes Hebrews just after Romans, attesting to the value of the Book and bearing witness to the early tradition that Paul might be its author. Modern interest in feminism has encouraged some commentators to propose that the sermon was written by Priscilla/Prisca, a learned woman described in Ac 18; 1Co 16:19; 2Tm 4:19. However, the writer of Hebrews clearly refers to himself as a man (e.g., the participle for "tell" in 11:32 is masculine). The authorship of the Letter remains a mystery.

Rhetoric and Doctrine. The writer of Hebrews, or his scribe, had an excellent education in classical oratory. Recent study of Hebrews has demonstrated that it is written in high Greek style, which distinguishes it from Paul's more common Greek style. The writer's doctrine depends on the apostles (2:3) and has important connections to Paul's use of the OT (cf. 10:38; Rm 1:17; Gal 3:11) and John's theology of the Word (cf. Jn 1:1–2; 10:30; 14:11; Heb 1:3; 7:3; 13:8). But the writer includes many unique insights and shows an interest in the priesthood that is not found in other apostolic writers.

Use of the Old Testament. Scripture itself teaches that the revelation of God was delivered under "covenant," or "testament," first given to Abraham and confirmed/renewed through Moses (Gn 17:9; Ex 2:24; chs. 3–6; Lv 26:42; Dt 1:8; 29:12–13; Jsh 24). Although many covenants are described in the Old Testament, Jeremiah saw the covenant given to Abraham and confirmed through Moses as the covenant (Jer 31:32), which the people of Israel broke. He then prophesied a second covenant, or "new covenant" (Jer 31:31–33; cf. Is 59:20–21; Gal 3:17). . . . . The two great covenants of Scripture—the old and the new—relate to each other as prophecy and fulfillment.

The first covenant pointed forward to the second, which would fulfill God's plan of redemption. The relationship of old and new, of prophecy and fulfillment, likewise reveals the unity of the Scripture.

Sabbath Rest. Hebrews wonderfully explains how the OT Sabbath (Saturday) foreshadowed the rest and peace of Christian faith and of heaven. In contrast with modern Adventists, who scare people with warnings that God will judge them for worshiping on Sunday rather than Saturday, Hebrews properly focuses on receiving the benefits of God's Word based on repentance and faith, not on observance of a calendar. (Cf. 10:1 and notes; Col 2:16–17.)

Christ's Death and Atonement. Hebrews argues forcefully that the crucifixion of Jesus is the one and only sacrifice for sins, which is not repeated or honored by further sacrifices. His death was a necessary payment and ransom for the sins of all people (cf. ch. 9). Christ is our sympathetic High Priest and one Mediator for salvation.

Melchizedek. Following the example of Ps 110:4, the writer of Hebrews provides an extensive comparison between this ancient priest of Salem (Jerusalem) and Jesus. The Dead Sea Scrolls and other early Jewish literature show a similar interest in the priesthood of Melchizedek, who was viewed as the first to establish priestly services at or near the site where the temple was built (Jos, *War* 6:438). Using Melchizedek as an illustration is one reason why the audience for Hebrews is considered to be a Jewish-Christian congregation. For the history of Melchizedek, cf. Gn 14.

Martyrs and Saints. Ch. 11 provides an early example of a martyr list, a composition that was popular during the Time between the Testaments (cf. Wis 10; Ecclus 44–50; 1Macc 2:51–60) and eventually led to the martyr and saint calendars beloved by early Christians. Remembering the martyrs and saints has three blessings for God's people: (1) their stories lead us to praise and thank God; (2) their examples strengthen our faith in God's mercy for us; and (3) with God's help, we may imitate their faith and virtues (Ap XXI 4–7). Believers who have gone to heaven may intercede for God's Church and pray against her enemies (cf. Zec 1:12; Rv 6:9–10), as do the angels. However, God never teaches His people to worship or pray to angels or saints, for such devotion belongs to God alone (cf. Ac 10:25–26; 14:8–15; Rv 19:10; 22:8–9; see Ap XXI 8–9).

Christian Discipline. Success and prosperity are popular themes for many preachers and writers today. However, their message often contradicts the Holy Scriptures. The writer of Hebrews, like Job, demonstrates that suffering is not necessarily proof of God's wrath; prosperity is not necessarily proof of His favor (Heb 12). God often works through suffering for the good of His people.

Blessings for Readers

In the Letter to the Hebrews, you will learn how to appreciate the OT most deeply and apply it to your life. As you read Hebrews, reflect on the great changes Jesus brought about when He fulfilled the laws and the promises of the old covenant. Take note of how all of Holy Scripture bears witness to this great work, which Jesus accomplished on the cross for your salvation. Because He stands now in heaven, interceding for you, pray for God's help and blessings with all boldness.

Outline

I.   Introduction/Theme: Christ Is the True and Final Revelation of God (1:1–3)
II. Jesus' Superiority (1:4–10:18)
    A. Over the Angels (1:4–2:18)
    B. Over Moses (3:1–4:13)
    C. Superiority of Jesus' Priesthood: Jesus, the New Melchizedek (4:14–7:28)
    D. Superiority of Jesus' Sacrifice (8:1–10:18)
III. Exhortation to Faithfulness (10:19–12:29)
    A. Invitation to Faithfulness (10:19–39)
    B. OT Examples of Faith: Following in the Faith of Our Fathers (ch. 11)
    C. Jesus as the Ultimate Example of Faithfulness (12:1–13)
    D. Warning against Disobedience, Using OT Examples (12:14–29)
IV. Final Exhortations (13:1–19)
V.   Blessings and Greetings (13:20–25)

PART 1

INTRODUCTION/THEME: CHRIST IS THE TRUE AND FINAL REVELATION OF GOD (1:1–3)

ESV	KJV
1 ¹Long ago, at many times and in many ways, God spoke to our fathers by the prophets, ²but in these last days he has spoken to us by his Son, whom he appointed the heir of all things, through whom also he created the world. ³He is the radiance of the glory of God and the exact imprint of his nature, and he upholds the universe by the word of his power. After making purification for sins, he sat down at the right hand of the Majesty on high,	*1* ¹God, who at sundry times and in divers manners spake in time past unto the fathers by the prophets, ²Hath in these last days spoken unto us by his Son, whom he hath appointed heir of all things, by whom also he made the worlds; ³Who being the brightness of his glory, and the express image of his person, and upholding all things by the word of his power, when he had by himself purged our sins, sat down on the right hand of the Majesty on high:

Introduction to Ch. 1 Though it is classified as an Epistle and grouped with other Epistles when in the NT, Hebrews is structured differently than many of these other Letters. Other Epistles commonly begin by stating the identity of the writer and the recipients. This is typically followed by a greeting. Hebrews begins differently, with powerful words about God and the revelation of His Word. The author does not identify himself, choosing instead to speak immediately about the work of God. The unique structure and presentation of this book is, in many ways, more like a sermon with a letter attached (cf. a similar possibility that 1 John is an apostolic sermon and 2 and 3 John are cover letters for the written sermon). Considered that way, these powerful opening words function like the beginning

15

of a sermon. They strongly assert that God has revealed Himself in Holy Scripture, thus confessing the divine authority of the Word. The first hearers and readers of Hebrews would have initially applied that assertion to the OT. Since the author will make repeated reference to the teachings of the prophets, this is an important truth to emphasize. But Christ is the center of both testaments. The resurrected Christ showed His disciples how the OT spoke about Him (Lk 24:27). He is also, of course, the subject of the NT. All Scripture testifies to Him and His work. But God's supreme self-revelation is the incarnation. Christ Jesus is Himself the revelation of God. As the second person of the Trinity, God Himself, this revelation in the incarnate Christ is superior to all others. Ch. 1 shows His supremacy to the prophets (1:1–3) and begins to demonstrate His supremacy to the angels (1:4ff.). As Hebrews continues, this theme will be expanded to show His supremacy over all others. God's people rejoice in these truths for Christ Jesus is the Savior of the world.

1:1 *Long ago at many times.* There is an epic ring to these words. The story of God's gracious work goes back to the very beginning of time and even before that, into eternity. God spoke with Adam in the Garden (e.g., Gn 1:15) and continued to speak to His people in various generations as He sent His prophets. He did not simply send His message once, but repeatedly communicated to His people in *many times.* Moreover, He spoke to them *in many ways.* God used various means to communicate to the prophets. These included speaking directly to them (e.g., Ex 3:1–4) and coming to them in visions and dreams (e.g., Nu 12:6, 8). Faithful prophets responded by conveying God's message to the people. Their message was delivered in diverse ways. They did this through oral proclamation (e.g., Jgs 6:8–10), by means of written words (e.g., Hab 2:2), and through dramatic, prophetic actions (e.g., Ezk 4). Still today, God continues to speak to us in their prophecies which are preserved in Holy Scripture. *God spoke . . . by the prophets.* While God used the prophets as His messengers, they themselves were not the source of the message. Peter reflects this when he writes, "For no prophecy was ever produced by the will of man, but men spoke from God as they were carried along by the Holy Spirit" (2 Pt 1:21). Inspired by God, their words and deeds were full of God's power and brought about God's will. *to our fathers.* These are our forebears in the faith, the faithful saints who lived by faith in the Savior that God had promised. Some of these will be specifically highlighted as examples of faith in ch. 11. Commenting on God's revelation to the prophets, Bengel wrote:

> The creation was revealed in the time of Adam; the last judgment in the time of Enoch; and so from time to time knowledge was given more fully unfolded. He also spoke . . . in divers modes of revelation, in dreams and visions. [He] refers to the matter . . . [and] to the form. In both there is an antithesis to one total and most perfect communication of God to us in Jesus Christ. The very multitude of prophets shows, that they "prophesied in part;" therefore, says he, you ought not to be frightened at the novelty of Christianity. . . . For a very considerable space of time there had arisen no prophets, in order that the Son might be the more an object of expectation. (Bengel 4:337–38)

1:2 *in these last days.* While some Christians use this language to speak only of future events, God's Word shows a broader meaning. The last days had already come when this Epistle was written—and we live in *these* days. The last days are the time of the definitive revelation of God's will in Christ (cf. Ac 2:14–21). In other words, since God has revealed His plan of salvation in Christ, His Church ever lives in the last days. Recognizing that we live in the last days, God's people know that their God is near. Thus the coming of God Incarnate is the pivotal moment of the last days. Previously, God spoke through the prophets but now, in Christ, *God has spoken* directly and immediately. Thus the words of the prophets and the words of Jesus are in distinct categories. This anticipates the establishment of the Bible as OT and NT. Recognizing this difference does not diminish the importance of the prophets who were God's agents in revealing His inspired Word. But it does recognize that Christ, the Word made flesh (Jn 1:14), is God's supreme revelation. The prophets faithfully recorded what God said and spoke in His name. Words like "thus says the LORD" (e.g., Is 43:1) demonstrate that they understood their role. In contrast, Christ, who is God, speaks directly, saying, "I tell you" (e.g., Mt 6:25). *by His Son.* Jesus is the eternal Son of God, the only-begotten Son, the Second Person of the Trinity. This description asserts His deity (cf. Jn 3:16; Mt 14:33; Mk 15:29). The supremacy of Jesus and His revelation is affirmed because He is God. Similarly, the words *appointed the heir* mark Jesus' unique status. An heir inherits all that belongs to his or her parents. As God's only begotten Son, Jesus is the rightful heir of *all things*, but He does not hoard His inheritance. Instead, He freely shares the Father's mercy, forgiveness, and new life with the brothers and sisters that are adopted into God's family through His saving work. *through whom also He created.* The Son was not created by the Father, but always existed with Him and the Holy Spirit (Jn 1:1). Creation is a work of the triune God. The Father, with the Holy Spirit, created all that exists, seen and unseen, by His Son, the Word of the Father (cf. Jn 1:3; Heb 3:3). *the world.* The Gk word used here (*aiōn*) literally means "the ages" or "eternity." In this context it brings the sense of "everything that has ever been created" including even time itself. All created things were made through Christ, as we confess in the Nicene Creed, "by [Christ] all things were made." Jesus is consequently supreme to all created things.

1:3 This verse asserts the full deity of Christ. He is *the radiance of the glory of God.* God the Father, invisible and dwelling in "unapproachable light" (1Tm 6:16), has revealed the light of His glory in Christ Jesus like rays from the sun. Scripture describes both the Father and the Son as "light" (cf. Eph 5:8; 1Jn 1:5; Jn 1:9; 8:12; and the Nicene Creed's affirmation that He is "Light of Light.") Noting that all things were created through Jesus (v. 2) asserted His deity; here the claim is reinforced by associating divine glory with Jesus, the Incarnate God. God's glory (Gk *doxa*) is His brightness, radiance, and splendor. In the OT, God's "glory" can describe His visible presence among His people (e.g., Ex 16:7). God's glory was manifest in a pillar of cloud by day and a pillar of fire by night (Ex 13:21). But Christ's incarnation is an even greater manifestation of God's glory. God was visibly present in His Incarnate Son. *the exact imprint of His nature.* Yet another affirmation of Christ's deity. As a wax seal reveals every detail of the metal stamp impressed upon it, Jesus is the exact expression of the Father's nature (Gk *hypostasis*), being eternally begotten of the Father. He possesses and reveals all that is divine. To see Jesus is to see the Father (Jn 14:9; cf. Col 1:15; 2Co 4:4). Luther reflects on this profound description, saying:

> These two words [imprint, nature] lead us to understand that the Father and the Son are of two kinds and distinct according to the Person, but one and undivided according to the substance. The word 'image' indicates that the Son is not the Father, but the image of the Father and a different Person. The phrase 'of his substance' indicates that he is not separate from the Father according to nature, but is together with him in one Godhead and

of equal substance, and is thus an image of the Father's substance, not made or having a beginning at a previous time, but having become and been from eternity, just as the divine substance was neither made nor had a beginning but has been from eternity . . . For the divine substance is eternal, whereas whatever has a beginning is temporal. (LW 34:222)

John Calvin likewise wrote about these profound words, noting both what they reveal and also the limitations of human language to fully describe God:

[These] are words borrowed from nature. For nothing can be said of things so great and so profound, but by similitudes taken from created things. There is therefore no need refinedly to discuss the question how the Son, who has the same essence with the Father, is a brightness emanating from his light. We must allow that there is a degree of impropriety in the language when what is borrowed from created things is transferred to the hidden majesty of God. But still the things which are evident to our senses are fitly applied to God, and for this end, that we may know what is to be found in Christ, and what benefits he brings to us.

It ought also to be observed that frivolous speculations are not here taught, but an important doctrine of faith. We ought therefore to apply these high titles given to Christ for our own benefit, for they bear a relation to us. When, therefore, thou hearest that the Son is the brightness of the Father's glory, think thus with thyself, that the glory of the Father is invisible until it shines forth in Christ, and that he is called the impress of his substance, because the majesty of the Father is hidden until it shews itself impressed as it were on his image. They who overlook this connection and carry their philosophy higher, weary themselves to no purpose, for they do not understand the design of the Apostle; for it was not his object to shew what likeness the Father bears to the Son; but, as I have said, his purpose was really to build up our faith, so that we may learn that God is made known to us in no other way than in Christ: for as to the essence of God, so immense is the brightness that it dazzles our eyes, except it shines on us in Christ. It hence follows, that we are blind as to the light of God, until in Christ it beams on us. It is indeed a profitable philosophy to learn Christ by the real understanding of faith and experience. The same view, as I have said, is to be taken of "the impress;" for as God is in himself to us incomprehensible, his form appears to us only in his Son. (Calvin 35–36)

He upholds the universe by the word of His power. God creates the universe and continues to uphold it in His continual work of preservation. Again underscoring the deity of Christ, both of these acts are ascribed to Him. Jesus, the Word who called creation into being (Gn 1; Jn 1:2), continues to uphold all creation by His divine word (cf. Col 1:17). His identification with the work of creation and the ongoing work of preservation are both further indications of His identity. Jesus does the work of God because Jesus is God. *purification for sins.* Having established Jesus' identity as true God, the author now turns to His redemptive work. The blood of sacrificed animals cleansed both the OT temple's altar and God's people from the defilement caused by sin (Lv 16:19, 30). Jesus alone makes the final, complete purification of our conscience (cf. Heb 9:14). These few words are a brief introduction to the critical topic of the significance of Jesus' sacrifice. Here they introduce a major theme of the book. The author will address this topic in detail in chs. 8–10. Luther glories in the significance of what our Savior has done for us since the Lord graciously accomplishes what we are unable to do. "We should despair of our penitence, of our purification from sins; for before we repent, our sins have already been forgiven. Indeed, first His very purification, on the contrary, also produces penitence in us, just as His righteousness produces our righteousness" (LW 29:112). *He sat down.* As with "making purification for sins," these words foreshadow a topic that will be addressed in more detail later in the book. Christ's sitting down indicates that His work was complete (cf. 10:11–14; Mk 16:19). *at the right hand.* The right hand of God does not refer to a physical location but rather represents the fullness of God's authority and glory (cf. Ps 110:1). In the OT, the chief court official was seated at the king's right hand as a symbol of his trusted status, power, and authority. The one at God's right hand has God's own power and authority. God is referred to as *the Majesty on high*, a Hbr. idiom that would have been familiar to the Jewish readers of this Epistle.

1:1–3 in Devotion and Prayer God communicates with His people. He wants us to know Him. We do not deserve this, but He graciously chooses to speak to us. Clearly, He is determined that we hear Him. He does not simply speak once and then leave us alone. Though His people often fail to listen, close their ears to His voice, or distort what He says, God keeps reaching out with His Word. He sends His prophets again and again. His messengers use various methods to communicate. Again and again they bring His word. At many times—in many ways—God spoke. Even one time and one way was more than humanity deserved, but God still sent the prophets. Sometimes His people listened and sometimes not. And still, God kept trying. In these last days, He has spoken by His Son. Jesus Christ is the revelation of God. He Himself is the message, the Word made flesh. He has made God known to us, for He is God. And still God keeps giving. Jesus spoke God's Word and then gave Himself as the atoning sacrifice for the sin of the world. His completed work has redeemed us. This is what God reveals. In these last days, He speaks forgiveness, life, and salvation in Jesus' name. He speaks to you. Listen to Him! •

In many times and various ways God's voice was clearly heard As prophets, by the Spirit sent, Proclaimed the holy word.

But in the fullness of God's time The Father sent His Son The Word to speak the word to us The sole-begotten One.

As You have promised, may Your word Like rain upon the earth Accomplish all that You desire Bring many to rebirth.

All glory to our God above And praise to Jesus be And glory to the Spirit, blest Through all eternity. Amen. (Steven P. Mueller, 2009)

PART 2

JESUS' SUPERIORITY (1:4–10:18)

Over the Angels (1:4–2:18)

ESV	KJV

[4]having become as much superior to angels as the name he has inherited is more excellent than theirs.
 [5]For to which of the angels did God ever say,
 	
 "You are my Son,
   today I have begotten you"?
 Or again,
 	
 "I will be to him a father,
   and he shall be to me a son"?
 	
 [6]And again, when he brings the firstborn into the world, he says,
 	
 "Let all God's angels worship him."
 	
 [7]Of the angels he says,
 	
 "He makes his angels winds,
   and his ministers a flame of fire."
 	
 [8]But of the Son he says,
 	
 "Your throne, O God, is forever
   and ever,
   the scepter of uprightness is
     the scepter of your kingdom.
 [9]You have loved righteousness and
   hated wickedness;
   therefore God, your God, has
     anointed you with the oil
     of gladness beyond your
     companions."
	[4]Being made so much better than the angels, as he hath by inheritance obtained a more excellent name than they.
	 [5]For unto which of the angels said he at any time, Thou art my Son, this day have I begotten thee? And again, I will be to him a Father, and he shall be to me a Son?
	 [6]And again, when he bringeth in the firstbegotten into the world, he saith, And let all the angels of God worship him.
	 [7]And of the angels he saith, Who maketh his angels spirits, and his ministers a flame of fire.
	 [8]But unto the Son he saith, Thy throne, O God, is for ever and ever: a sceptre of righteousness is the sceptre of thy kingdom.
	 [9]Thou hast loved righteousness, and hated iniquity; therefore God, even thy God, hath anointed thee with the oil of gladness above thy fellows.
	 [10]And, Thou, Lord, in the beginning hast laid the foundation of the earth; and the heavens are the works of thine hands:
	 [11]They shall perish; but thou remainest; and they all shall wax old as doth a garment;

[10]And,

"You, Lord, laid the foundation of
the earth in the beginning,
and the heavens are the work of
your hands;
[11]they will perish, but you remain;
they will all wear out like a garment,
[12]like a robe you will roll them up,
like a garment they will be
changed.
But you are the same,
and your years will have no end."

[13]And to which of the angels has he
ever said,

"Sit at my right hand
until I make your enemies a
footstool for your feet"?

[14]Are they not all ministering spirits
sent out to serve for the sake of those
who are to inherit salvation?

2 [1]Therefore we must pay much
closer attention to what we have
heard, lest we drift away from it. [2]For
since the message declared by angels
proved to be reliable, and every transgression or disobedience received a
just retribution, [3]how shall we escape
if we neglect such a great salvation?
It was declared at first by the Lord,
and it was attested to us by those
who heard, [4]while God also bore
witness by signs and wonders and
various miracles and by gifts of the
Holy Spirit distributed according to
his will.

[5]Now it was not to angels that God
subjected the world to come, of
which we are speaking. [6]It has been
testified somewhere,

"What is man, that you are mindful of him,

[12]And as a vesture shalt thou fold
them up, and they shall be changed:
but thou art the same, and thy years
shall not fail.
[13]But to which of the angels said
he at any time, Sit on my right hand,
until I make thine enemies thy footstool?
[14]Are they not all ministering spirits,
sent forth to minister for them who
shall be heirs of salvation?

2 [1]Therefore we ought to give the
more earnest heed to the things
which we have heard, lest at any time
we should let them slip.
[2]For if the word spoken by angels
was stedfast, and every transgression
and disobedience received a just recompence of reward;
[3]How shall we escape, if we neglect
so great salvation; which at the first
began to be spoken by the Lord, and
was confirmed unto us by them that
heard him;
[4]God also bearing them witness,
both with signs and wonders, and
with divers miracles, and gifts of the
Holy Ghost, according to his own
will?
[5]For unto the angels hath he not
put in subjection the world to come,
whereof we speak.
[6]But one in a certain place testified, saying, What is man, that thou
art mindful of him? or the son of man
that thou visitest him?
[7]Thou madest him a little lower than
the angels; thou crownedst him with
glory and honour, and didst set him
over the works of thy hands:
[8]Thou hast put all things in subjection under his feet. For in that he put
all in subjection under him, he left
nothing that is not put under him.

or the son of man, that you care for him?
⁷You made him for a little while lower than the angels;
you have crowned him with glory and honor,
⁸putting everything in subjection under his feet."

Now in putting everything in subjection to him, he left nothing outside his control. At present, we do not yet see everything in subjection to him. ⁹But we see him who for a little while was made lower than the angels, namely Jesus, crowned with glory and honor because of the suffering of death, so that by the grace of God he might taste death for everyone.

¹⁰For it was fitting that he, for whom and by whom all things exist, in bringing many sons to glory, should make the founder of their salvation perfect through suffering. ¹¹For he who sanctifies and those who are sanctified all have one source. That is why he is not ashamed to call them brothers, ¹²saying,

"I will tell of your name to my brothers;
in the midst of the congregation I will sing your praise."

¹³And again,

"I will put my trust in him."

And again,

"Behold, I and the children God has given me."

¹⁴Since therefore the children share in flesh and blood, he himself likewise partook of the same things, that through death he might destroy the one who has the power of death, that is, the devil, ¹⁵and deliver all those

But now we see not yet all things put under him.

⁹But we see Jesus, who was made a little lower than the angels for the suffering of death, crowned with glory and honour; that he by the grace of God should taste death for every man.

¹⁰For it became him, for whom are all things, and by whom are all things, in bringing many sons unto glory, to make the captain of their salvation perfect through sufferings.

¹¹For both he that sanctifieth and they who are sanctified are all of one: for which cause he is not ashamed to call them brethren,

¹²Saying, I will declare thy name unto my brethren, in the midst of the church will I sing praise unto thee.

¹³And again, I will put my trust in him. And again, Behold I and the children which God hath given me.

¹⁴Forasmuch then as the children are partakers of flesh and blood, he also himself likewise took part of the same; that through death he might destroy him that had the power of death, that is, the devil;

¹⁵And deliver them who through fear of death were all their lifetime subject to bondage.

¹⁶For verily he took not on him the nature of angels; but he took on him the seed of Abraham.

¹⁷Wherefore in all things it behoved him to be made like unto his brethren, that he might be a merciful and faithful high priest in things pertaining to God, to make reconciliation for the sins of the people.

¹⁸For in that he himself hath suffered being tempted, he is able to succour them that are tempted.

who through fear of death were subject to lifelong slavery. [16]For surely it is not angels that he helps, but he helps the offspring of Abraham. [17]Therefore he had to be made like his brothers in every respect, so that he might become a merciful and faithful high priest in the service of God, to make propitiation for the sins of the people. [18]For because he himself has suffered when tempted, he is able to help those who are being tempted.

Introduction to 1:4–2:18 Following the powerful assertions of Christ's divine identity and work in vv. 1–3, Hebrews launches immediately into its first topic: Christ is superior to the angels. In fact, there is no grammatical break between the introduction and this first section. What v. 4 says about Christ's supremacy to the angels is textually connected to His sitting at the right hand of the divine Majesty (v. 3). This section's focus on Christ's relationship to angels raises interesting questions. While we do not know the specific context of the anonymous author and recipients of this sermon/letter (see Anonymous, pp. 11–12), it is easy to discern some of their challenges by what is written to them. This section makes it clear that some struggled with biblical and nonbiblical teachings of angels, as well as the significance of such teaching to the person and work of Christ. It may be that some were struggling with gnostic ideas that considered spiritual beings to be better than beings with a physical existence. Since angels are pure spirit, does this make them better than Jesus who took on human flesh? Does Christ's assumption of a human nature impose a lesser status upon Him? By returning readers to Scripture, the author shows the consistent biblical teaching about angels and about the Christ. This is no theoretical discourse, but he clearly shows how these doctrines impact our own life and faith.

1:4 *superior to angels.* Angels, although holy and great, were created by God. Since, as v. 3 has already reminded us, Jesus is the one through whom all things were created, He is, therefore, the creator of the angels. The creator is obviously greater than the things that He made. Moreover, Jesus, through His suffering and humility, resurrection and exaltation, showed all creation that He was truly the eternal Son of the Father and that He was and is far above any creature. At the completion of His work, He "sat down at the right hand of the Majesty on high" (v. 3). No angel has such a lofty position—it belongs to God alone. Furthermore, their respective names testify to His supremacy. These created beings have the name "angel" which means "messenger." They serve at God's will. But in contrast, *the name He has inherited,* that is, the title "Son" that is His by virtue of His eternal relationship with the Father, is vastly superior. It expresses the wonder that Jesus, the Son of Mary, is also the Son of God from eternity. By nature and by work, Jesus is "far above . . . every name that is named not only in this age, but also in the one to come" (Eph 1:21). His is the name that "is above every name" (cf. Php 2:1–11). No angel has a name like His. Hus notes the significance of His supremacy when he writes: "Christ alone is the head of the universal church" (*The Church*, p. 27). Similarly, Wesley said: "The Jews gloried in their law, as it was delivered by the ministration of angels. How much more may we glory in the gospel, which was given, not by the ministry of angels, but of the very Son of God!" (Wesley, 565).

1:5–13 Christ's supremacy to the angels is not a new teaching. As is done repeatedly in this Epistle, the author marshals evidence from the OT to demonstrate the consistency of God's Word and its fulfillment in Christ. God spoke by the prophets (v. 1), so the prophetic word is thoroughly cited to support his claims. Here seven passages from the OT (five of them from the Psalms) are presented to show that the Messiah was foretold to be the Son of God. As such, He is superior to the angels. This is not only true in these last days (1:2); it was true in the time of the prophets and it is eternally true.

1:5 The first of the string of OT quotations, Ps 2:2 foreshadows Christ, who is not a created being but is the creator, the very *Son* of God. As the only *begotten* Son, He Himself is God. One creates or makes things that are different than oneself. One begets someone of the same nature. God begets God; everyone and everything else is created. This affirmation of Christ's deity consequently demonstrates His supremacy to everything else. This makes the question *To which of the angels . . . ?* rhetorical. It is obvious that no angel was ever addressed in such words; they apply to Christ (cf. Ac 13:33). This assertion is reinforced by citing 2Sm 7:14, showing the relationship of Father and Son. While that verse was originally spoken of David,

2Sm 7:13 shows a messianic meaning when it says, "I will establish the throne of his kingdom forever." Thus it is no surprise that Hebrews sees these words referring to God the Father and God the Son.

1:6 *the firstborn.* A firstborn son stood in a special position. He would receive an inheritance double that of his brothers (Dt 21:16–17) and generally was in a position of leadership over them. A king's firstborn son was typically the successor to the throne. Because Jesus is the "firstborn" of the Father, the glory, honor, and power of the Father also belong to Jesus. (Cf. Col 1:15 where Jesus is called "the firstborn of all creation.") The quotation of Dt 32:43 (cited from the LXX) underscores this. Not only is Jesus the firstborn; the angels are told to worship Him. Rm 8:29 calls Jesus "the firstborn among many brothers." This recognizes His unique status as God's only begotten Son but also notes the fruits of His work: that through Him many people are adopted into God's family.

1:7 Angels are a wonderful part of God's creation. God, who "makes the clouds his chariot" and "rides on the wings of the wind" (Ps 104:3), has made the angels (which literally means "His messengers") *winds* and *a flame of fire.* In Ps 104:4, the source of this quotation, these words describe the angels that accompany God and demonstrate His glory. They are poetically depicted as powerful natural phenomena. In this context "flame of fire" may refer to lightning bolts. While there is a sense of mystery and awe that is associated with these beings, they remain creatures and are not divine. This contrasts with Jesus' status as the firstborn Son who shares in the divine nature of His Father.

1:8–9 Ps 45, quoted here, is a royal psalm in which the king receives the promises made by God (cf. 2Sm 7:13). God made extraordinary promises to David. While He was faithful in keeping those promises, they see their ultimate fulfillment in Jesus, the descendant of David. *Your throne, O God* recognizes both its source and the divine king who will occupy the throne. His eternal throne endures *forever and ever.* Only Jesus truly establishes and occupies an eternal throne, and His reign brings God's own righteousness and joy. This remarkable passage is a stark contrast to what was just said of the angels in v. 7. It is true that angels are honored as winds and fire, but the Christ is the eternal king who loves *righteousness* and reigns with *uprightness.* In the OT, kings were *anointed* as a sign of their office (1Sm 16:12; 1Ki 1:34), as were priests (Ex 40:13) and sometimes prophets (1Ki 19:16). The Hbr. word "Messiah" means "anointed one" as does the Gk "Christ." Ac 10:38 says, "God anointed Jesus of Nazareth with the Holy Spirit and with power." This is uniquely true of Him. He is anointed *beyond* all others—with the ultimate anointing as the Lord's Christ.

1:10–12 Ps 102, quoted here, is the prayer of a person who is suffering from physical distress and derision from his enemies. The psalmist cries out to the omnipotent divine creator who *laid the foundations of the earth in the beginning,* a clear allusion to Gn 1:1. God does not merely create various things and creatures, but the very foundations of the earth (cf. Jb 38:4–11). He creates from nothing, calling all into being by His word of command. But His creation is not limited to the earth; rather, *the heavens are the work of Your hands.* All things that exist, "visible and invisible," as the Nicene Creed says, are created by God. As in v. 2, the author clearly indicates the role of God the Son in creation. This work demonstrates that He—the Creator—is categorically different than His angelic creatures. The psalmist is part of God's creation and so he contrasts his own vulnerable, transitory life with God and His eternal kingdom. The natural world, created by God, is not eternal. It will *perish . . . wear out like a garment.* Human beings, too, will perish and wear out. The psalm, however, hints at something more. The world *will be changed.* Like a *robe* or a *garment* that is taken off and exchanged for another when it is worn beyond usefulness, God will change His creation. As Peter writes, "we are waiting for new heavens and a new earth" (2Pt 3:13). We trust this promise because it comes from our God who says, "Heaven and earth will pass away, but my words will not pass away" (Mt 24:35). This description of the temporal nature of creation is given to reveal just how different Christ is from His creation. Not only is He the creator; His very nature marks Him as different from all other beings. *You are the same.* The Son of God is immutable in nature and character (cf. 13:8; Mal 3:6). Consequently we can confidently trust what He says. The reliability of God's promises will be considered again in 7:21. Finally, this passage confesses that *Your years will have no end.* God is eternal and since Jesus is the God-man, He shares this attribute and is eternal. The principle reason this passage is cited here is to show the supremacy of Jesus to the angels—and it has certainly demonstrated that truth. Jesus is the eternal, immutable Creator.

1:13 This is the first citation of Ps 110, a messianic psalm that is frequently cited in Hebrews and is the most-quoted psalm in the entire NT. Jesus Himself quotes it against the Pharisees who are puzzled by its meaning (e.g., Mt 22:42–46). It will be pivotal as Hebrews discusses the priesthood of Jesus (cf. 5:6). Here it is cited, with these other passages from the psalms, to demonstrate the uniqueness of Christ and His supremacy to the angels. No angel and no other creature was ever given such an invitation. *sit at My right hand.* The "right hand" is a metaphor for the highest position of trusted power and authority. The repetition of "right hand" from 1:3 (see note there) brackets this section of biblical teaching on the angels. Jesus is the One who sits at the right hand of God the Father Almighty. Here, the citation continues, *until I make Your enemies a footstool.* In the ancient Near East a conqueror might literally place his foot on his vanquished enemies to indicate his dominance and triumph. This occurred, for example, in Jsh 10:24: "when they brought those kings out to Joshua, Joshua summoned all the men of Israel and said to the chiefs of the men of war who had gone with him, 'Come near; put your feet on the necks of these kings.' Then they came near and put their feet on their necks." The combination of sitting at God's right hand and the placing of enemies underfoot affirms Christ's divine nature and office. He is the Son of God and superior to all other beings.

1:14 *ministering spirits . . . serve.* This verse concludes the author's teaching about the supremacy of Jesus over the angels. Having seen the remarkable statements about Christ that are not made of the angels, the conclusion is obvious: Jesus, the Son of God, is greater than the angels. But does that mean that angels are nothing? No, they are servants of God, sent by Him, and a blessing to His people. Indeed, they are *ministering spirits.* They are sent to *serve.* This is their purpose and calling. They obey the will of God, their Master (cf. Ps 91:11; 103:20–21). What's more, the service is directed at *those who are to inherit salvation.* That means they are sent to us, those who are blessed by the Father, through the work of Christ, to inherit the treasures won for us by Jesus (Mt 25:34). As children inherit from their parents, so Christians inherit with Christ all that the Father has to give. Jesus, our elder brother, includes us by grace in His family with its riches. We thank God for the angels, but must not give them the honor or status that belong to God alone.

1:4–14 in Devotion and Prayer Don't mistake the servant for the Master! It is appropriate for us to be thankful when we are blessed by others. When, for example, a present is delivered to us, we may express our appreciation to the servant who drove the delivery truck and carried the package, but we do not mistake them for the person who sent this gift. We know that it was not given to us by the deliverer. That person came at the request of the sender. We rightly recognize and thank the person who gave the gift. Because God's people are sinful, when we encounter the many blessings that come from God Himself, we may, at times, become confused. We may be tempted to confuse the servant who delivers gifts with the God who gives them. When God sends us faithful ministers, they serve with His gifts on His behalf. It is appropriate for us to thank such servants and be grateful for them, but not to confuse them with God. Our pastors and other servants of the Gospel minister with His gifts; the glory belongs to God alone. Similarly, God's angelic servants seem to have confused the recipients of this Letter, and they may still confuse some Christians today. We may be tempted either to give them too much credit or, on the other hand, we may overlook the wonderful gift God gives us in the angels. But God still keeps giving His various gifts, and He keeps sending His servants to help His people. So thank God for the angels! They are a blessing to His people. They "guard us" in all our ways and "bear us up" (Ps 91:11). They are "ministering spirits sent to serve for the sake of those who are to inherit salvation" (Heb 1:14). What a gift! But do not confuse the servant for the Master who sent him. When St. John was tempted to worship an angel, God's angelic servant responded "You must not do that! I am a fellow servant with you and your brothers the prophets and with those who keep the words of this book. Worship God" (Rev 22:9). We are not to worship the angels nor to put them in God's place. Rather, we worship with them. "With angels and archangels and with all the company of heaven, we laud and magnify" God's glorious name, evermore praising Him who is holy. • Lord Jesus Christ, eternally begotten Son of God, You are the creator and sustainer of the universe. We thank You for Your gift of the holy angels who guard us. Strengthen our faith that we may receive Your gracious gifts with glad hearts and join with the host of heaven to worship You now and forever. Amen.

31

2:1 *Therefore . . . closer attention.* The superiority of Christ to the angels, demonstrated with ample evidence from the OT (1:5–13), has consequences. As He is superior to the angels, so His Word is supreme. Ancient Israel once listened to the Law which was delivered by angels (cf. v. 2). How much more should Christians give their whole attention to the Word that has been delivered by Jesus, God's eternal Son. The message He brings is worthy not only of attention, but of the very closest attention. Without Christ and His Gospel, we have nothing. *what we have heard.* This is the Gospel of Jesus, the Son of God, whose sacrifice cleanses us from sin. This Gospel is the "power of God to salvation to everyone who believes" (Rm 1:16). *lest we drift away.* The loss of faith is not always a dramatic rejection; it often starts as one begins to move away from God and His truth. The author describes this as "drifting." As a boat that is cut free from its moorings can slowly float away with the passing tide and become lost, so a Christian who does not hear God's Word may soon find themselves far away from Him. St. Paul notes this danger with similar terms in Eph 4:14, warning that Christians not be "tossed to and fro by the waves and carried about by every wind of doctrine, by human cunning, by craftiness in deceitful schemes." Hebrews would have us mindful of this danger so that we are not complacent but eager to receive God's Word with glad and faithful hearts.

2:2 *the message declared by angels.* While the Exodus account does not specify the role of angels in delivering the Law, which was spoken by God (Ex 20:1), the role of the angels is mentioned by Stephen (Ac 7:38, 53) and Paul (Gal 3:19). Evidently, some were using such ideas to overstate the role of the angels, who actually are "ministering spirits" (1:14) and subject to Christ. Here the author is expanding on the contrast of the previous verses. As Christ is superior to the angels, so the Gospel is superior to the Law. *reliable.* This word can also mean "valid," "in force," or "guaranteed." This description is an affirmation of the divine source and authority of the Law. It is God's Word and therefore is holy and true. The Law is not to be taken lightly or ignored. In fact, this is the reason why *every transgression or disobedience received a just retribution.* God's Law is authoritative. Any violation of the Law merits the appropriate punishment, including the final punishment of death (Rm 6:23) and damnation. Whether intentional or not, whether by commission or omission, whether seen by other people or known only to God, any violation of the Law merits judgment. If we have only the Law, all stand condemned and are without hope, for all have sinned.

2:3 *how shall we escape if we neglect such a great salvation?* Under the Law, humanity stands condemned and has no hope. But according to God's grace and mercy, Jesus' sacrifice frees people from the curse of the Law (cf. Gal 3:13). This is a free gift of God. He is our life and only hope. Yet we must remember that God's grace is specifically located in Christ. God freely gives salvation, but He gives it in the work of His Son. "There is salvation in no one else, for there is no other name under heaven by which we must be saved" (Ac 4:12). If this gift God has given is neglected, that is, if there is no regard for what He has done, no faith in Him and His work, there is no other means of salvation. Those who despise Christ will not escape the just punishment for their sin. Note that the author speaks these words inclusively: both he and his readers are addressed by these cautioning words. The warning is for us and for the entire world: Jesus is the only Savior. Only He can deliver us. Do not turn away from Him! *declared at first by the Lord.* Jesus declared the Gospel of Salvation in His preaching and enacted it in His work. (cf. Lk 19:10; Jn 3:16–17; 14:6). *attested to us by those who heard.* The eyewitnesses to Jesus testified to His teaching (cf. Lk 1:2; Ac 5:32). We have received their testimony in the books of the NT. These words suggest that the writer of Hebrews was not St. Paul or one of the Twelve, because they were directly called by Jesus and received the Word directly from Him. In contrast, the author states that he heard this message through those who first heard Jesus.

2:4 *God also bore witness.* The Gospel was revealed by Jesus Himself (v. 3). Eyewitnesses heard Him and saw His work and faithfully handed on their testimony (v. 3). In addition to this, the Father and the Holy Spirit attested to the message of salvation through *signs and wonders and various miracles.* (Cf. Ac 2:22, 43; 1Jn 5:7–8; see also notes at 10:5–18). While we may first think of specific miraculous signs when we hear such words, the writer also includes, as evidence, the broader category of *gifts of the Holy Spirit.* Literally this simply says, "and the Holy Spirit distributed according to His will." This may means the "gifts" of the Holy Spirit as the ESV translates, for God chooses to bless His people with everything needed to live by faith. (Cf. Rm 12:6–8; 1Co 12–14; Gal 5:22–23; Eph 4:11–12). God gives gifts to His people to be used for the good of the Church. It may also be taken more broadly to say that the gift of the Holy Spirit Himself is God's testimony to the truth. While both ideas are consistent with Scripture, we do well to remember that the Spirit's first and most important gift is faith (cf. 1Co 12:3; Jn 14:26). This meaning also accords with the rest of this passage: do not neglect the gift of faith in Christ that has been given by the Holy Spirit. Taken together, this passage demonstrates that the entire Trinity is concerned with our salvation and testifies to us and that God strives to keep us in the faith.

2:1–4 in Devotion and Prayer The admonitions of Hebrews found here and in other passages can sound like strict warnings, and indeed they are! The Gospel is an amazing gift, but it is exclusive. Jesus is "the way, and the truth, and the life." No one comes to the Father except through Him (Jn 14:6). Without Jesus, we are on our own, trapped in the hopelessness of our sin, and deserving only judgment. Thanks be to God that He has not left us in this state. Jesus Himself secured our salvation and reveals it to us. The apostles testify to Him and to His vicarious death and resurrection which they witnessed. God has given us His inspired Word through these witnesses, and by His Holy Spirit He continues to testify to His Church through pastors, teachers, and the witness of other Christians as they proclaim that Word and exercise the gifts of the Spirit in service. God surrounds us with His Gospel, speaking it to us again and again so that we do not turn to our own hopeless devices and push His gifts away. He provides all that is needed for us to receive this precious gift of salvation. • Lord Jesus, thank You for Your salvation and for revealing Your Gospel to me. By Your Holy Spirit, keep me in the faith. Let me not close my ears to Your voice but always attend to Your gracious Word of forgiveness, life, and salvation. Bless me that I may help share that grace with others who need to hear. Amen.

2:5 The holy angels watch over God's people. He has given His angels to watch over and protect believers (Ps 91:11–12) and has appointed certain angels to watch over the nations of this world (cf. Dn 10:13). But the Son of God has greater authority than they do. He has authority over the whole of creation, including the angels. Any authority they have has been given to them by God who is supreme. He reigns eternally. The present age and also the *world to come*, all things in the future, are *subjected* to Him. Christ is supreme.

Calvin compared the original dominion of man over creation and the subjection of all things to Christ, saying:

I indeed allow that man was at first put in possession of the world, that he might rule over all the works of God; but by his own defection he deserved the loss of his dominion, for it was a just punishment for ingratitude as to one thus favoured, that the Lord, whom lie refused to acknowledge and faithfully to worship, should have deprived him of a right previously granted to him. As soon, then, as Adam alienated himself from God through sin, he was justly deprived of the good things which he had received; not that he was denied the use of them, but that he could have had no right to them after he had forsaken God. And in the very use of them God intended that there should he some tokens of this loss of right, such as these,—the wild beasts ferociously attack us, those who ought to be awed by our presence are dreaded by us, some never obey us, others can hardly be trained to submit, and they do us harm in various ways; the earth answers not our expectations in cultivating it; the sky, the air, the sea, and other things are often adverse to us. But were all creatures to continue in subjection, yet whatever the sons of Adam possessed would be deemed a robbery; for what can they call their own when they themselves are not God's? (Calvin 56–57)

Similarly, Bengel wrote concerning the difference in authority between the angels and the Christ:

God subjected both angels and all things, not to the angels, of whom nothing was written to that effect [implying any such intention], but to man, or the Son of Man, Jesus Christ. The angels had more to do in the Old Testament; but in the New Testament, when human nature was exalted by Christ, the angels are our fellow-servants. I ventured to say, more to do; and it may be also supposed from the antithesis, that greater reverence was due to the angels in the Old Testament than in the New Testament, where they are now our fellow-servants. And from this very circumstance, that they are our fellow-servants, we understand that they are not inactive under, the New Testament, but merely that they act under a different relation from that under which they acted under the Old Testament. (Bengel 4:351–52)

2:6–8 Ps 8, quoted here, reflects on the apparent insignificance of human beings in contrast to the great significance that God gives to them. The parallelism of the psalm carries a much deeper meaning when it is remembered that Jesus calls Himself the Son of Man (e.g., Mk 2:10).

35

2:6 *testified somewhere.* We are accustomed to fast and easy access to specific references from Scripture and so may be surprised at this generic reference. Here the author may be citing from memory or from notes, since finding specific references in a scroll was difficult. Though he often quotes Scripture, he does not provide specific references but in most cases simply notes the book that they came from. Chapter and verse numbers were later additions to the text, made in order to facilitate easier use. The writer's freer style of quoting is an example of the human side of the inspired Scriptures. He, and his readers, undoubtedly recognized the words of the psalm even without a reference. *What is man . . . the son of man.* These words may originally have been seen simply as poetic parallelism. A richer meaning becomes evident when they are read in light of Christ, the Son of Man. The humble tone indicates that the psalmist recognizes the relationship of humanity to its creator. Why should God pay any attention to such creatures? We have no right to think that He would be *mindful* of us, much less *care for* us. Yet we marvel at the gracious truth that God does, in fact, care for His creation and for humankind.

2:7 *for a little while lower.* In the psalm's parallelism this applies both to "man" and "the son of man." As the angels were charged with protecting human beings (see note, v. 5), humans are lower than the angels. Since the Son of God assumed human flesh and became part of His creation during the time of His humiliation, He did not always or fully use His divine prerogatives and attributes. Thus the Lord was, in a sense, lower than the angels. But neither is a permanent state. Jesus resumed the full exercise of His divine attributes in His exaltation and the angels are subject to Him. Furthermore, because of His work, humanity will once more be restored to be the crown of God's creation. The "little while" will come to an end in heaven. Jesus is already *crowned with glory and honor,* recognized for who He is. "God has highly exalted him . . . at the name of Jesus every knee should bow, in heaven and on earth and under the earth, and every tongue confess that Jesus Christ is Lord, to the glory of God the Father" (Php 2:10–11). As part of creation, the angels, too, bow before Him and confess that He is Lord.

2:8 *subjection.* Ps 8:6 speaks of human beings, who have dominion over the earth and its creatures (cf. Gn 1:28). Being fully human, Jesus also shares in this dominion over creation. Yet He is also fully divine and, being God, He has still greater dominion. All creation is subject to its Creator. *under His feet.* These words recall the imagery of victory in Ps 110:1 and cited in 1:13. Here it is not only His enemies but all things that are under Him. Everything in creation is subject to Christ; there are no limits to this, since *He left nothing outside of His control.* When the child of God looks at the world, he or she may question this statement since it doesn't always seem to align with our observations. In the midst of life's challenges, we are tempted to think that God is not in control. The author of Hebrews notes this, saying *we do not yet see everything in subjection.* Our observation, however, is incomplete. By faith alone (cf. Heb 11:1–3), we confess Jesus' authority over our own lives and His authority over all things, even though life may, at times, seem out of control. (Cf. 1Co 15:25; Php 3:21.) What we see *at present* is temporary; God is bringing everything under subjection to Christ and we will fully see this at His return.

2:9 *made lower than the angels.* This repeats the idea quoted in v. 7 and makes the application to Jesus explicit. These words do not refer to Jesus' incarnation, which is not for "a little while" but eternal. They speak of what is known as the doctrine of Christ's humiliation. Before His resurrection and ascension, Jesus did not always or fully choose to demonstrate or utilize His divine power, attributes, and prerogatives, and so appeared lower than the angels. By taking the form of a servant, He appeared to be less authoritative than those glorious beings. Still, even while He was in His state of humiliation, the angels are upheld by His word (1:3), as is the rest of creation. Christ's entered His state of humiliation in order to save us. Bengel wrote:

> The apostle takes away from the Jews the offensive scandal (stumbling-block) of the cross: and so refutes the argument, which might be drawn from the sufferings of Christ against His glory, and that glory the source of glory to us also, as that he even inverts it [turns it into an argument for, instead of against, Christ]. He shows that the suffering of death is so far from obstructing the glory and honour of the Messiah, that it rather confirms them to us. Whence he infers, that the fact of Jesus being "made lower than the angels," which was only for a little, did not refer to the circumstance that He should continue under the power of death, but that, after He had once suffered death to the utmost. He should have everything made subject to Him. It is Jesus to whom the humbling

and crowning, as described in the psalm, apply. It is therefore the same Person, to whom also the power over all appropriately belongs, which (power) follows close after, in the gradation of the psalm. (Bengel 4:356)

crowned with glory and honor. Through Jesus' death and resurrection, His true status as God's Son was revealed to the sinful world, and God the Father exalted Him (cf. Php 2:9–11). In His state of exaltation, Christ no longer restrains the use of His divine attributes and prerogatives but fully uses them for the sake of His Church. *because of the suffering and death.* There was nothing accidental about the work of Christ. His status and exaltation are not in spite of His suffering. On the contrary, Christ is exalted because of His suffering and death. God's character is clearly revealed in the suffering of Christ on behalf of sinners. *by the grace of God.* This is God's nature and character: He is gracious. God has freely provided His Son as the sacrifice for the sin of the world (Jn 19). *taste death for everyone.* Jesus' death has drained the cup of sin and death that poisoned every person (cf. Rm 5:12–17). Because of Christ's vicarious death, anyone who keeps His word "will never taste death" (Jn 8:52). *for everyone.* The significance of Jesus' sacrifice is not dependent on anything in mankind. He died to reconcile not only believers but also the whole world to God (2Co 5:19; cf. Jn 12:32).

2:10 *it was fitting.* God's actions do not always fit humanity's expectations. Fallen human logic may think that God cannot or should not suffer on behalf of His creatures. The suffering of God scandalizes and offends those who presume to decree what is fitting for God. St. Paul recognized this truth, saying, "the wisdom of the cross is folly to those who are perishing" but "the foolishness of God is wiser than men, and the weakness of God is stronger than men" (2Co 1:18, 23). But the shocking truth is that God chooses to act in our best interest at the cost of the suffering and death of Christ. When God's gracious character and self-revelation are known, it is evident that such actions accord perfectly with His nature. Given who He is, these deeds consistently reveal His nature. It is fitting—His gracious nature is seen through this work. *He . . . by whom all things exist.* These words refer to God the Father, who created all things through His Son (1:2–3). Here the author is saying that the Father makes the founder of salvation—Jesus—perfect through suffering. The combined images of creation and redemption further emphasize God's giving character.

for whom. Creation belongs to the Creator. While God in His good-ness and grace gives many gifts to His creatures, it is important to remember that it all belongs to Him. St. Augustine appropriately in-cludes humanity among the things that belong to God as he reflects, "You have formed us for Yourself, and our hearts are restless until they find rest in You" (*NPNF*1 1:45). God can do whatever He wills with His creation. It is His, but He chooses to become part of His cre-ation, to suffer as part of it, in order to redeem it for Himself. In this work, He is *bringing many sons to glory.* Jesus' glory will be shared with all whom God leads in faith (cf. Rm 8:30). He has earned the glory but, by His grace, He shares it with Christians. He brings us to His eternal kingdom where we will dwell with Him in glory. *sons.* This word (Gk *huios*) includes both males and females and applies to persons of all ages. It is a relational description, describing chil-dren that belong to Him. God is not bringing slaves to Himself but His own beloved children. *the founder.* (Gk *archēgos*, author, leader). This is Jesus Himself (cf. 12:2). Faith is a gift of God and was estab-lished by the work of Christ. It all comes from Him, apart from any human contribution. *perfect through suffering.* This does not mean that there was something lacking in Jesus or that He was inferior or unholy in any way. "Perfect" (Gk *teleioō*) is based on the word for "end." It means "brought to its conclusion, finished, or complete." The work of Christ was finished in His passion (cf. Jn 19:30, "it is finished"). As God's eternal Son, Jesus demonstrated complete obe-dience to the Father through His suffering. As a test may demonstrate that a student has perfect or complete knowledge of a topic, the cross showed that Jesus completely obeyed the Father's will. Jesus' Passion led to His exaltation and glory. John Wesley notes that this passage speaks of Christ's perfection or completeness and that this is different than our salvation:

> What is here said of our Lord's being made perfect through suf-ferings, has no relation to our being saved or sanctified by [our] sufferings. Even he himself was perfect, as God and as man, before ever he suffered. By his sufferings, in his life and death, he was made a perfect or complete sin-offering. But unless we were to be made the same sacrifice, and to atone for sin, what is said of him in this respect is as much out of our sphere as his ascension into heaven. (Wesley, 568)

2:11 *sanctifies.* This means to make holy. Sinners are declared holy and righteous because of Christ's saving work (cf. 13:1; 10:10, 14). Humans do not sanctify themselves; God sanctifies us. We are *those who are sanctified.* While we passively receive this sanctification, which is earned by Christ, we yet have commonality with Him since the sanctifier and the sanctified both have *one source.* Because through Jesus the Father adopts us as His "sons" (v. 10), Jesus and Christians have God as their Father. We have been graciously adopted into His family (Rm 8:15). Additionally, Jesus, as a true human being, shares descent with us from the one human father, Adam. We are united to Christ in creation and, even more profoundly, in redemption. *not ashamed to call them brothers.* Jesus is ready to confess before the Father and all creation that all who believe in Him are truly His family (cf. Mt 12:48–50; 25:40). Since He has sanctified us by His blood, we stand with Him in righteousness.

2:12–13 These verses provide OT quotations that emphasize Jesus' solidarity with mankind.

2:12 In Ps 22, David prays to God because he is suffering from persecution and distress. He ends with the confident confession of the Lord's righteousness (Ps 22:22) that is quoted here. Jesus, David's descendant and heir, prayed a portion of this psalm on the cross (Mt 27:46; Mk 15:34). It is fitting that this psalm, spoken from the cross, shows that we are His *brothers* and that our Savior has told us of God's *name.* Jesus, the Son of God and our brother, reveals the Father to us (cf. 1:2 and note; Jn 1:18).

2:13 These words from Isaiah (8:17–18) speak of the trust that the prophet and his family had in the face of coming judgment. They also describe Jesus, who while suffering judgment for humanity's sin, placed His trust completely in His Father. As the eternal Son of God, Jesus says, *I will put My trust in Him.* Since He is "bringing many sons to glory" (v. 10), the redeemed, who are *the children God has given,* now also put their trust in God. Jesus has bound Himself to those who place their trust in Him, and God has placed us in His unfailing care (Jn 17:2). These words show that the work of Christ is, in fact, effective: some have received His gifts and are now the children of God. Accordingly, John Calvin wrote,

> How much soever the doctrine of the Gospel may be a stone of stumbling to the household of the Church, it is not yet God's will that it should wholly fall; on the contrary, he bids it to be sealed

among his disciples: and Christ, in the name of all his teachers as the head of them, yea, as the only true Teacher, who rules us by their ministry, declares that amidst this deplorable ingratitude of the world, there shall still be some always who shall be obedient to God (Calvin 69).

2:14 *children share in flesh and blood.* This verse shows the critical need for Christ's incarnation. The children that God entrusted to Jesus (v. 13) are human beings and therefore are flesh and blood. Though fallen, our physical nature is part of God's creation that He once proclaimed "very good" (Gn 1:31). *partook of the same things,* that is, of "flesh and blood." Jesus became, and still remains, a real human being and truly is our brother. Although no other human has ever existed without physical flesh and blood, Christ Jesus preexisted as the eternal Son of God. In the fullness of time, He voluntarily took on our flesh for our salvation (cf. Jn 1:14). Through the incarnation, Jesus truly shares our human nature and experience, yet without sin. As the Lutheran reformers confessed,

> He did not receive a foreign nature, but our own flesh in the unity of His person. In this way He has become our true Brother. . . . Christ redeemed human nature as His work, sanctifies it, raises it from the dead, and gloriously adorns it as His work (FC Ep I 5–6).

Jesus partakes in our human nature, and has given His people a further gift in that Christians and their Lord also share the unique fellowship of His body and blood in the Lord's Supper (1Co 10:16–17). *through death . . . destroy.* Without the Incarnation, without taking on real flesh and blood, the Son of God would not have been able to die. His human nature was accompanied with the possibility of mortality. All other human beings face death as a consequence for sin; our Lord did not deserve death, but willingly chose to die as the sacrifice for the sin of the world (cf. Jn 1:29) Jesus' death absorbed God's judgment against sin. In this great reversal, Jesus, who knew no sin, bore all sin and the condemnation of death on the cross. *the power of death.* Death has a claim on those who sin (Rm 6:23), but that power has been destroyed by Jesus (cf. 1Co 15:54–56; 2Tm 1:10). Bengel wrote that Jesus' death is

> a paradox. Jesus suffered and overcame death; the devil, wielding death in his hand, succumbed. Jesus in turn imparts to us life through His flesh and blood; John vi. He assumed our nature, that His body might be delivered up, and His blood poured out.

41

Therefore the delivering up of the body and the pouring out of the blood are the facts which are chiefly had regard to: John vi. 51. . . . Death was the executioner and minister of the devil as a cruel master, delivering up men to him whom he led away in sin: but Jesus dying made them dying His own, Rom. xiv. 9. . . . His power was manifest: who it was that lurked beneath this power as wielding it, escaped the notice of mortal men. (Bengel 4:365–66)

the devil. Satan uses God's Law to bring accusations against those who have sinned. He tempts people to regard only their own works and not those of the Savior. But Jesus destroyed the devil and his works, as Luther wrote, "The devil's work is to crush us under his feet and, because of our sin, to dispatch us from life into death. . . . [Christ's] works are truly divine works such as: to justify, to restore to life, to save" (LW 13:135). As death is defeated, so is Satan (cf. 1Jn 3:8; Jn 16:11). Jesus is victorious over all.

2:15 *deliver.* Captive to sin and death, we are unable to free ourselves. Christ comes to free us. *all those.* This includes every other human being. Jesus comes for all, because all were in *lifelong slavery.* All who sin face death as a consequence of sin (Rm 6:23). Fear is an appropriate response by sinners who recognize their inability to deliver themselves. No excuse or rationalization can remove the fact that death awaits all mankind. The *fear of death* is a natural response of those who have no hope. Christ comes to deliver His people from that fate. Our only hope is God's deliverance in Him. We are bound in this fear unless God speaks His word of mercy in Christ (cf. Rm 8:15).

2:16 *surely it is not angels He helps.* Previous references to the angels demonstrated the superiority of Christ over them. Here another distinction is made: Christ came to redeem human beings, not angels. When the author speaks of *the offspring of Abraham,* he is not only referring to those of Jewish ancestry, for all who have faith in the Savior are the offspring of Abraham (cf. Gal 3:6–9, 26–29). In Abraham, through the work of His descendant Jesus, "all families of the earth shall be blessed" (Gn 12:3).

2:17 *therefore.* In order to redeem human beings, the Savior needed to be fully human Himself. Since humans are flesh and blood, the Savior *had to be* flesh and blood. He needed to fully share our nature. As Gregory of Nazianzen wrote, "that which He has not assumed He has not healed; but that which is united to His Godhead is also saved" (*NPNF2* 7:440). *like His brothers in every respect*. Jesus was, and is, a real human being who has shared in every aspect of human life, including the temptation to sin. The Incarnation is not partial. He did not become partially human or assume only portions of our existence and experience. Jesus embodies everything that it means to be truly human. He is perfectly human. Embedded in this argument is a further difference between Jesus and the angels. Jesus is not an angel; He is fully God and fully Man. There is no one like Him. Anticipating a substantial theme of this book, the reason here given for the Incarnation is so that Jesus could *become a merciful and faithful high priest*. As High Priest, Jesus intercedes for us and brings our needs to the Father because He knows the reality of human weakness. He is able to do this because, as High Priest, He sacrificed Himself for us and presents us, clothed in His righteousness, to the Father. He shows mercy by doing this for us and, in fulfilling all of His Father's will, was truly faithful. *In the service of God*. Jesus' sacrifice is given to God the Father and is not compelled by Satan or any other power. It is given by God, to God. Jesus went to the cross willingly, thwarting Satan's purposes (1Co 2:8; 1Jn 3:8). He does so out of love for His people and not out of selfish interest. *propitiation*. This word (Gk *hilaskomai*) describes reconciliation (as the KJV translates it), appeasement, or making one favorably inclined. Jesus' priestly work mercifully reconciles sinners with God. His perfect life, sacrificial death, and victorious resurrection removes the stain of sin, bringing human beings into a right relationship with the Father. This is what He does as our "merciful and faithful high priest." Bengel wrote concerning Christ's priesthood:

> Nowhere, except in the 110th Psalm, and Zech. vi. 13, and in this epistle, is Christ expressly called a Priest; and it is only in this epistle that the priesthood of Christ is professedly discussed. Whence it is evident, how extraordinary in its character, and how necessary, is this book of the New Testament. However, in all these passages, which are even of the Old Testament, there is added the mention of the kingdom, which is oftener spoken of elsewhere without the priesthood. Nay, on the Cross, on which this Priest offered His sacrifice, He had the title (inscription) of King. The priesthood, as well as the kingdom, is appropriate (belongs fittingly) to this First-begotten. (Bengel 4:369)

for the sins of the people. These words again emphasize the high priesthood of Christ. As the Levitical High Priests brought sacrifices and interceded for Israel, Jesus, our Great High Priest, offered the ultimate sacrifice of Himself and continues to intercede for His Church.

2:18 *He . . . has suffered . . . is able to help.* Jesus became truly human for us (v. 14). While He did not commit sin, He "in every respect has been tempted as we are" (4:15). These truths assure us personally. Even as He resisted temptation, He suffered the effects of our sin. Jesus has shared our experiences and truly understands our plight. This shared experience is a source of hope and strength to those who suffer and are *tempted* to doubt, despair, or other sins. Christ resisted all temptations and then gave His life as a propitiating sacrifice for all. He delivers us from temptation (cf. Mt 6:13), strengthens us in trial, and also shares His victory over sin with us.

2:5–18 in Devotion and Prayer How can we fathom what Jesus has done for us? What words could ever express the wonder of His grace or be sufficient gratitude for this amazing gift? Because of our sin, we deserved to live in slavery to the fear of death (v. 15), but God does not give us what we deserve. Instead of destroying His fallen creation, the Son of God became part of it. Calling us His brothers, He was made like us in every respect (v. 17). He endured temptation and suffering (v. 17) but committed no sin. He mercifully and faithfully served as our High Priest to make propitiation for our sin and reconcile us to the Father (v. 17). We sometimes are tempted to ask, "Who can understand what I am facing?" Jesus truly can. He has experienced every temptation and trial that we experience and endured them all without sinning. He who alone perfectly resisted all temptation exchanges our sin for His righteousness. Our High Priest declares that we are holy, righteous, and free! He will never forsake us but always intercedes for His people, and He will always help us when we are tempted. • Lord Jesus Christ, You became human to be our Savior. You faced all temptation without sin, but bore my sin to the cross. You have delivered me from slavery to the fear of death and have called me, and all Your people, Your brother. Bless and strengthen me, merciful Savior, that I may turn from sin, trust in You, and rejoice in all You have done for me. Amen.

Over Moses (3:1–4:13)

ESV	KJV
3 ¹Therefore, holy brothers, you who share in a heavenly calling, consider Jesus, the apostle and high priest of our confession, ²who was faithful to him who appointed him, just as Moses also was faithful in all God's house. ³For Jesus has been counted worthy of more glory than Moses—as much more glory as the builder of a house has more honor than the house itself. ⁴(For every house is built by someone, but the builder of all things is God.) ⁵Now Moses was faithful in all God's house as a servant, to testify to the things that were to be spoken later, ⁶but Christ is faithful over God's house as a son. And we are his house if indeed we hold fast our confidence and our boasting in our hope. ⁷Therefore, as the Holy Spirit says, "Today, if you hear his voice, ⁸do not harden your hearts as in the rebellion, on the day of testing in the wilderness, ⁹where your fathers put me to the test and saw my works for forty years. ¹⁰Therefore I was provoked with that generation, and said, 'They always go astray in their heart; they have not known my ways.' ¹¹As I swore in my wrath, 'They shall not enter my rest.' " ¹²Take care, brothers, lest there be in any of you an evil, unbelieving heart, leading you to fall away from the living God. ¹³But exhort one another every day, as long as it is called "today," that none of you may	*3* ¹Wherefore, holy brethren, partakers of the heavenly calling, consider the Apostle and High Priest of our profession, Christ Jesus; ²Who was faithful to him that appointed him, as also Moses was faithful in all his house. ³For this man was counted worthy of more glory than Moses, inasmuch as he who hath builded the house hath more honour than the house. ⁴For every house is builded by some man; but he that built all things is God. ⁵And Moses verily was faithful in all his house, as a servant, for a testimony of those things which were to be spoken after; ⁶But Christ as a son over his own house; whose house are we, if we hold fast the confidence and the rejoicing of the hope firm unto the end. ⁷Wherefore (as the Holy Ghost saith, To day if ye will hear his voice, ⁸Harden not your hearts, as in the provocation, in the day of temptation in the wilderness: ⁹When your fathers tempted me, proved me, and saw my works forty years. ¹⁰Wherefore I was grieved with that generation, and said, They do alway err in their heart; and they have not known my ways. ¹¹So I sware in my wrath, They shall not enter into my rest.) ¹²Take heed, brethren, lest there be in any of you an evil heart of unbelief, in departing from the living God.

be hardened by the deceitfulness of sin. [14]For we have come to share in Christ, if indeed we hold our original confidence firm to the end. [15]As it is said,

"Today, if you hear his voice, do not harden your hearts as in the rebellion."

[16]For who were those who heard and yet rebelled? Was it not all those who left Egypt led by Moses? [17]And with whom was he provoked for forty years? Was it not with those who sinned, whose bodies fell in the wilderness? [18]And to whom did he swear that they would not enter his rest, but to those who were disobedient? [19]So we see that they were unable to enter because of unbelief.

4 [1]Therefore, while the promise of entering his rest still stands, let us fear lest any of you should seem to have failed to reach it. [2]For good news came to us just as to them, but the message they heard did not benefit them, because they were not united by faith with those who listened. [3]For we who have believed enter that rest, as he has said,

"As I swore in my wrath, 'They shall not enter my rest,' "

although his works were finished from the foundation of the world. [4]For he has somewhere spoken of the seventh day in this way: "And God rested on the seventh day from all his works." [5]And again in this passage he said,

"They shall not enter my rest."

[6]Since therefore it remains for some to enter it, and those who formerly received the good news failed to enter because of disobedience, [7]again he appoints a certain day, "Today,"

[13]But exhort one another daily, while it is called To day; lest any of you be hardened through the deceitfulness of sin.

[14]For we are made partakers of Christ, if we hold the beginning of our confidence stedfast unto the end;

[15]While it is said, To day if ye will hear his voice, harden not your hearts, as in the provocation.

[16]For some, when they had heard, did provoke: howbeit not all that came out of Egypt by Moses.

[17]But with whom was he grieved forty years? was it not with them that had sinned, whose carcases fell in the wilderness?

[18]And to whom sware he that they should not enter into his rest, but to them that believed not?

[19]So we see that they could not enter in because of unbelief.

4 [1]Let us therefore fear, lest, a promise being left us of entering into his rest, any of you should seem to come short of it.

[2]For unto us was the gospel preached, as well as unto them: but the word preached did not profit them, not being mixed with faith in them that heard it.

[3]For we which have believed do enter into rest, as he said, As I have sworn in my wrath, if they shall enter into my rest: although the works were finished from the foundation of the world.

[4]For he spake in a certain place of the seventh day on this wise, And God did rest the seventh day from all his works.

[5]And in this place again, If they shall enter into my rest.

[6]Seeing therefore it remaineth that

saying through David so long afterward, in the words already quoted,

"Today, if you hear his voice, do not harden your hearts."

⁸For if Joshua had given them rest, God would not have spoken of another day later on. ⁹So then, there remains a Sabbath rest for the people of God, ¹⁰for whoever has entered God's rest has also rested from his works as God did from his.

¹¹Let us therefore strive to enter that rest, so that no one may fall by the same sort of disobedience. ¹²For the word of God is living and active, sharper than any two-edged sword, piercing to the division of soul and of spirit, of joints and of marrow, and discerning the thoughts and intentions of the heart. ¹³And no creature is hidden from his sight, but all are naked and exposed to the eyes of him to whom we must give account.

some must enter therein, and they to whom it was first preached entered not in because of unbelief:

⁷Again, he limiteth a certain day, saying in David, To day, after so long a time; as it is said, To day if ye will hear his voice, harden not your hearts.

⁸For if Jesus had given them rest, then would he not afterward have spoken of another day.

⁹There remaineth therefore a rest to the people of God.

¹⁰For he that is entered into his rest, he also hath ceased from his own works, as God did from his.

¹¹Let us labour therefore to enter into that rest, lest any man fall after the same example of unbelief.

¹²For the word of God is quick, and powerful, and sharper than any twoedged sword, piercing even to the dividing asunder of soul and spirit, and of the joints and marrow, and is a discerner of the thoughts and intents of the heart.

¹³Neither is there any creature that is not manifest in his sight: but all things are naked and opened unto the eyes of him with whom we have to do.

Introduction to 3:1–4:13 Since there were evidently some who had more regard for the angels than for their Creator, the first section of Hebrews demonstrated Jesus' superiority to these spiritual beings (1:4–2:18). The book now proceeds to prove His superiority to Moses. Moses was understandably held in high regard. He served God's people as prophet and deliverer during a critical time in their formation as a nation. By God's power, Moses delivered Israel out of slavery and led them to the Promised Land. Moses saw God, and as a mediator, he conveyed God's Word to Israel, authoring the Torah. Naturally such a prophet would be held in esteem by those who believed his message. But Moses was a servant in God's house, while Jesus is the

Son of God. Moses delivered Israel to the Promised Land and Joshua led them into it (3:8), but Jesus delivers all of God's people from sin and death and into the true, eternal promised land (3:1–6). Because of their rebellion, many Israelites did not enter the Promised Land. This serves as a warning to Christians lest we rebel against God and fail to enter the eternal promised land of heaven (3:7–4:18).

3:1 *Therefore . . . consider Jesus.* Heb 2:14–18 focused the reader's attention on the saving work of Jesus, which is not conducted for angels but for human beings. These words now return our attention to the main topic of this section—the supremacy of Jesus—and provide another example of His supremacy. Jesus is greater than Moses. *holy brothers you who share in a heavenly calling.* Our kinship with fellow Christians is based on our common adoption by God the Father, through faith in His Son (cf. Jn 1:12–13; Gal 4:4–7). In this calling we are not holy because of our own efforts—indeed, left to ourselves, we are dead in our trespasses and sins. Rather, we are declared holy because Christ credits His righteousness to us. As God, heaven is His, but He shares that with us—not by our own efforts, but by God's sharing His holiness with us (cf. 1Pt 1:15). We have been declared holy for Christ's sake and should gladly recognize our fellow redeemed as those God declares holy. Not only are we brothers and sisters, we recognize that we ourselves, along with our fellow Christians, have been baptized. Our sins have been forgiven. We are holy. We all have a heavenly calling—the call to faith. *the apostle and high priest of our confession.* Priests in the OT offered sacrifices, and they also revealed God's will through their teaching. In the NT, God sent apostles to speak on His behalf. Jesus is the High Priest and Apostle who fully reveals God's will and fulfills both testaments. He offers Himself as the final sacrifice for the sins of the world, and He reveals God and His will to humanity. This is the only time in the NT that Jesus is called *apostle*, which means "sent one," though in Jn 20:21, Jesus uses the verbal form of apostle in regard to Himself, saying, "as the Father has sent [Gk *apostellō*] me, even so I am sending you." *confession.* We believe and confess that Jesus is the Son of God and the Savior of the world. He is our High Priest and is God's apostle to us. The Gk word for "confess" (*homologia*) literally means "same words." We say the same thing that God has said: we believe that Jesus is from God and is our High Priest. We confess our faith in Him to God, to one another, and before the world.

3:2 *faithful to Him who appointed.* An apostle brings a message from the one who sends them. If the sender's message is to be trusted, the messenger must accurately convey it. Faithfulness is critical. Jesus, the apostle (v. 1) of the Father, faithfully reveals God's gracious plan to humanity. This fulfilled the Father's will: He appointed Jesus to do this work (Ac 3:20). *just as Moses.* Moses was the greatest OT prophet, and even though he was sinful, he is an example of a faithful leader. Moses saw God in part (Ex 33:20), but Jesus is the only-begotten Son of God and therefore reveals God to us in ways that Moses could not (Jn 1:18). Moses was *faithful in all God's house*, both in the tabernacle and among the people of Israel, the household of faith in Moses' time. Even more was Jesus faithful to the Father who appointed Him as High Priest and apostle. While Hebrews is demonstrating the superiority of Jesus to Moses, this does not lessen Moses' importance. Moses was a prophet, called and sent by God. He was faithful in his office.

3:3 There are strong parallels between Moses and Jesus, but they are not equal and there is no doubt who is greater. Jesus has been *counted worthy of more glory than Moses.* These words clearly assert Jesus' supremacy to Moses and are backed up with a simple truth. *the builder . . . has more honor.* One might be impressed by the designs of an architect and the craftsmanship of a builder, but we would never say that the house they designed and built was greater than they are. Likewise, the creator has more honor than what is created, because what is created depends on the creator for existence. Confusing the Creator and creation is idolatry. Jesus is the Creator of all things, including Moses and Israel. He is therefore worthy of greater honor. Luther explains this, noting that Moses was, in fact, preparing God's people for their coming Lord:

> Whatever Moses ordered at God's command he did to be prepared for the personal rule of Christ, who was to dwell among them as in His own house. . . . Moses and the priesthood count for nothing, compared with Christ. They are under obligation; and since He is the true Lord, they must hand over the keys to Him and serve Him (LW 13:305).

3:4 *every house is built by someone.* This is the essence of what is called the "cosmological argument" for the existence of God. What is the source of creation? It had to come from somewhere or be created by someone. Hebrews doesn't give a full explanation here, but simply affirms *the builder of all things is God.* All creation owes its being and daily life to God. As part of creation, human beings—including Moses—owe their existence to the Son of God through whom God created everything (1:2). Again, this shows that Jesus is superior to Moses and worthy of greater honor.

3:5 *faithful as a servant.* A servant does the will of the master without necessarily knowing what the master has in mind. A master expects that his servants will obey him. Moses was a reluctant servant (e.g., Ex 3:11) but he did follow God's call to serve. God called Moses to speak His Word—*to testify*—and since he delivered God's Word to Israel as God called him to do, God decreed that Moses was "faithful in all my house" (Nu 12:7). Yet Moses was not God; he was a servant of God (cf. Ex 14:31; Dt 34:5; Ps 105:26). He testified concerning *things that were to be spoken later.* Among these things was the coming of the Messiah (cf. Dt 18:15, 18). While Moses was faithful in testifying, God the Father makes the fullness of His will known through Jesus the Son (cf. Jn 15:15).

3:6 *over God's house as a son.* Jesus knows the will of the Father and speaks with His full authority. Moses is part of creation and a servant; Jesus is the Creator and the Son of God. While some aspects of their work are similar, Jesus is categorically greater than Moses. *we are His house.* Moses served among God's house, the people of Israel. Through Christ, the Church is now the house of God, the place where God dwells (cf. 1Co 3:16; 6:19; 2Co 6:16; Eph 2:21; 1Pt 2:5). *hold fast . . . our hope.* This call to a strong, confident faith has Christ as its object. He is our confidence and our hope. We truly are His house—His dwelling place—if we have faith in Him. Since all this is by His grace and not our own works, He is our reason for *boasting* (cf. 1Co 1:31; Rv 3:11).

3:1–6 in Devotion and Prayer In His grace and mercy, God sent Jesus, the Word made flesh, to this earth to dwell among us (Jn 1:14). We have been redeemed by His gracious work. We have been called to faith and into the communion of the Church by His Spirit. He now proclaims: "You are God's temple . . . God's Spirit dwells in you" (1Co 3:16). Our Creator, worthy of all honor, praise, and worship, has become part of His creation in order to serve us. He faithfully carried out His Father's will. Because of His death and resurrection, all who receive His gift of faith are declared holy. We share a heavenly calling. We boast not in ourselves but in what Jesus has done for us, to

His glory. • Lord Jesus, our Creator and Redeemer, You were faithful when we were faithless. By Your blood, You have made us Your dwelling place. Hold us in Your grace that Your Church may be Your holy Temple, to the glory of Your name. Amen.

Introduction to 3:7–4:13 These verses again show the author's deep knowledge of the OT. He exhorts the reader through a series of OT examples concerning the Sabbath and the inheritance of the Promised Land. Moses revealed God's will regarding the Sabbath to Israel and led them to the border of the Promised Land. Jesus' work surpasses the service of Moses in giving His people true rest and leading us to the true promised land—heaven.

3:7–11 This citation from Ps 95:7–11 alludes to the rebellion of God's people in the wilderness—especially the rebellion depicted in Nu 14. There the people faithlessly refused to enter the Promised Land after spies brought back a disheartening report about the land. They lacked faith in God's power and guidance and fell under judgment.

3:7 *the Holy Spirit says.* The Scriptures, written by men, were inspired by the Holy Spirit and are His words (cf. 2Tm 3:16). When God speaks, listen. One can always use such words in regard to Scripture: God says . . . Here the writer uses this introduction to encourage his readers to hear the words of Ps 95 as an exhortation to them personally. *Today . . . do not harden.* These words are quoted again in v. 15 and 4:7. In each case, they introduce a stern warning. Do not ignore what God says; take His Word to heart! He speaks today, so listen today.

3:8 *do not harden your hearts.* A hardened heart does not function as it should and can be fatal. A spiritually hardened heart does not listen to what God says; it does not receive His Word with gladness; it does not believe. The unbelief and hardening described here originates in humans. Human beings harden their own hearts when they turn away from God and His gifts. We are warned lest we act like unbelieving Israel of old who did not respond to God in faith. They did this in *rebellion . . . on the day of testing.* (Cf. Nu 14 where Israel grumbled against Moses and against God, wishing that they were back in slavery. The consequence of their unbelief was that none of them entered the Promised Land except Joshua and Caleb.) It was indeed a day of testing, but they failed the test in unbelief and doubt.

3:9 *your fathers put Me to the test.* Again, the blame lies solely with the unbelieving people. God was faithful to them, giving ample evidence of His care, but Israel did not believe. One consequence of their rebellion is that they were not allowed to enter the Promised Land then but instead would wander the desert for *forty years* before their children would be allowed to enter the land that God had prepared for them.

3:11 *They shall not enter My rest.* The Israelites who rebelled against God died during the forty years in the wilderness and did not enter the Promised Land (Nu 14:22–23). They had no permanent home for the rest of their earthly lives but were wandering nomads. Luther applies their circumstances to the Church, saying, "We wretched men have lost that bliss of our physical life through sin, and while we live we are in the midst of death. And yet, because the Sabbath command remains for the church, it denotes that spiritual life is to be restored to us through Christ" (LW 1:80).

3:12 *an evil, unbelieving heart.* The Israelites in Nu 14 had such hearts. Refusing to trust that God would give them the Promised Land, they did not receive the gift. They refused to believe God's promises and trust in His powerful care. This is applied to the reader who is admonished to *take care* that they not share the same unbelief. We are warned not to doubt *the living God,* for He actively looks into the hearts of all people and makes a just judgment (Heb 10:30b–31; cf. Mt 16:16). Because of their unbelief, Israel wandered in the desert for forty years. Those who *fall away* from faith in God have no hope of entering the eternal promised land. This is a matter of utmost seriousness.

3:13 *exhort . . . every day.* Given the reality of temptation, it is important to recognize that God gives us responsibility to help our fellow Christians and to seek their exhortation in our lives. Since we constantly face temptation, this is a daily need. The first readers of this Letter may have gathered daily in their homes for prayer, which would have given them natural opportunities to encourage one another in this way (cf. 10:24–25). Yet even if we do not follow that daily discipline, we still are called to seek exhortation and graciously exhort our fellow believers. *as long as it is called today.* Repeating the language of v. 7 (which will return again in 4:7), this emphasizes the importance of immediate attention. The time to believe, to resist temptation, and to encourage one another is now. Do not delay until tomorrow, for we do not know if this is our last day. God graciously calls us now. Listen to Him and encourage your fellow Christians. *hardened.* As in v. 7, this is related to turning away from God into sin. Giving in to temptation and *the deceitfulness of sin* is behind one's hardening of his or her own heart. There is no one to blame but ourselves. Refusal to trust God is coupled with a refusal to accept what is true. An unbelieving heart will willingly accept deception. Sin, which appears alluring and desirable, is self-destructive (cf. Rm 7:11). Regarding this important calling to exhort our fellow believers, Calvin wrote, "Unless our faith be now and then raised up, it will lie prostrate; unless it be warmed, it will be frozen; unless it be roused, it will grow torpid. He would have us then to stimulate one another by mutual exhortations, so that Satan may not creep into our hearts, and by his fallacies draw us away from God" (Calvin 88).

3:14 Verse 1 reminded us that since we "share in a heavenly calling" with our brothers and sisters in the faith (cf. note at 3:1), we are moved to consider Jesus our Great High Priest. Now, in the midst of this exhortation, we are reminded of the means by which we remain in faith and resist the temptation to harden our hearts and fall away. Together with our fellow believers we *share in Christ.* In our Baptism, we have been united with our Savior, been baptized into his death, and died to sin, and we now walk in newness of life. We, too, will rise with Him (cf. Rm 6:1–14). He exchanged His righteousness for our sinfulness. We are united with Him and with all who share that faith. The author describes this as *our original confidence.* God gives us faith and preserves in faith. God, in Christ Jesus, forgives sin. This phrase may be the call to holiness and the hope of future glory given in Baptism (1Pt 3:21). Be strong in the faith that God has given you. Through it, we are united to Christ and are delivered from sin, death, and the power of the devil. *firm to the end.* Faith is not a one-time event. God calls us to believe and sanctifies and keeps us in the faith. It is He who strengthens (cf. Rm 16:25). We are called to walk in this new life (Rm 6:4)—to live in it and enjoy the gifts that God gives. This exhortation is repeated in verses like "The one who endures to the end will be saved" (Mt 10:22) and "Be faithful unto death, and I will give you the crown of life" (Rv 2:10). God draws us to Him and promises His salvation to all who belong to Him. We have good reason for confidence and hope.

3:15 See note, vv. 7–11. This repetition underscores the urgency of the author's warning. Luther ponders this, saying, "Since we have begun happily, just as they had—let us fear, lest by defecting we abandon 'the beginning of the substance,' as they abandoned it and deserted" (LW 29:158).

3:16–18 *who? . . . those who left Egypt led by Moses.* Hebrews' warning is a pointed one. The Israelites who had been led out of Egypt saw and heard wondrous things. They witnessed great miracles. Their lives were spared by the blood of the Passover lamb. God gave them a prophet and God Himself led them. These people *heard.* They knew God's will. They had no excuse, and yet they *rebelled* against that will. They *provoked* God with their sinful disobedience again and again during the forty years that they wandered in the wilderness. God richly provided for all of their needs and cared for them. Yet despite receiving such marvelous blessings, they were *disobedient.* The result of this was that they were unable to enter the *rest* of the Promised Land. They missed out on even greater blessings than they had already seen, due to their acts of unbelief. This narrative is recalled here as an example to remind readers that those who have experienced God's goodness should not become complacent, but rather should persevere in the faith. Those who forsake God will lose their rest and inheritance. See note, 1:14.

3:19 *unable . . . because of unbelief.* Hebrews gets to the heart of the matter: their sin was a symptom of the absence of faith. God's offer was sincere; He was willing to give His people rest in the Promised Land, but His people were unwilling to receive it. The people's unbelief—their lack of confidence in the promises of God—rendered them incapable of experiencing the blessings that flow from trust. God forgives all who trust in Him, but "without faith it is impossible to please him" (11:6).

4:1 *Therefore.* This simple word calls us to connect ourselves to the story of God's people. This is not historical trivia; we live in just such a story. As Israel was led by God, so are we. Let us learn from their mistake and trust our God because the *promise . . . still stands.* Israel's story is recounted as a warning to believers today, but it is not too late. God's promise of forgiveness and peace remains true and can be lost only if we refuse it. He still wants us to enter His rest. *let us fear.* We should carefully watch that our trust is in the promise of God in Christ Jesus rather than in human understanding. We, who

54

have received His gracious salvation, are to guard against unbelief and complacency that could lead us to neglect our calling to faith. *lest any of you.* Note well how carefully the author draws all of his readers into his warning. "Let us fear." "Lest any of you." This is not a warning to be taken lightly—all Christians are called to persevere in the faith. Use the gifts that God gives you. *should seem to have failed.* Since only God can see the heart, the author is careful not to usurp His place and pronounce God's judgment upon another person. We may be too prone to conclude that a weak or struggling fellow believer lacks faith when God sees faith. The author warns lest Christians be overly self-confident and think there is no danger of falling, yet it is God alone who can judge whether a person trusts in Christ for salvation. Outward appearances can, at times, be deceiving. While we are to lovingly watch out for our brothers and sisters and care for them, here the caution is for each of us.

4:2 *good news.* This word (Gk *euangelizō*) is the verbal form of the word "Gospel." God's good news is always an undeserved gift. It came to Israel just as it came to us. Israel did not receive God's blessings because of their own goodness but because of God's gracious character. Part of God's gift to Israel was an earthly blessing: the gift of the Promised Land. God's even greater Good News to Israel and to His Church is the gift of new life in Christ. Israel's earthly disobedience kept them from the Promised Land for forty years, and those who did not have faith would not enter the eternal promised land. They heard the *message* (literally, "the word," Gk *logos*) but it *did not benefit them.* The promise was sincere. The word is efficacious. God is faithful to His promises. But when they rejected His gift of faith, they could not receive its benefits. *united by faith.* By faith, we receive the promises of God and become members of His household (3:2). Trusting in God's promise, we receive the gifts that God gives. The problem with Israel, and the problem that we are warned against, is that while God's promise is sincere, sinners may resist the promise. Without faith, the promise is not received. But not all reject it. Some did receive it and continue to receive it. We are united (KJV, "mixed") with our fellow believers of all times and places. We are united with the faithful of Israel and with the faithful today. In all times, God preserves His people and unites us in the true faith. The communion of saints includes all who trust the living God. Luther ponders these things, saying,

These three—faith, the Word, and the heart—become one. Faith is the glue or the bond. The Word is on one side; the heart is on the other side. But through faith they become one spirit, just as man and wife become 'one flesh' (Gen. 2:24). Therefore it is true that the heart is combined with the Word through faith and that the Word is combined with the heart through the same faith. (LW 29:160)

4:3 *we who believe.* Words of exhortation are not given to cause us to despair, but to strengthen us in faith. We *have believed.* God has called us by the Gospel and given us faith. Accordingly, by His grace, we *enter that rest.* The rest of God's people in the Promised Land foreshadowed the promise of a far greater new life of rest. This promise is fulfilled in Christ Jesus, who gives us an eternal home and rest. It is given to all who receive His gifts in faith. *They shall not enter.* The warning of Ps 95 is here repeated (cf. 3:11) and will be noted again (4:3), underscoring the seriousness of this admonition. *His works were finished.* This rest is rooted in God's seventh day of creation. As God's rest has existed from the foundation of the world, so His people throughout time have been free to enter this rest and peace. This rest in Christ is a greater one than had been previously understood. See note, v. 9.

4:4 This biblical rationale for the Sabbath is quoted from Gn 2:2 and is echoed in Ex 20:11; 31:17.

4:5 A third repetition of Ps 95:11, which speaks of God's judgment because of His people's refusal to enter the Promised Land. (Cf. 3:11; 4:3; Nu 16.) God established the Sabbath, the "rest" of the Promised Land, and the rest of heaven. It is His rest, which He shares.

4:6–7 The author now applies the argument he has been making. While some will disbelieve in *disobedience* to God, some will *enter it.* God will grant this promised rest to His faithful. *formerly received the good news.* See note, v. 2. Stated this way, it is a reminder that faith is an eternal calling. They once received it but later hardened their hearts and did not believe. We are not called to believe once but to believe and keep on believing in Christ by the Holy Spirit's gift of faith. *Today.* Note the urgency the author reveals in this verse. Do not think on the past, but on God's call to you now. God *appoints a certain day.* Do not presume that you are free to ignore God's gracious invitation until a time that you think it is convenient. We do not know our days or future. God always calls in the present.

He called Israel. He called *David*, who wrote about their experience while including himself in the call. And He calls us to faith today. Listen to Him. Believe. (See note, 3:7–11.)

4:8 *if Joshua had given them rest.* The author now broadens the narrative. This is not only about the Israelites who did not enter the Promised Land because of their rebellion. The promised rest was not merely release from Egyptian slavery and a new life in the Promised Land. Those who left Egypt died in the desert due to their disobedience (3:16–19). God still fulfilled His promises when the next generation did enter the Promised Land. Joshua led them into their new home at God's direction. But the rest they received there, though a blessing, was not the ultimate fulfillment of God's promise. That perfect rest was yet to come, for God had *spoken of another day later on*. That promise came through the second Joshua, Jesus, who saves His people from their sin (cf. Mt 1:25). Joshua or "Jehoshuah" means "the LORD is my salvation." In the Greek NT, Joshua and Jesus share the same name (cf. Ac 7:45). Cyril of Jerusalem shows this parallel: "Jesus the son of Nave [i.e., Joshua] was in many things a type of Him [Jesus]. For when he began to rule over the people, he began from Jordan, whence Christ also, after He was baptized, began to preach the gospel" (*NPNF*2 7:60).

4:9 *there remains a Sabbath rest.* God has fully completed the six days of His work in creation; thus, His Sabbath rest extends throughout time. In Christ, God's people enter into God's day of rest and experience the peace He gives. The promise of rest is not of a single day (Ex 20:8–11), nor even a lifetime in a new land; it is a promise of eternal rest and peace with God (cf. Rm 5:1). This rest remains for us.

4:10 *whoever.* This promise is inclusive. It applies to anyone who, by faith, receives God's gift of rest. *entered God's rest.* We truly enter the rest God promises when we enjoy the result of His completed work. Jesus, our "Joshua" (v. 8), gives us rest when He declares, "It is finished" (Jn 19:30). The benefits of Christ's completed work, received by faith, are distributed in the proclamation of the Gospel and the administration of the Sacraments. Receiving those gifts is receiving God's rest. We know that we have not deserved such blessings and that we never could deserve them. They are given to us as a gift. Accordingly, we rest from our *works*: there is nothing for us to do. Christ has earned our rest for us. (Cf. Rv 14:13.)

4:11 *strive to enter that rest.* This is not a call to try to save our-selves. Christ has already earned our salvation, and we rest from our works (v. 10). Instead, this is a call to receive the gifts He gives. We do this when we daily return to our Baptism, renouncing the devil and all evil, and by His gift of faith, trust God's mercy in Christ, who has prepared our eternal rest in heaven (Jn 14:2). *that no one may fall.* God preserves us in the faith. Use the means that He provides to sustain and strengthen faith. Through them, the Holy Spirit will keep us from falling (cf. Jude 24). We do not rely on our own strength, but trust in God's word and promise.

4:12 *the word of God.* The person striving to enter God's rest (v. 11) is equipped by the Word. God's Word remains forever and always accomplishes the work that He sends it to do (cf. Is 55:11). God's Word is *living.* It is more than just ideas or history; it gives life (Ps 119:25; cf. 1Pt 1:23) because it comes from the living God. Fur-thermore, God's Word is *active* (the Gk word *energēs* underlies the English word "energy"; it can also be translated "effective"). God's living Word always has the power to accomplish what God desires. God says, "Is not my word like fire . . . and like a hammer that breaks the rock in pieces?" (Jer 23:29). St. Paul reminds us that "the word of God . . . is at work in you believers" (1Th 2:13). Hebrews picks us a similarly powerful image: it is *sharper than any two-edged sword.* Even the sharpest sword can cut only through flesh and bone; God's Word cuts through any spiritual barriers that stand between human beings and God. It pierces to the *division of soul and of spirit, of joints and of marrow.* God's Word cuts to the innermost part of a human being. Nothing is hidden from Him or beyond the reach of His Word. *discerning the thoughts and intentions of the heart.* God's Word exposes the true state of a person's heart and reveals our standing before God. God does not merely know our words and actions but our entire self. He knows us fully—better than we know ourselves. The comparison to a sword emphasizes God's work in our lives through the Law, in keeping with the exhortation in 3:13. (See also the note at 3:7–4:13.) Nothing is hidden from God.

One of the great themes of the Reformation was a focus on the need to be faithful to Holy Scripture. The Lutheran reformers strong-ly proclaimed *Sola Scriptura*: Scripture alone is to be the source and norm of Christian teaching. So Luther writes of this power:

Christ's Word breaks through and wounds. It takes away every ground of trust and ascribes redemption solely to the blood of Christ; it pricks and wounds the soul. This is a health-bestowing wound, for these weapons kill in order to make alive. . . . It is, however, a fall that is happy and full of consolation, demonstrating the power and success of the Word. (LW 12:225)

Calvin likewise wrote concerning the powerful Word of God:

God's word is a discerner . . . for it brings the light of knowledge to the mind of man as it were from a labyrinth, where it was held before entangled. There is indeed no thicker darkness than that of unbelief, and hypocrisy is a horrible blindness; but God's word scatters this darkness and chases away this hypocrisy. Hence the separating or discerning which the Apostle mentions. (Calvin 104)

Bengel applied this text by first considering the division of soul and spirit and then noting how God addresses the whole person:

Hence it is evident that soul and spirit are not synonymous, but the spirit is in the soul. Man, contemplated according to his nature, consists of soul and body. Matt, x, 28: but when he has in him the working of God's word, he consists of spirit, soul, and body. The inmost parts, and the recesses in the spirit, soul, and body of man, are called by Synecdoche . . . joints and marrow (marrows). (Bengel 4:382).

Like the reformers, we should gratefully recognize the power and efficacy of God's Word and gladly receive it with faith.

4:13 *hidden.* There are no secrets from God, who is omniscient (2Ch 16:9; Jb 34:21; Ps 33:13–15). *naked and exposed.* Absolutely everything that we are is known to God. "Naked" brings to mind the fall into sin. Before the Fall, Adam and Eve "were both naked and were not ashamed" (Gn 2:25), but after they sinned, they recognized their nakedness and clothed themselves in fig leaves (Gn 3:7). Their clothing hid neither their bodies nor their sinfulness from their Creator. Furthermore, when Hebrews speaks of *no creature* being hidden, this not only shows God's complete knowledge but also, in the context of a piercing sword, suggests an animal prepared for slaughter. God replaced Adam and Eve's fig leaves with garments of skins (Gn 3:21). Their sin brought death into the world and they were now covered, by God's action, with the skin of another creature. All of this shows both the perfect knowledge of God and the horrible significance of sin. Before the power of God's Word we have no defense. The Almighty One knows all about us, and unless He has mercy, we will die. *we must give account.* If we stand on our own, we will surely be justly condemned for our sin. We are accountable to God, the eternal Judge who sees all, for all our thoughts, words, and deeds (cf. Rm 14:10–12). Only clothed in Christ's righteousness can we stand before Him in confidence.

3:7–4:13 in Devotion and Prayer Who can explain the unbelief of the Israelites? They saw miraculous signs and personally witnessed God's mighty deliverance. They were sustained in the wilderness, fed on manna, and given all that they needed to thrive. In their wilderness wanderings, God was ever faithful. He revealed Himself to them and formed them into a nation. He was leading them to a new home—the Promised Land—and told them of its great bounty. But sinners are always prone to turn in on themselves and away from their Lord. They grumbled against God and His prophet Moses. They doubted His promises, hardened their hearts, and tested His patience again and again. Responding to this repeated unfaithfulness, God finally decreed that that first generation would die in the wilderness. They themselves would not live in the Promised Land. Who can understand such obstinacy and unbelief? We can! Their story is our story. It serves, in part, as a warning to Christians who are tempted to make the same mistake. God has made us many great promises. He calls us to trust Him and to follow Him so that we may enter the rest that He has enjoyed and sanctified since the completion of creation. To receive that rest, He calls us to rest from our works. Since we are unable to save ourselves and since our own works are like filthy rags before God (Is 64:6), these will not give us a place in God's rest. But Christ's perfect work does! In Him we have rest from the accusation of the Law. The Holy Spirit gives us faith to trust in Christ's finished work and grants us peace with God that begins now and endures for all eternity. Learn from the story of the Israelites: trust God, who will keep His promises. He is faithful. • Lord Jesus, our deliverer and our God, by Your work on my behalf, You have won my salvation and freed me from sin, death, and despair. You are my rest. When I am weary and afraid, strengthen me that I may always look to You. Refresh me with Your Word and Sacrament. Send me Your Holy Spirit to preserve me in the faith until You bring me to the promised land that You have prepared for all who belong to You. Amen.

Superiority of Jesus' Priesthood: Jesus, the New Melchizedek (4:14–7:28)

ESV	KJV
[14]Since then we have a great high priest who has passed through the heavens, Jesus, the Son of God, let us hold fast our confession. [15]For we do not have a high priest who is unable to sympathize with our weaknesses, but one who in every respect has been tempted as we are, yet without sin. [16] Let us then with confidence draw near to the throne of grace, that we may receive mercy and find grace to help in time of need.	[14]Seeing then that we have a great high priest, that is passed into the heavens, Jesus the Son of God, let us hold fast our profession. [15]For we have not an high priest which cannot be touched with the feeling of our infirmities; but was in all points tempted like as we are, yet without sin. [16]Let us therefore come boldly unto the throne of grace, that we may obtain mercy, and find grace to help in time of need.
5 [1]For every high priest chosen from among men is appointed to act on behalf of men in relation to God, to offer gifts and sacrifices for sins. [2]He can deal gently with the ignorant and wayward, since he himself is beset with weakness. [3]Because of this he is obligated to offer sacrifice for his own sins just as he does for those of the people. [4]And no one takes this honor for himself, but only when called by God, just as Aaron was.	5 [1]For every high priest taken from among men is ordained for men in things pertaining to God, that he may offer both gifts and sacrifices for sins: [2]Who can have compassion on the ignorant, and on them that are out of the way; for that he himself also is compassed with infirmity. [3]And by reason hereof he ought, as for the people, so also for himself, to offer for sins. [4]And no man taketh this honour unto himself, but he that is called of God, as was Aaron.
[5]So also Christ did not exalt himself to be made a high priest, but was appointed by him who said to him, "You are my Son, today I have begotten you"; [6]as he says also in another place, "You are a priest forever, after the order of Melchizedek." [7]In the days of his flesh, Jesus offered up prayers and supplications, with loud cries and tears, to him who was able to save him from death, and he was heard because of his reverence. [8]Although he was a son, he	[5]So also Christ glorified not himself to be made an high priest; but he that said unto him, Thou art my Son, to day have I begotten thee. [6]As he saith also in another place, Thou art a priest for ever after the order of Melchisedec. [7]Who in the days of his flesh, when he had offered up prayers and supplications with strong crying and tears unto him that was able to save him from death, and was heard in that he feared;

learned obedience through what he suffered. ⁹And being made perfect, he became the source of eternal salvation to all who obey him, ¹⁰being designated by God a high priest after the order of Melchizedek.

¹¹About this we have much to say, and it is hard to explain, since you have become dull of hearing. ¹²For though by this time you ought to be teachers, you need someone to teach you again the basic principles of the oracles of God. You need milk, not solid food, ¹³for everyone who lives on milk is unskilled in the word of righteousness, since he is a child. ¹⁴But solid food is for the mature, for those who have their powers of discernment trained by constant practice to distinguish good from evil.

6 ¹Therefore let us leave the elementary doctrine of Christ and go on to maturity, not laying again a foundation of repentance from dead works and of faith toward God, ²and of instruction about washings, the laying on of hands, the resurrection of the dead, and eternal judgment. ³And this we will do if God permits. ⁴For it is impossible, in the case of those who have once been enlightened, who have tasted the heavenly gift, and have shared in the Holy Spirit, ⁵and have tasted the goodness of the word of God and the powers of the age to come, ⁶and then have fallen away, to restore them again to repentance, since they are crucifying once again the Son of God to their own harm and holding him up to contempt. ⁷For land that has drunk the rain that often falls on it, and produces a crop useful to those for whose sake it is cultivated, receives

⁸Though he were a Son, yet learned he obedience by the things which he suffered;

⁹And being made perfect, he became the author of eternal salvation unto all them that obey him;

¹⁰Called of God an high priest after the order of Melchisedec.

¹¹Of whom we have many things to say, and hard to be uttered, seeing ye are dull of hearing.

¹²For when for the time ye ought to be teachers, ye have need that one teach you again which be the first principles of the oracles of God; and are become such as have need of milk, and not of strong meat.

¹³For every one that useth milk is unskilful in the word of righteousness: for he is a babe.

¹⁴But strong meat belongeth to them that are of full age, even those who by reason of use have their senses exercised to discern both good and evil.

6 ¹Therefore leaving the principles of the doctrine of Christ, let us go on unto perfection; not laying again the foundation of repentance from dead works, and of faith toward God,

²Of the doctrine of baptisms, and of laying on of hands, and of resurrection of the dead, and of eternal judgment.

³And this will we do, if God permit.

⁴For it is impossible for those who were once enlightened, and have tasted of the heavenly gift, and were made partakers of the Holy Ghost,

⁵And have tasted the good word of God, and the powers of the world to come,

⁶If they shall fall away, to renew them again unto repentance; seeing they crucify to themselves the Son of

a blessing from God. ⁸But if it bears thorns and thistles, it is worthless and near to being cursed, and its end is to be burned.

⁹Though we speak in this way, yet in your case, beloved, we feel sure of better things—things that belong to salvation. ¹⁰For God is not unjust so as to overlook your work and the love that you have shown for his name in serving the saints, as you still do. ¹¹And we desire each one of you to show the same earnestness to have the full assurance of hope until the end, ¹²so that you may not be sluggish, but imitators of those who through faith and patience inherit the promises.

¹³For when God made a promise to Abraham, since he had no one greater by whom to swear, he swore by himself, ¹⁴saying, "Surely I will bless you and multiply you." ¹⁵And thus Abraham, having patiently waited, obtained the promise. ¹⁶For people swear by something greater than themselves, and in all their disputes an oath is final for confirmation. ¹⁷So when God desired to show more convincingly to the heirs of the promise the unchangeable character of his purpose, he guaranteed it with an oath, ¹⁸so that by two unchangeable things, in which it is impossible for God to lie, we who have fled for refuge might have strong encouragement to hold fast to the hope set before us. ¹⁹We have this as a sure and steadfast anchor of the soul, a hope that enters into the inner place behind the curtain, ²⁰where Jesus has gone as a forerunner on our behalf, having become a high priest forever after the order of Melchizedek.

God afresh, and put him to an open shame.

⁷For the earth which drinketh in the rain that cometh oft upon it, and bringeth forth herbs meet for them by whom it is dressed, receiveth blessing from God:

⁸But that which beareth thorns and briers is rejected, and is nigh unto cursing; whose end is to be burned.

⁹But, beloved, we are persuaded better things of you, and things that accompany salvation, though we thus speak.

¹⁰For God is not unrighteous to forget your work and labour of love, which ye have shewed toward his name, in that ye have ministered to the saints, and do minister.

¹¹And we desire that every one of you do shew the same diligence to the full assurance of hope unto the end:

¹²That ye be not slothful, but followers of them who through faith and patience inherit the promises.

¹³For when God made promise to Abraham, because he could swear by no greater, he sware by himself,

¹⁴Saying, Surely blessing I will bless thee, and multiplying I will multiply thee.

¹⁵And so, after he had patiently endured, he obtained the promise.

¹⁶For men verily swear by the greater: and an oath for confirmation is to them an end of all strife.

¹⁷Wherein God, willing more abundantly to shew unto the heirs of promise the immutability of his counsel, confirmed it by an oath:

¹⁸That by two immutable things, in which it was impossible for God to lie, we might have a strong consola-

7 ¹For this Melchizedek, king of Salem, priest of the Most High God, met Abraham returning from the slaughter of the kings and blessed him, ²and to him Abraham apportioned a tenth part of everything. He is first, by translation of his name, king of righteousness, and then he is also king of Salem, that is, king of peace. ³He is without father or mother or genealogy, having neither beginning of days nor end of life, but resembling the Son of God he continues a priest forever.

⁴See how great this man was to whom Abraham the patriarch gave a tenth of the spoils! ⁵And those descendants of Levi who receive the priestly office have a commandment in the law to take tithes from the people, that is, from their brothers, though these also are descended from Abraham. ⁶But this man who does not have his descent from them received tithes from Abraham and blessed him who had the promises. ⁷It is beyond dispute that the inferior is blessed by the superior. ⁸In the one case tithes are received by mortal men, but in the other case, by one of whom it is testified that he lives. ⁹One might even say that Levi himself, who receives tithes, paid tithes through Abraham, ¹⁰for he was still in the loins of his ancestor when Melchizedek met him.

¹¹Now if perfection had been attainable through the Levitical priesthood (for under it the people received the law), what further need would there have been for another priest to arise after the order of Melchizedek, rather than one named after the order of Aaron? ¹²For when there is a change in the priesthood, there is necessar-

tion, who have fled for refuge to lay hold upon the hope set before us:

¹⁹Which hope we have as an anchor of the soul, both sure and stedfast, and which entereth into that within the veil;

²⁰Whither the forerunner is for us entered, even Jesus, made an high priest for ever after the order of Melchisedec.

7 ¹For this Melchisedec, king of Salem, priest of the most high God, who met Abraham returning from the slaughter of the kings, and blessed him;

²To whom also Abraham gave a tenth part of all; first being by interpretation King of righteousness, and after that also King of Salem, which is, King of peace;

³Without father, without mother, without descent, having neither beginning of days, nor end of life; but made like unto the Son of God; abideth a priest continually.

⁴Now consider how great this man was, unto whom even the patriarch Abraham gave the tenth of the spoils.

⁵And verily they that are of the sons of Levi, who receive the office of the priesthood, have a commandment to take tithes of the people according to the law, that is, of their brethren, though they come out of the loins of Abraham:

⁶But he whose descent is not counted from them received tithes of Abraham, and blessed him that had the promises.

⁷And without all contradiction the less is blessed of the better.

⁸And here men that die receive tithes; but there he receiveth them, of whom it is witnessed that he liveth.

ily a change in the law as well. ¹³For the one of whom these things are spoken belonged to another tribe, from which no one has ever served at the altar. ¹⁴For it is evident that our Lord was descended from Judah, and in connection with that tribe Moses said nothing about priests.

¹⁵This becomes even more evident when another priest arises in the likeness of Melchizedek, ¹⁶who has become a priest, not on the basis of a legal requirement concerning bodily descent, but by the power of an indestructible life. ¹⁷For it is witnessed of him,

"You are a priest forever,
    after the order of Melchizedek."

¹⁸For on the one hand, a former commandment is set aside because of its weakness and uselessness ¹⁹(for the law made nothing perfect); but on the other hand, a better hope is introduced, through which we draw near to God.

²⁰And it was not without an oath. For those who formerly became priests were made such without an oath, ²¹but this one was made a priest with an oath by the one who said to him:

"The Lord has sworn
    and will not change his mind,
'You are a priest forever.' "

²²This makes Jesus the guarantor of a better covenant.

²³The former priests were many in number, because they were prevented by death from continuing in office, ²⁴but he holds his priesthood permanently, because he continues forever. ²⁵Consequently, he is able

⁹And as I may so say, Levi also, who receiveth tithes, payed tithes in Abraham.

¹⁰For he was yet in the loins of his father, when Melchisedec met him.

¹¹If therefore perfection were by the Levitical priesthood, (for under it the people received the law,) what further need was there that another priest should rise after the order of Melchisedec, and not be called after the order of Aaron?

¹²For the priesthood being changed, there is made of necessity a change also of the law.

¹³For he of whom these things are spoken pertaineth to another tribe, of which no man gave attendance at the altar.

¹⁴For it is evident that our Lord sprang out of Juda; of which tribe Moses spake nothing concerning priesthood.

¹⁵And it is yet far more evident: for that after the similitude of Melchisedec there ariseth another priest,

¹⁶Who is made, not after the law of a carnal commandment, but after the power of an endless life.

¹⁷For he testifieth, Thou art a priest for ever after the order of Melchisedec.

¹⁸For there is verily a disannulling of the commandment going before for the weakness and unprofitableness thereof.

¹⁹For the law made nothing perfect, but the bringing in of a better hope did; by the which we draw nigh unto God.

²⁰And inasmuch as not without an oath he was made priest:

²¹(For those priests were made without an oath; but this with an oath by

to save to the uttermost those who draw near to God through him, since he always lives to make intercession for them.

²⁶For it was indeed fitting that we should have such a high priest, holy, innocent, unstained, separated from sinners, and exalted above the heavens. ²⁷He has no need, like those high priests, to offer sacrifices daily, first for his own sins and then for those of the people, since he did this once for all when he offered up himself. ²⁸For the law appoints men in their weakness as high priests, but the word of the oath, which came later than the law, appoints a Son who has been made perfect forever.

him that said unto him, The Lord sware and will not repent, Thou art a priest for ever after the order of Melchisedec:)

²²By so much was Jesus made a surety of a better testament.

²³And they truly were many priests, because they were not suffered to continue by reason of death:

²⁴But this man, because he continueth ever, hath an unchangeable priesthood.

²⁵Wherefore he is able also to save them to the uttermost that come unto God by him, seeing he ever liveth to make intercession for them.

²⁶For such an high priest became us, who is holy, harmless, undefiled, separate from sinners, and made higher than the heavens;

²⁷Who needeth not daily, as those high priests, to offer up sacrifice, first for his own sins, and then for the people's: for this he did once, when he offered up himself.

²⁸For the law maketh men high priests which have infirmity; but the word of the oath, which was since the law, maketh the Son, who is consecrated for evermore.

Introduction to 4:14–5:10 Hebrews has demonstrated Jesus' superiority to the angels (1:4–2:18) and to Moses (3:1–4:13). It now turns to a critical point: Jesus is the supreme priest, an argument that will continue through 5:10. Like other high priests, Jesus is from among the people and can sympathize with them since He shares their experience; but unlike all others, He has no sin (4:14–5:3). Like other priests, Jesus does not appoint Himself but was appointed to this office by God (5:4–6). While other priests offered sacrificial animals, Jesus Himself suffered to bring salvation to His people (5:7–10). He truly is superior to all other priests.

4:14 *a great high priest.* Since we are fully exposed before God and must give Him an account (v. 13), our sin and inability to save ourselves is evident. Our only hope is for God to save us, and He does, providing both sacrifice and priest in the person of His Son. Jesus Christ is the only one who can truly represent us to the Father and truly represent the Father to us. *passed through the heavens.* Fully divine and fully human, Jesus is uniquely able to provide everything that we need. He was God from all eternity (cf. Jn 1:1) who, in the fullness of time, became incarnate. As we confess in the Nicene Creed, "He came down from heaven." Having completed His work, He ascended to heaven (Ac 1:9; Eph 4:10). Jesus bridged the otherwise infinite gap between God and humanity. He is thus uniquely equipped and appointed to be our mediator to the Father. *Son of God.* Unlike all other priests, Jesus Himself is divine. As God, He has complete access to the Father, which He uses on our behalf as He pleads for us. *hold fast.* Christ alone is our High Priest. He alone is our hope. Accordingly, Christians cling to Christ in faith since He has already demonstrated His grace and power. As the reformers proclaimed, Christ alone (*solus Christus*) is the Savior of the world. *our confession.* The Gk word *homologia* means "same words." We speak the same words as God, agreeing with what He tells us and sharing these divine truths with our fellow believers as together we confess the "same words" (cf. Rm 10:9; 1Tm 6:12). The content of this confession is Christ and His work. Focused upon Him, Melanchthon states:

> The apostle tells us to come to God, not with confidence in our own merits, but with confidence in Christ as the High Priest. The apostle requires faith. . . . [Also,] Peter says we receive forgiveness of sins through Christ's name, that is, for His sake. It is not for the sake of our merits, not for the sake of our contrition, attrition, love, worship, or works. He adds: *When we believe in Him.* Peter requires faith. For we cannot receive Christ's name except by faith. (Ap IV 82–83)

4:15 *sympathize with our weaknesses.* "Sympathize" simply renders the Gk word in English letters. This word connotes compassion. The KJV renders this: Jesus is "touched with the feeling of our infirmities." See note, 2:17. *weaknesses.* (KJV "infirmities") This is a broad word that refers to the effects of a condition or illness. Jesus understands our state and has compassion on us, willing to provide what we need and doing whatever is necessary to accomplish it.

tempted as we are. Cf. Mt 4:1–11; Mk 1:12–13; Lk 4:1–13 for accounts of Jesus' temptation. When Christ took on human flesh, He chose to endure all human afflictions, including temptation. He faced all manner of temptations faced by humans. While some specific temptations are recorded, Hebrews is clear to say that Jesus' temptation was comprehensive. He was *in every respect . . . tempted as we are.* He experienced all that we do, sharing not only our flesh but our experience as well. *yet without sin.* This is a crucial difference. All other humans succumb to temptation, but Jesus did not. Temptation may be resisted. The perfect, incarnate Son of God did what other human beings were unable to do. He experienced genuine temptation in its full strength but did not give in. He remained wholly faithful to His Father.

4:16 *confidence.* Recognizing what Jesus has done, we come before God boldly and in confident faith. We know what the outcome will be, because Christ is our Great High Priest (cf. 10:19; Eph 3:12). He has promised grace and mercy. *the throne of grace.* These words evoke the place where sacrifice was offered on the Day of Atonement (Lv 16:2–3). God receives the sacrifice offered as a substitute for sinful people. All other sacrifices, however, pointed forward to their fulfillment. On the cross, Christ offered the greatest and final sacrifice, fulfilling all others. Those who place their trust in Christ, rather than fleeing from God, can come to Him expecting mercy, healing, and life (see SC, Lord's Prayer). This is the gracious character of our God. Luther confesses thus concerning the confidence Christians have in God's grace:

> Those who cling to God alone should be sure that He will show them mercy. In other words, He will show them pure goodness and blessing, not only for themselves, but also to their children and their children's children, even to the thousandth generation and beyond that. This ought certainly to move and impel us to risk our hearts in all confidence with God [Hebrews 4:16; 10:19–23], if we wish all temporal and eternal good. For the supreme Majesty makes such outstanding offers and presents such heartfelt encouragements and such rich promises. (LC I 39–40)

Luther further teaches that "God desires nothing more seriously from us than that we ask Him for much and great things. In fact, He is angry if we do not ask and pray confidently" (LC III 56–57). *receive mercy and find grace.* This is what we confidently expect and find in faith. Because of the work of Christ, those who trust in Him receive God's forgiveness. They do not receive what their sins deserve but rather what Christ has earned. Concerning this precious gift, Luther writes:

> Jesus Christ is our mediator, our throne of grace, and our bishop before God in heaven, who daily intercedes for us and reconciles all who believe in him alone, and who call upon him; that he is not a judge, nor cruel, except for those who do not believe in him, or who reject his comfort and grace; [and] that he is not the man who accuses and threatens us, but rather the man who reconciles us [with God], and intercedes for us with his own death and blood shed for us so that we should not fear him, but approach him with all assurance and call him dear Savior, sweet Comforter, faithful bishop of our souls, etc. (LW 50:20–21)

5:1 *chosen from among men.* The high priest had to be one of the people. He represented them all to God as their mediator. But no man could decide on his own initiative to be the high priest. He had to be *appointed.* God instituted the priesthood and its regulations. God chose the sons of Aaron, and on the basis of this election, they fulfilled their priestly office (cf. Ex 28:1; Nu 3:10). Their calling was not an internal feeling but rather external to them. It came from God. He had to authorize them in this office, which they exercised *on behalf of men.* God did not need the priests or the sacrifices; sinners did. He appointed the priests because of human need. *to offer gifts and sacrifices for sins.* Priests offered such things according to God's Word. It is important to note that ordinary high priests offered something other than themselves to atone for sin (cf. 8:3) and that all other high priests needed sacrifices for themselves as well (v. 3).

5:2 *deal gently . . . He Himself is beset with weakness.* Even though he stands between God and the people as an intermediary, the high priest is also one of the people. He himself is a sinner. While this presents some challenges that need to be addressed (v. 3), it also has the benefit that he can more readily understand the need of others. He, too, is a sinner. The high priest, like other worshipers, was weighed down by weakness in the face of temptation. One who needs and receives mercy can compassionately deal with others who need mercy. We see the same thing in our ministers today. They are not perfect but sinners in need of forgiveness—just like those they serve. Faithful ministers recognize this and therefore can be compassionate with those who struggle. Jesus, our Great High Priest, who is fully human but not sinful, can do this perfectly.

5:3 *sacrifice for his own sins.* The high priest, being a sinner, had to make atonement for his own sins as well as for the sins of the people (cf. Lv 9:7; 16:6; Heb 7:27). He was *obligated* to do this, as the sacrifice was the divinely appointed means of forgiveness and reconciliation. If his sin was not covered, he could not approach God's presence to serve His people. He was also obligated to sacrifice for the people. God gave him this holy responsibility.

5:4 *honor.* It was, and is, an honor to serve God. To be high priest was a particularly great honor, since he alone would enter into the presence of God's glory and represent the whole nation. But no one could *take this honor for himself.* The only way one could fill this office was to be *called by God.* See note, v. 1. Even Aaron, the first high priest, did not take this office on himself but was appointed by God.

5:5 *Christ . . . did not exalt Himself.* As God, Jesus is worthy of all glory and honor. He could rightly insist on being exalted and demand to be worshiped. But He did not seek honor and glory for Himself. Instead, for the sake of sinners, He lived among us in meekness. He humbled Himself, even to death on a cross. God the Father has therefore exalted Him to the highest place (Php 2:5–11; cf. Jn 8:54). *appointed.* The Father appointed Jesus to serve as the true High Priest. He alone is authorized to fulfill this office. The quote from Ps 2:7 was addressed to the earthly king of God's people. Yet it also prophesied a greater fulfillment—the enthronement of Christ, the only begotten Son of God, after His ascension.

5:6 *Melchizedek,* a key figure in the priestly argument of Hebrews, is introduced here through this quote from Ps 110:4. Melchizedek was a priest and king who blessed Abraham and received offerings from him (cf. Gn 14:18–20). Although Melchizedek could not be from Aaron's lineage, having lived before Aaron was born, Melchizedek was, nevertheless, a true priest. In a similar way, Jesus is a true priest, even though He was not from Aaron's lineage (cf. v. 10). This argument will be developed further in ch. 7.

5:7 *the days of His flesh.* This phrase refers to the time of Jesus' ministry on earth when He was visibly present among His disciples. Even after His ascension, Jesus remains true man and has flesh and blood (cf. Lk 24:40). *offered.* The word for offering prayers is the same as for offering sacrifice. This emphasizes the priestly nature of Jesus' work, which includes intercessory prayer and sacrificial suffering. Luther writes of Christ's sacrificial work, saying,

> That is the true sacrifice. . . . It deserves to be praised to the utmost and to have every honor given to it, especially over against those other false, lying sacrifices of our own works, which were invented to deny and blaspheme this sacrifice. He is also the Priest who ought to be called a priest above all others. What man can praise and exalt Him enough? . . . No matter how great or burdensome sin, wrath, hell, and damnation may be, this holy sacrifice is far greater and higher! (LW 13:319–20)

with loud cries and tears. In the Garden of Gethsemane, Jesus prayed, "My Father, if it be possible, let this cup pass from Me; nevertheless, not as I will, but as You will" (Mt 26:39). From the cross He cried "with a loud voice, . . . 'My God, my God, why have You forsaken me?'" (Mt 27:46), and before dying, He committed His spirit to the Father with a loud voice (Lk 23:46). Jesus' genuine humanity is evident in the fact that He faced suffering and in the way in which He faced suffering. *able to save Him from death.* While Jesus did, in fact, die to fulfill the Father's will that we might be redeemed, He also trusted that His Father would bring Him through death to resurrection and new life. Jesus was saved from death because He rose again, conquering death and the grave. *heard because of His reverence.* Jesus lived with pure devotion to the Father. His prayers conformed fully to the Father's will and were heard (cf. Mt 26:39; Jn 17). Luther discusses Jesus' prayer, saying:

> In the same manner He also fulfilled the third part of the priestly office: intercessory prayer. Along with, and beyond, His sacrifice Christ also prayed to God the Father in our behalf. Isaiah 53:12 speaks of this function of His priestly office: 'He bore the sins of many, and made intercession for the transgressors.' . . . By means of such prayer He won for us and communicated to us the power and merit of His sacrifice, that is, forgiveness of sins, righteousness, and eternal life. Prayer like that is valid forever and works its power in all Christendom. In short, He continues to exercise this office as our Mediator and Advocate before God. (LW 13:320)

Bengel contemplated the juxtaposition of Christ's sufferings with His complete trust in His Father, saying:

71

When the cup [of suffering] was presented, there was also presented to the soul of the Saviour the horrible image of death, which was joined with sorrow, ignominy, and cursing, and was of a lingering nature, and He was moved to pray for the removal of the cup. But the purity of filial affection in the Saviour with the exercise of holy reason and moderation instantly softened that horror, and subsequently absorbed it completely, as the serenity of His mind returned. "And He was heard," not that He should not drink the cup, but that He should now drink it without any horror; whence also He was strengthened by an angel. (Bengel 4:388)

Similarly, John Wesley wrote about the anguish of Christ and His willing obedience:

What he most exceedingly feared was the weight of infinite justice; the being "bruised" and "put to grief" by the hand of God himself. Compared with this, everything else was a mere nothing; and yet, so greatly did he ever thirst to be obedient to the righteous will of his Father, and to "lay down" even "his life for the sheep," that he vehemently longed to be baptized with this baptism, Luke 12:50. (Wesley 573)

Calvin considered our own prayers in light of Christ's prayer, pondering the truth that God hears the prayers of His people even when we see no direct evidence of this, and the types of things for which we should pray. He writes:

God often hears our prayers, even when that is in no way made evident. For though it belongs not to us to prescribe to him as it were a fixed rule, nor does it become him to grant whatsoever requests we may conceive in our minds or express with our tongues, yet he shews that he grants our prayers in everything necessary for our salvation. So when we seem apparently to be repulsed, we obtain far more than if he fully granted our requests. (Calvin 123)

5:8 *He learned obedience.* Nothing was lacking in Jesus, nor was there anything that needed to be corrected in Him. "Learned" comes from the same Gk root as the word "disciple." Jesus experienced and demonstrated, as true man, what it is to obey the will of the heavenly Father. As God's Son, He did not need to do this, which is why this sentence is introduced with *although He was a son.* He was obedient and underwent suffering for His people who are disobedient and unable to fulfill God's will. He did this *through what He suffered.*

5:9 *made perfect.* As in 2:10 (see note there), "perfect" (Gk . *teleioō*) means "brought to conclusion, finished, or complete." Jesus' work of salvation, earned through His suffering and death, is complete and perfect. *source of eternal salvation.* Ac 4:12 says "there is salvation in no one else for there is no other name under heaven given among men by which we must be saved." Jesus alone is our source of salvation. He is "the way, and the truth, and the life" (Jn 14:6). This is an exclusive claim. Salvation is free, but it is only found in Jesus Christ. *eternal salvation.* Jesus' deliverance is not limited to small matters or merely to earthly problems. Jesus delivers from sin, death, and the devil. Through Him we have eternal life. *to all who obey Him.* This word means to listen to and do what He says. This is referring not to obedience of the Law's demands, but to faith. Faith hears and believes the message of Christ. Rm 1:5 speaks in this same sense when it refers to the "obedience of faith."

5:10 *designated.* Jesus did not choose this for Himself but was solemnly acclaimed by the Father (see notes, 1:2; 3:2; 5:1). *the order of Melchizedek.* See note, v. 6. This bracketing verse returns us to the central idea that Christ sacrificed Himself for us as both victim and High Priest. This is how He secured our salvation. The priesthood of Melchizedek and Jesus will be addressed in more detail in ch. 7.

4:14–5:10 in Devotion and Prayer "No one understands what I am going through! They do not know how hard it is to face this situation. It feels like everyone is judging me, but they haven't walked in my shoes. If they only knew what this is like, they might understand." Have you ever thought such things or spoken such complaints? Most people have. Words like these may be self-pitying words of complaint. We may say such things to excuse behavior that we know should make us ashamed. Often they simply are reflecting feelings of despair. But sometimes they may be correct. The people who surround us may not really know what we are going through or how difficult a situation really is. If they haven't had a similar experience, how could they really know what it is like? But God knows. This is not a sentimental platitude but a statement of grace. He truly knows because the Son of God became fully human for us. He shares our complete humanity and knows the weaknesses that we experience. He knows what it is to be tempted because He has been tempted as we are. But unlike us, He did not give in to temptation. He resisted temptation—for you! Obedient to His Father's will, He suffered—for you! Alone, forsaken, and condemned for our guilt, He died—for you! He knew that God would deliver Him from death and that because of what He has done, God would deliver you from death too. What great news! God not only understands all that we go through and sympathizes with our weaknesses, but He takes care of our greatest enemies as well. He is our source of eternal salvation. He lives and intercedes to the Father—for you! Truly, He helps us in all our needs. • Lord Jesus, our true and great High Priest, You did everything needed for me. Come to me in my weakness and infirmity and grant me Your strength. Come to me when I am tempted and give me Your will. Come to me with Your grace and forgiveness. Come to me when I am dying and give me Your life. Amen.

Introduction to 5:11–6:20 These challenging verses comprise the central admonition of the Letter to the Hebrews. The author rebukes his readers and draws them back from spiritual collapse and to spiritual maturity. He speaks bluntly and directly because he loves his readers and wants them to grow in faith and rely on Christ Jesus alone.

5:11 *hard to explain . . . dull of hearing.* This introduces a stinging rebuke. The teaching presented here is important and not too complicated, but the hearers are slow to listen and understand. The Gk word for "dull" also means "sluggish" or "lazy." They are not making any effort to hear and understand, probably because the topic is uncomfortable to them. This is what makes the topics being presented *hard to explain.* The problem does not lie with the topic nor the writer but with the readers.

5:12 *by this time.* The readers apparently had been Christians for some time but they are surprisingly immature given their time in the faith. The author is clearly disappointed in their lack of growth in understanding. *teachers.* (Gk *didaskalos*) In the NT this is sometimes used as another word for "pastor" or it may refer to a distinct calling as a theological teacher (cf. Ac 13:1; 2Tm 1:11). The ability to teach is critical for pastors (e.g., 1Tm 3:2; 2Tm 2:24), and this work is so important to the church that James warns, "Not many of you should become teachers, my brothers, for you know that we who teach will be judged with greater strictness" (Jas 3:1). Given the importance of teaching in the NT, this admonition is striking: by now they should be mature enough that they are able to teach others the truths of the Christian faith, but the opposite is the case. While they should be mature enough and knowledgeable enough to be teachers, they are, in fact, in need of someone to teach them the basics! These teachings are described as *the basic principles of the oracles of God.* "Oracles" (Gk *logion*) typically refers to a collection of sayings, particularly sayings that have authority. We should probably understand this as a synonym for Scripture. The "basic principles" of these oracles are key points of apostolic teaching, such as the examples listed in Heb 6:1–2. While the basics are always important, we are called to grow in knowledge of God's Word. *milk.* Newborns thrive on their mothers' milk but are weaned and introduced to solid food as they grow. In the ancient world milk was considered food for children and for the ill. When he says "you need milk" we might hear, "all you can handle is baby food. What does that make you? Can you only handle spiritual baby food?" (cf. 1Co 3:1–2). *solid food.* As a child grow, she is introduced to a wider range of foods that nourish, satisfy, and delight. Likewise, with maturity, a Christian student of Scripture is better prepared to understand more challenging passages and apply them correctly to life's more difficult issues. An immature student may fall into doubt or fear, or perhaps most dangerously, pride.

5:13 *unskilled in the word.* Here the point is made clearly. The immature have a minimal knowledge of Scripture. If they do not grow in faith, they may be unable to keep the truths of Scripture straight and they will easily fell into error. They simply may not know what God is telling them because they are not listening to Him when He speaks in His Word.

5:14 *mature.* Again the message is clear: "grow up!" An infant in the faith may have a basic knowledge of Christian teaching. Trusting in Christ, they have a saving faith, even if they only know the basics. But we are not called to limit our knowledge but to grow and mature. Scripture repeatedly calls us to maturity in the faith (e.g., Eph 4:13). God knows that this will be a blessing to His people. He wants us to mature for our own benefit and for the benefit of others. *powers of discernment trained by constant practice.* Discernment is recognizing the differences between things and judging what is good and what is not in ways that are pleasing to God. In the example used here, adults, by experience, have developed palates that can discern subtle differences in food and drink. Palates are refined with practice and experience. Similarly, spiritually mature people have been exposed to the breadth of Holy Scripture. They have read, studied, and pondered the Word of God. With a solid knowledge of Scripture, they can properly discern and receive the "solid food" of advanced teaching. See note, v. 12. *distinguish good from evil.* The spiritually mature are able to distinguish true teaching from false teaching, and good behavior from wickedness. This builds them up in God's truth and protects them from false, destructive teachings.

6:1 *leave.* The author is certainly not telling us to "leave behind" or "abandon" biblical teaching. We always need the full counsel of God including the foundational teachings of our faith. (This is the sense in which Peter uses the concept of "milk" in 1Pt 2:2 "Like newborn infants, long for the pure spiritual milk, that by it you may grow up into salvation.") Rather, Hebrews is saying "go deeper. For now, let us move on to other topics that will help you grow in faith." These are all teachings from Scripture and we are called to learn. *the elementary doctrine of Christ.* This means the basic, foundational teachings of the Christian faith. See note, 5:12. *maturity.* Cf. 5:14. *foundation.* The fundamental doctrines or basic beliefs. These remain important, but they are not the total teaching of the Christian faith. If you are building a house, you need a good foundation but there is more to the house than just the foundation. Foundational Christian teachings are of critical importance, but God teaches us throughout His Word. Other biblical teachings are built upon this foundation. These other teachings are also important. So Calvin wrote:

> As the foundation is laid for the sake of what is built on it, he who is occupied in laying it and proceeds not to the superstruction, wearies himself with foolish and useless labour. In short, as the builder must begin with the foundation, so must he go on with his work that the house may be built. Similar is the case as to Christianity; we have the first principles as the foundation, but the higher doctrine ought immediately to follow which is to complete the building. (Calvin 131)

repentance. Rejecting and turning away from those actions that do not flow from faith in Christ. *dead works.* Without faith and without God's approval, all our works are useless and indeed lay a foundation of false confidence before God (cf. Is 64:6). In this sense, it does not matter what other people think of our works, or how proud we are of what we accomplish. "Without faith it is impossible to please [God]" (11:6). *faith toward God.* Trust in the promises of God, especially the promise of forgiveness in Christ Jesus. Hebrews is not in any way disparaging repentance and faith; it is calling us to grow in this faith.

6:2 *washings.* The Gk for "washing" is *baptismos* which means "to wash" or "apply water." This word is used when describing washing objects (e.g., Mk 7:3–4) or baptizing people (e.g., 1Pt 3:21). Here it is used in the plural. This may mean there were questions or disputes about the meaning of the baptism of John the Baptizer and of Christian Baptism. There may also have been confusion regarding various OT commands about ritual washings and whether they still needed to be performed. If the readers truly knew the Scriptures, they would have no difficulty discerning between Christian Baptism, which is instituted by Christ as a means of grace, and other washings (cf. Acts 19:4–5). *the laying on of hands.* This may refer to a number of different things. In this context, it may refer to a liturgical action that likely accompanied baptismal prayers. Hands were also laid on the sick when God was asked for healing (Mk 5:23; Ac 9:12) and on those being set aside for ministry in Christ's Church (e.g., 1Tm 4:14). *resurrection of the dead.* The raising, in the body, of all those who have died (cf. 1Co 15), is a basic, critical doctrine that was frequently discussed. *eternal judgment.* The final judgment after the resurrection of all the dead (cf. Mt 25:31–46). All of these things are important teachings, but immaturity either focused on them exclusively, to the neglect of other biblical teachings, or else immature believers could not even keep these basic teachings straight.

6:3 *if God permits.* Acknowledging God's direction and timing, the author intends to talk about other things, but recognizes that he may need to discuss even these basic topics with immature Christians.

5:11–6:3 in Devotion and Prayer The Christian faith is so simple that a little child can articulate its truths. Having been instructed in the faith, they can confess their faith in age-appropriate ways. We marvel at their sincerity and recognize them as a fellow child of God. We, too, are called to have a child-like faith, trusting our dear Father in heaven. But do we distort that to fabricate an excuse? Are we tempted to believe and know as little as possible, thinking, "that's good enough"? Do we seek a minimalistic Christianity? This is not the response of living faith. Hebrews has a simple message for those who have such an attitude: "Grow up!" For your own sake, listen to your Lord and God. Go deeper into His Word. You will find a richness and depth of grace that will nourish and sustain you for a lifetime. You will find yourself better equipped to live as His child. You will be better able to serve your neighbor. You won't be leaving behind that child-like faith; you will instead discover just how wonderful it is. God calls us to a rich diet of His Word that will nourish, delight, and satisfy us. He calls us to be His children who are growing in faith. • God, my Father, thank You for making me Your child. Thank You for all that Jesus has done for me. Grant that I never lose a child-like faith. Grant me Your Holy Spirit that I may also grow in faith, grow in knowledge of Your will, and gladly serve my neighbor. In Jesus name. Amen.

Introduction to 6:4–6 This is a particularly challenging text and prone to misinterpretation and misapplication. God's Law rightly condemns sin and crushes sinners. It is rightly applied to those who are secure in their sins and to those who see no need for God's salvation. But applied to those who already know their guilt and despair of their sins, the Law continues to crush and to kill. Such repentant sinners need to hear the Gospel—what God has done for them in the person and work of Christ. These words are written to Christians who seem to think that sin is no threat to them and that they can leave the Christian faith when they like, sin as they please, and then return to seek forgiveness later. Such an immature attitude reveals a spiritual problem and is, in fact, a serious threat to the person. The Lutheran reformers say:

> Remember that God punishes sin with sins. This means that because of their self-confidence, lack of repentance, and willful sins, He later punishes with hardheartedness and blindness those who had been converted. . . . This punishment should not be interpreted to mean that it never had been God's good pleasure that such persons should come to the knowledge of the truth and be saved (FC SD XI 83).

In regard to this passage's most challenging words, that it is *impossible . . . to restore them again to repentance,* Martin Luther writes: "If anyone has fallen away from Christ, who is the true sacrifice for sins, and seeks another way or mode to be saved and go to heaven, he will never go there, he will not succeed" (StL 7:959). These words teach that no mere person can bring back those who, having received faith, fall away from it and seek a way of salvation other than Christ. But God is no mere person, and "with God all things are possible" (Mt 19:26). If you have loved ones who have fallen away, continually pray for them, that God may restore them. Continue to love them and share the Gospel with them. While they cannot convert themselves and we cannot convert them, with God, all things are possible.

6:4 *impossible*. The author is sternly warning those who are being tempted. Do not arrogantly think that you can temporarily forsake your faith to indulge your sinful nature. Humans cannot convert themselves—this is the work of God alone (1Co 12:3; Eph 2:8). However, we may be prone to misunderstand the word "impossible." This word translates the Gk *adynatos*. The Gk prefix *a* changes a word to negative. *Dynatos* is the word for power, or ability. *Adynatos* literally means "not power," "powerless", or "no ability." A person does not have the power or ability to convert himself. If a Christian renounces the faith, they simply do not have the ability to choose to return. The unconverted never have this power—only God can work faith. The warning is clear: do not forsake your faith, thinking that you can return to it when you please. As an unbeliever, you will not have the ability to choose to believe. But lest we despair, God reminds us that He can bring the dead to life, turn enemies into sons, and convert the unbelieving into believers. It is impossible for us, but all things are possible for God (cf. Mt 19:26). *Once . . . enlightened*. In other words, once they have come to faith in Christ by the work of the Holy Spirit. Christ is the light of the world (Jn 8:12). Light is a common biblical description of the gifts of God, who has "called you out of darkness into His marvelous light" (1Pt 2:9; cf. 10:32; Eph 1:18; Col 1:12–13; 1Jn 1:5–7). *tasted the heavenly gift*. A second description of the repentance (cf. Ac 11:17–18) and faith (Eph 2:8) worked by God. God's gift of grace is an objective reality (Eph 2:8) that is experienced and recognized by those who are converted (cf. Ps 34:8). *shared in the Holy Spirit*. A third description of God's gift of faith. Those baptized into Christ have called out to God the Father through the Spirit (cf. Rm 8:15), and without the Holy Spirit, no one can say, "Jesus is Lord" (1Co 12:3). They have seen these gifts in their own lives. Knox compared this passage to Jesus' warning about looking back from the plow (Luke 9:62). He wrote the following appeal in his "Letter to the Faithful in London":

O, dear brethren, remember the dignity of our confession: you have followed Christ; you have proclaimed war against idolatry; you have laid hand upon the truth, and have communicated at the Lord's table; will you now suddenly slide back? Will you refuse God, and make a compact with the devil? Will you tread the most precious blood of Christ's testament under your feet? which assuredly you do as oft as ever you present your bodies amongst idolaters before that blasphemous idol. God, the Father of all mercies, for Christ his Son's sake, preserve you from that sore temptation, whose dolours and dangers sorrow will not suffer me to express! (Knox 34–35)

6:5 *tasted the goodness of the word of God.* Those spoken of here are not ignorant concerning what God says. Having received God's Word of mercy and grace in the Gospel and Baptism, they have continued to receive the blessings of God's Word and have seen God working through it for their good. The Gospel is the "power of God for salvation to everyone who believes" (Rm 1:16). God's inspired Word is "profitable for teaching, for reproof, for correction, and for training in righteousness" (2Tm 3:16). God does not bring us to faith and then leave us to ourselves; He continues to bless us and equip us with everything we need. *powers of the age to come.* God's miraculous intervention in their lives now anticipates the greatness of the blessings of heaven. It is as if heaven has invaded earth (cf. Col 1:13). God has bestowed amazing blessings on His children. They have seen His gifts and His faithfulness.

6:6 *fallen away.* Somehow, despite having received such abundant blessings (described, in part, in vv. 4–5), they have irrationally turned away from them, rejecting God's gift of repentance and faith. *restore them.* This completes the statement begun in v. 4 with "it is impossible." The intervening phrases make the extent of their rejection clear. They know what they are leaving behind. Having abandoned faith, they once again lack the ability to convert themselves and to restore themselves to the faith they once held. This is beyond any human being's ability, for without the Holy Spirit, we are dead in our trespasses (Eph 2:1) and cannot save or convert ourselves. *crucifying once again.* The author shows that unbelief is not the rejection of an idea but is, in fact, rejection of Christ Himself. Like the crowds calling for Jesus' crucifixion, those who fall away actively reject Christ's mercy and forgiveness (cf. 10:29). This is done *to their* *own harm.* They cannot inflict any further harm or suffering upon Christ, who has already died for the sins of the world. The damage is to themselves. They are turning away from their only hope into condemnation and death. *holding Him up to contempt.* This is the opposite of confessing Christ. It is speaking and acting as if the sacrifice of Christ has no power. These are difficult words to hear, but this severe warning is not given to drive us to despair but rather to move us to rely on Christ alone. This is what Luther reflects when he says,

> I have already been preaching Christ and fighting against the devil in his false teachers for a number of years; but I have experienced how much difficulty this business has caused me. For I cannot repel Satan as I would like. Nor can I finally grasp Christ as Scripture propounds Him to me, but the devil often suggests a false Christ to me. Thanks be to God, however, for preserving us in the Word, in faith, and in prayer! We know that one should walk in humility and fear in the sight of God and not presume upon our own wisdom, righteousness, doctrine, and courage. One should rely on the power of Christ. When we are weak, He is strong; and through us weaklings He always conquers and triumphs. To Him be glory forever. Amen. (LW 26:196)

6:7–8 Similar imagery of fruitful and unfruitful land is a frequent motif in Scripture (e.g., Is 5:1–7).

6:7 *receives a blessing from God.* God blessed the land He created to be fruitful (Gn 1:11). According to His design, the land produces a crop after the rain. This is a blessing to the land itself, which is empowered to be fruitful. It is also a blessing to those who will enjoy its produce. When they also have *cultivated* the land, caring for it and working to grow a specific group, they expect to harvest and enjoy the fruits of that crop. Similarly, God's children, who have received the saving and empowering waters of Baptism, produce the fruit of faith (Jn 15:5). This is a blessing to them but also a blessing to their neighbors, who benefit from the fruit they produce. Both of these are by God's design.

6:8 *thorns . . . cursed.* Thorns were part of the curse that followed Adam's sin (Gn 3: 18–18). Those who receive God's gifts through faith but then fall away will fail to bear the fruit of God's Spirit. They become like weeds, sapping resources while producing nothing. Those who fall away may try to sow doubt or discord among other believers. *worthless and near to being cursed.* Note the pause in these words. The curse is not necessarily immediate. Judgment is near, but there may yet be time for God to work and for the straying to repent. *its end is to be burned.* Just as thorns and thistles, being unproductive, are cut down and burned, so those who fail to trust God's Word will face His judgment (cf. Mt 3:12; Jn 15:6; Lk 13:6–9). There is no other source of salvation than the one they have rejected. God is patient, but His patience has a limit. Again, remember that these words are written to warn us: these are serious matters. Remember what God has given you, rejoice, and be faithful to Him.

6:9 *sure of better things.* The warning of the previous verses is an important one, but it is not God's only message. The author comforts his readers. Confident in their faith, he is likewise confident that God will bestow spiritual blessings on them that flow from a life of trust in Christ Jesus. He is confident that these better things *belong to salvation.* He warned them so that they would not be tempted to leave these wonderful blessings.

6:10 This verse reminds the recipients of some of the fruit that their faith is producing. God has begun His work of salvation among them and will remember His own demonstration of love and service through them. Surely He will also show His righteousness in bringing their salvation to completion (cf. Eph 1:13–14). Notice that the fruits of faith are not self-serving; they are seen in their *work.* This is not implying that works earn salvation but is speaking of the work that they do, in response to faith, in serving other people. Further evidence is seen in the *love* that they show to others and in their service to their fellow Christians, who, having been justified, are holy and therefore are called the *saints.* The fruit of faith is not directed inwardly but outward, toward our neighbor. God recognizes this work and graciously remembers and honors such service as if it was done to Him (cf. Mt 10:42; 25:40). This, too, is a gracious gift from God.

6:11 *earnestness to have the full assurance of hope.* The author does not want his warning (vv. 4–8) to be misapplied. Those who trust in Christ can and should have complete confidence in the promises of God. He will always be faithful to His children and will keep them in the faith. This, too, like the works done for the neighbor, is a fruit of faith and a gift of God.

Revelation and Assurance

Randall C. Zachman, in *John Calvin as Teacher, Pastor, and Theologian: The Shape of His Writings and Thought* (Grand Rapids, MI: Baker Academic, 2006), draws a distinction between Luther and Calvin on the topic of revelation and assurance (Zachman, 176). He notes that Luther describes seeing the opposition of the world while hearing and believing what God reveals in His Word. The revelation of the Word alone (*sola Scriptura*) gives faith and thereby causes one to see the invisible things of God with assurance. For example, in commenting on Hebrews 6, Luther wrote:

> How beautifully [the author of Hebrews] combines the two, faith and patience! For faith causes the heart to cling fast to celestial things and to be carried away and to dwell in things that are invisible. (LW 29:185)

The Word creates faith that sees the things of God despite the angry opposition of the world. Similarly, Melachthon wrote against "vagrant speculations," affirming that one needs to see God in Christ, revealed in the Gospel (Zachman 47).

Calvin, like Luther and Melanchthon, decried the speculative theology of the scholastics.

> [The Schoolmen] have in a manner drawn a veil over Christ, to whom, if our eye is not directly turned, we must always wander through many labyrinths. . . . Faith consists not in ignorance, but in knowledge— knowledge not of God merely, but of the divine will. We do not obtain salvation either because we are prepared to embrace every dictate of the church as true . . . but when we recognize God as a propitious Father through the reconciliation made by Christ, and Christ as given to us for righteousness, sanctification, and life. (*Institutes of the Christian Religion*, Henry Beveridge, trans. [Edinburgh, 1945–46], 3.2.2)

However, Calvin further sought assurance by combining what one sees in both creation and in the Word. Reason interprets creation and faith hears and receives what God says in the Word. For Calvin, these two are living images of God that human beings can grasp, sources of divine revelation that bring assurance (Zachman 176). He appealed to both reason and Scripture.

Among heirs of the Reformation, Wesley described assurance in yet a different manner. He was perhaps reacting to the increase of rationalism in his day as well as the physical responses to preaching and teaching that accompanied revivalism. He wrote:

> The full assurance of faith relates to present pardon; the full assurance of hope, to future glory. The former is the highest degree of divine evidence that God is reconciled to me in the Son of his love; the latter is the same degree of divine evidence (wrought in the soul by the same immediate inspiration of the Holy Ghost) of persevering grace, and of eternal glory. So much, and no more, as faith every moment "beholds with open face," so much does hope see to all eternity. But this assurance of faith and hope is not an opinion, not a bare construction of scripture, but is given immediately by the power of the Holy Ghost; and what none can have for another, but for himself only. (Wesley 575)

Wesley emphasized an immediate revelation above and beyond what God said through the Word or that one could discern in creation. Wesley's view thus prepared the way for emphasis on miracles, signs, and wonders as assurances of God's presence and of salvation. In other words, Wesley looked for something more than the "bare construction of scripture" that Luther found so deeply assuring. ❧

6:12 *sluggish.* Or "lazy," this is the same word used in 5:11 (where the ESV translates it "dull" of hearing). This repetition brackets the warning of this section. The author has shown that the greatest danger to those who dull their ears to the Word of God is the loss of faith, which leads to a loss of hope. Don't let this happen! Instead, be *imitators of those who . . . inherit the promises.* Follow the good example of those who lived by faith in God. (This theme is developed further in ch. 11.) Like them, we can inherit the promises by faith.

6:4–6:12 in Devotion and Prayer So often we are tempted to act as if God's will for our lives is a burden or a limitation that constrains our ability to enjoy life. Faced with a temptation, we ask: "How far can I go before I get in trouble? What is the absolute limit of behavior that will let me have the maximum "fun" without the consequences being too severe?" We think we can skirt the very edges of danger. "What do I really have to avoid?" "What is the minimum that I have to do or believe to be safe?" These are foolish, immature questions. They do not reflect a meaningful relationship with, or understanding of, the God who has created us to be His own people. God's will is not given to limit our pleasure but rather to show us what true joy is. He does not restrict in order to annoy us but rather to lead us into an abundant, meaningful, and satisfying life. Our sinful nature is always looking for the wrong things. So Hebrews warns us: "Watch out! There's real danger in what you are doing! Don't let your pursuit of happiness rob you of any hope for happiness at all." Our Lord Jesus has given us great gifts of life and salvation. We have tasted His gifts and seen that they are good. We have been blessed not only by Him directly but also by the love and service of the saints, who were responding to His love in their lives. Listen to the call of God: I am with you; stay where I have lovingly planted you. Nourished in your baptism, fed at the table, strengthened by My Word, stay with Me and with My people. Here you find great blessings. Here you find great joy. And here you will grow in faith and maturity and see even greater blessings. • Gracious Father, You have blessed me with many gifts. Thank You for all of these gifts, especially for the gift of my Savior, Jesus. By Your Holy Spirit, keep me united with my Savior. Grant that I remain in Him and He with me, that I might bear much fruit to the glory of Your name. As You have blessed me, make me a fruitful blessing to others. Give me a confident faith and bring me at last to Your kingdom where I will see the fullness of Your blessings. In Jesus' name. Amen.

Introduction to 6:13–20 The previous verse commended imitation of the faithful, who inherit God's promises. This section demonstrates the reliability of God, who has made those great promises to His people.

6:13 *God . . . swore by Himself.* God was not compelled to promise Abraham that He would bless and multiply him. The blessing itself was already an astonishing, undeserved gift. Yet God chose to give certainty, not only making the promise but swearing an oath that He would fulfill what He promised. Such a solemn oath is a vow to do something and is typically made before witnesses so that one cannot later claim that no oath was taken. In ideal circumstances, an oath is made before an authority who can aid in its enforcement, if necessary. There is no greater witness than God Himself, so accordingly He invokes His own authority and character when He makes a solemn promise. God is utterly reliable in His promises since "He is unchangeable in will and essence" (FC SD XI 75). The allusion referenced here is found in Gn 22:16–18, where God gave His absolute guarantee in promising His blessing to Abraham.

6:14 *bless . . . multiply.* God blessed humanity through the command to "be fruitful and multiply" (Gn 1:28). He reiterated this, emphasizing it as a blessing, in Abraham's call. Given the age of Abraham and Sarah, this was indeed a blessing. Because of God's blessing, Abraham's descendants would become a great nation (cf. Gn 12:2).

6:15 *patiently waited.* Verse 12 called Christians to patiently wait for God's promised inheritance. Abraham believed God's promise, even though its fulfillment took much longer than he expected. Because God is always faithful to His promises, Abraham's patience was not in vain. He did obtain *the promise* in God's own time.

6:16 *swear by something greater.* Oaths are taken upon something in which people rely for blessing or security in life. They were often part of a greater covenant, which included promises and blessings but also consequences if the oath is broken. Oaths are not to be taken falsely (Lv 19:12) or made lightly. Scripture teaches that they must be fulfilled (cf. Nu 30:2; Dt 23:21; Ec 5:4). *an oath is final for confirmation.* When oaths are taken as seriously as they were in the biblical world, the oath actually verifies the claims of the one taking it. Oaths may be taken legitimately in certain cases, but Jesus warns against the misuse of oaths in Mt 5:33–37.

6:17 *God decided to show more convincingly.* The impetus to make such a promise is entirely from God's will. He was not compelled to do this. God's statement should have been sufficient, but He underscores His promises to give His doubting people greater confidence. *the heirs of the promise.* God's promise to make Abraham a great nation passed through him to his descendants, who saw the fulfillment of God's promise. This is not limited to biological descent, for all those who place their faith in Christ are heirs of Abraham and therefore heirs of the promise made to him (cf. Gal 3:29). *unchangeable character of His purpose.* Unlike human beings, God's purpose does not change due to time or circumstance (cf. Mal 3:6; Pr 19:21).

6:18 *two unchangeable things.* These are God's purpose, which He communicated to His people, and His oath that promised fulfillment. God's stress on the validity of this promise gives His people even more confidence. Cf. v. 17. *it is impossible for God to lie.* God's promise and oath are unbreakable. "God is not a man, that He should lie, or a son of man, that He should change his mind. Has He said, and will He not do it? Or has He spoken and He will not fulfill it?" (Nu 23:19; cf. Ti 1:2) He doesn't just tell the truth, He is the Truth (Jn 14:6). We can be absolutely certain that God will remain true to His Word. *fled for refuge.* Not to a place, but to God Himself. He freely gives His protection from evil to all those who call out to Him (cf. Pss 34:8; 46:1; 91:2). *hold fast.* The character of God strengthens our faith. God gives us the gift of faith, and in that faith, we cling to our faithful Lord. *the hope set before us.* Knowing that God's Word is true, we have confidence in all of His promises. This includes the hope of sharing with Jesus, by the Holy Spirit's power, the eternal blessings of life with the Father.

6:19 *anchor of the soul.* As an anchor holds a ship in position during a storm, so the sure and certain hope of eternal life gives us stability in the sufferings and temptations of life. *hope that enters into the inner place behind the curtain.* This begins to reintroduce the theme of the priesthood, which will be developed in ch. 7ff. The "inner place" is the Most Holy Place in the tabernacle (and later, the temple). It contained the ark of the covenant and was the place where God caused His glory to dwell for the good of His people. Lv 16:2 warns against improperly entering the Most Holy Place. The high priest would enter annually on the Day Atonement, but only after carefully following God's directions for purification. Our hope—

Christ Jesus, our Great High Priest—has entered the Most Holy Place to make atonement for us. In Him we have access to the gracious and sanctifying presence of God.

6:20 *a forerunner on our behalf.* Jesus, as both true man and true God, has prepared the path to the Father for us. He has gone to the Father, and because of His priestly work, we are now reconciled to the Father and will enter into His presence eternally. Jesus is the Way to the Father (Jn 14:6). *high priest forever.* As God, Jesus is eternal, thus His priestly office is eternal. God's unchangeable, gracious character is demonstrated in Christ's eternal priesthood. *the order of Melchizedek.* See note, 5:6.

6:13–20 in Devotion and Prayer "Promises are made to be broken." That is often the cynical conclusion of those who have been disappointed by the unfaithfulness of others. Promises are just words and easy to ignore, twist, or break. Often, when people try to emphasize their promises by oaths and swearing, we become even more suspicious. Will they really keep their promises? Too often, promises are broken or neglected. But God doesn't take His promises lightly. He does not waver in fulfilling them. He always keeps His promises. When He called Abraham, He called an old, childless man. But God promised Abraham that He would become a great nation. Abraham believed God's promise, and he was not disappointed. Abraham and Sarah had a son, and through Isaac, Abraham's line grew into a great nation. God promised Abraham that all the nations of the earth would be blessed through Him, and they have been, for Jesus, the world's Redeemer, was descended from Abraham. But even this was not the extent of God's lavish promise. All who trust in Christ Jesus share in the blessing of life promised to Abraham. You are a child of Abraham and an heir of the promise. Because God is faithful, you receive the confidence and hope that enters into God's presence through Christ. We have access to the Father through Jesus. We live in a restored, holy relationship with Him because our Savior has covered us in His righteousness. This is God's promise to you: You are forgiven. You are His heir. In Christ, You will live in Him forever. • Heavenly Father, thank You for sending Jesus as the fulfillment of Your promise and for making me Your child. Bless me so that I may confidently and firmly believe Your promise. Make me a blessing to other people so that, through me, they may know Jesus. Amen.

Introduction to 7:1–10 In 5:6, 10, and 7:1, Jesus is called an eternal priest "after the order of Melchizedek." This phrase, from Ps 110:4, now begins to be explored in detail. The author builds on the scant details about Melchizedek that are found in Scripture to show how his life and work foreshadows the work of Jesus, our Great High Priest.

7:1 *king . . . priest*. Melchizedek was both a priest and a king at the same time. This foreshadowed the unity of true kingship and priesthood that is fulfilled in Christ. (cf. Gn 14:18–20; Ps 110:4). *Salem*. Josephus clarifies this when he writes that "they afterward called Salem Jerusalem" (Ant.1.180). Salem is listed in parallel with Zion in Ps 76:2. The name "Salem" comes from the word for "peace," which means that, in a sense, Melchizedek was the "king of peace" (v. 2). Another early name for this city is Jebus (Jgs 19:10–11). *Most High God*. (Gk *theou tou hypsistou*; Hbr. *'ēl 'ēl-yōn*; cf. Gn 14:18). This is the one true God, the God of Abraham. God is called the Most High in Pss 7:17; 9:2; 18:13; 46:4. *slaughter of the kings*. This battle (recounted in Gn 14:13–16) occurred before the encounter between Abraham and Melchizedek. Abraham became involved when those kings took Abraham's nephew Lot captive and plundered his possessions. Abraham engaged them to deliver Lot and retrieve his property. *blessed him*. This was a priestly action by Melchizedek for Abraham. Melchizedek also brought Abraham bread and wine (Gn 14:18). Calvin reflects on this event, saying:

> It is indeed no wonder that he dwells so minutely on this subject. It was doubtless no common thing that in a country abounding in the corruptions of so many superstitions, a man was found who preserved the pure worship of God; for on one side he was nigh to Sodom and Gomorrah, and on the other to the Canaanites, so that he was on every side encompassed by ungodly men. Besides, the whole world was so fallen into impiety, that it is very probable that God was nowhere faithfully worshipped except in the family of Abraham; for his father and his grandfather, who ought to have retained true religion, had long before degenerated into idolatry. It was therefore a memorable fact, that there was still a king who not only retained true religion, but also performed himself the office of a priest. (Calvin 155)

7:2 *apportioned a tenth part*. Abraham recognized Melchizedek's priestly status by offering him a tithe of the spoils of battle. This was not payment for the blessing but a response to a blessing already given and received. *king of righteousness . . . king of peace.* In Hebrew, *by translation of his name,* Melchizedek means "King of Righteousness." Since Salem comes from the word for peace, King of Salem means "King of Peace." These significant titles foreshadow the office of Christ Jesus.

7:3 Since the Levitical priesthood is directly connected to ancestry, genealogies are important to priestly discussions. So it is remarkable that nothing is known about Melchizedek aside from the brief reference in Gn 14:18–20 and in further allusions to this story. In later years, after the establishment of the Levitical priesthood, a priest could not take office until he was validated as having appropriate Levitical descent. But since Melchizedek predates Aaron, it is impossible for him to meet this standard and it cannot apply to him. This is critical evidence of the legitimacy of specific non-Levitical priests. However, this verse builds on Melchizedek's story in a different manner. Since there was no established priestly ancestry for Melchizedek, there is no record of his parents (*he is without father or mother*) or other ancestry (*without . . . genealogy*). Neither his birth nor death are recorded (*having neither beginning of days nor end of life*). On this basis, Hebrews draws a parallel to Jesus, who, as the Son of God, is eternal—He has no beginning of days and He lives eternally. As there is no recorded end to Melchizedek's priesthood, he *continues a priest forever,* so to speak. Likewise, there is no end whatsoever to the eternal priesthood of Christ. The Son of God truly is an eternal priest. Melchizedek is, in this and other ways, a type of Christ. Remarking on the parallels, Bengel makes this interesting comment:

> The Son of God is not said to be made like to Melchisedec, but the contrary (vice versa); for the Son of God is more ancient, and is the archetype; comp. viii. 5, [where in like manner heavenly things are set forth as more ancient than the things belonging to the Levitical priesthood]. (Bengel 4:403)

7:4 *how great.* Jews considered their ancestor Abraham to be an exceedingly great man, so Abraham's tithe to Melchizedek demonstrates the priest-king's greatness. *this man.* Melchizedek. *the patriarch.* Abraham was the common ancestor of the Israelites—the biological source of their great nation. Even more, he is the patriarch of all who, like him, are justified by faith (cf. Rm 4:11, 16; Gal 3:7). *Tenth.* See v. 2.

7:5–6 *commandment . . . to take tithes.* Levitical priests received the tithe from their fellow Israelites as a matter of law. This was an obligation and responsibility that God gave to the Israelites (cf. Nu 18:21; 2Ch 31:4). *from their brothers.* The Levites and those of other tribes were all of equal descent from Abraham. They received the tithes to support their priestly office, which was exercised on behalf of all Israel. *But this man . . . received tithes.* Unlike the Levites, Melchizedek was not an heir of Abraham and had no legal claim to Abraham's possessions. Neither had God commanded Abraham to give a tithe to this priest. Nonetheless, Melchizedek received the patriarch's tithe, showing his God-given authority as priest and king. Furthermore, his status is shown in his ability to bless great Abraham. Abraham *had the promises,* but the priest still *blessed him.*

7:7 *the inferior is blessed by the superior.* The fact that Melchizedek blessed the patriarch Abraham and received his tithe suggests that Melchizedek is, in some sense, even greater than Abraham.

7:8 *in the one case.* This refers to the Levites. They receive the tithes according to God's command. These priests are *mortal.* When they die, another takes their place. *he lives.* Since no death is recorded for Melchizedek, and since there is no recorded end to his office, his priestly office is, in a sense, without end (cf. v. 3; Ps 110:4). Melchizedek foreshadows Christ, who truly lives forever and intercedes for His people as an eternal priest (cf. Jn 6:57; Rv 1:17–18).

7:9–10 *one might even say that Levi himself.* As the patriarch of all Israelite priests who followed him, Levi rightly received tithes, as did his priestly descendants. *in his loins.* Before Levi was born, his ancestor Abraham paid a tithe to Melchizedek. Levi was, in a sense, genetically present in Abraham. When Abraham paid the tithe, he demonstrated the legitimacy and supremacy of Melchizedek to Levi.

7:1–10 in Devotion and Prayer Thankful for God's blessings and deliverance in battle, Abraham first received a blessing from God through His priest Melchizedek. He responded in faith and gave a tithe to Melchizedek. Abraham honored the priest's office and supported God's servant when he did this. In later generations, the Israelites were commanded to give a tithe to the Levitical priests in response to God's blessings and to support the priests' holy calling. We, too, encounter a priest—one even greater than Melchizedek or the Aaronic priests—Jesus the Great High Priest. Through this ultimate priest we freely receive wondrous, undeserved blessings from

God. Christ our Great High Priest is truly a priest forever and serves to lead us to His kingdom. In response, we are blessed to offer to God a portion of what He has given us. We give freely and gladly, knowing that all blessings come from Him and mindful that we have received infinite blessings through the priestly work of Jesus. • Lord Jesus, You are my Priest who sacrificed Yourself for me and who continues to intercede for me. You are my king of righteousness and king of peace. Thank You for the life You have given me in Your kingdom. Thank You for clothing me in Your righteousness. Grant me Your peace. Amen.

Introduction to 7:11–28 Hebrews continues to explore the idea of priesthood, comparing Jesus to Melchizedek and to the Levites. This is done to demonstrate the legitimacy and superiority of Jesus' priesthood.

7:11 *perfection.* The word used here (Gk *teleiōsis*) also means "fulfillment" or "completion." The sacrifices offered by the Levitical priesthood were established by God, but needed to be repeated for the forgiveness of further sins. The sacrificial system was a gift of God that foreshadowed what was completed in Christ. In Him alone do we find the fullness and true substance of salvation (Col 2:17). Likewise, *the law* which accompanied the Levitical priesthood was unable to bring perfection or completeness. It is good and holy, but sinners are incapable of keeping it. Thus the *order of Aaron*, and the Law that accompanied it, was not the final solution. God provided this perfect solution: Christ, who is a true priest in the *order of Melchizedek*. And the fact that God did this demonstrates the superiority of Christ's priesthood. If the Levites and the Law had been sufficient, there would have been no need for Christ.

7:12 *change in the priesthood . . . change in the law.* The Aaronic priesthood was part of the greater revelation of the Law. This Law included stipulations for sacrifice and the rituals and ceremonies of worship. Its fulfillment depended on the Levitical priesthood. Yet these were not a permanent solution, as repeated sin required repeated sacrifice. A change of priesthood, to Christ, was accompanied by a change in the Law: it was fulfilled.

7:13–14 *descended from Judah.* This is the crux of a difficult theological challenge that the Hebrews would have recognized immediately. The Messiah was to be from the tribe of Judah, a descendant of David. But Moses *said nothing about priests* from Judah, and no one from Judah *has ever served at the altar*. On the contrary, priests had to come from the tribe of Levi. They had to be descendants of Aaron. How, then, could one person be both priest and king? The only way this could be true would be if there was another priesthood—one with different stipulations. This conundrum is the reason Hebrews discusses Melchizedek in such detail.

7:16–17 *another priest in the likeness of Melchizedek*. The challenge posed in v. 15 is resolved by the Melchizedekian priesthood. Jesus is this other priest. His priesthood is *not on the basis of a legal requirement concerning bodily descent*. Bodily descent was, in fact, a requirement of the Levitical priesthood. Not being from Levi, Jesus did not meet this requirement. But neither did Melchizedek! The requirement of descent cannot apply to those who exist before the law of descent was given. Because Melchizedek lived long before Levi and the Levitical law, he was exempt from this requirement. Likewise, because Jesus is the eternal Son of God, He lived before the Levitical requirement. He therefore needs no Levitical genealogy to be a priest. Rather, His priesthood is based on His *indestructible life*. The Son of God has always existed. Though He died as a sacrifice on Calvary, He rose again and lives eternally. This is His indestructible life. Jesus Christ, the eternal Son of God, serves as the true, eternal High Priest of all people.

7:17 Ps 110:4 is quoted once again to demonstrate Christ's priestly office. It prophetically speaks of Christ forever glorified at the right hand of the Father. (See note, Heb 1:3.) He truly is priest forever.

7:18 *former commandment set aside . . . weakness and uselessness*. The commandment regarding Levitical priests was replaced by Christ's effective, gracious priesthood. Though God's Law is holy, it was unable to bring sinners to salvation since they are unable to fulfill its demands of perfection (cf. Rm 8:3). The Law certainly had, and has, its uses, but it is insufficient and worthless for our greatest need—we cannot be saved by the Law.

7:19 *the law made nothing perfect*. The Law could not make sinners perfect, though it demanded perfection (Lv 19:2). "Perfect" (Gk *teleioō*) means to be complete, brought to its finish or end, or without defect. Proper sacrifice, offered by the priest, forgave sins, but it required repetition whenever sin inevitably recurred (cf. 9:9; 10:1; Ac 13:39). In response, God *introduced* a *better hope*, a superior answer to sin. This better hope is Christ, for the fullness of redemption could only come through His priestly suffering and glory. Our perfect Priest gives us access to the Father, who declares us holy for Christ's sake. The new covenant fulfills the old covenant and offers a lasting solution to the weaknesses of the Levitical priesthood. This is the hope that we hold fast (6:18), and through it, we *draw near to God*. God gives us His gift of faith, through which we "with confidence draw near to the throne of grace, that we may receive mercy and find grace to help in time of need" (4:16). We cry, "Lord, have mercy," confident that He will graciously help us in our weakness.

7:20 *not without an oath.* Just as God swore an oath to Abraham (6:13–20) to give greater assurance of His promises, God likewise assures us of His promise that Christ is our Priest. God has made Christ a priest by oath (cf. v. 21; Ps 110:4). Levitical priests were not established with such an oath. This is unique to Christ and strengthens our assurance.

7:21 Ps 110:4 is cited again, this time emphasizing God's promise concerning the unending priesthood of Jesus. The Father Himself has declared that Jesus is an eternal priest.

7:22 *guarantor of a better covenant.* This is the only time that "guarantor" (Gk *engyos*) is used in the NT. A guarantor is a person who would pledge something as a guarantee that he would fulfill the other person's obligations. This was sometimes done when a person would go into debt. The guarantor would offer their wealth, their freedom, or sometimes even their own life if the debtor did not meet their obligations. We see similar situations today when a loan is co-signed or when someone posts bail for an accused criminal. God has promised a new, better covenant. The life of Jesus is the guarantee that He will fulfill His promise. We will receive the fullness of God's mercy and new life in this new, *better covenant.* Jesus guarantees it.

7:23–24 *former priests . . . death . . . He continues forever.* The Levitical priests themselves were sinners and therefore mortal. There were, therefore, *many* such priests who served, but none of them brought the final solution. None could *continue in office* forever, since they died. But our High Priest, Christ, has passed through death to life. He lives forever and His priesthood likewise *continues forever.* It is permanent because Jesus lives eternally. His priesthood and promises will never end.

7:25 *save to the uttermost.* Nothing is lacking in the salvation Jesus brings. He saves "to the uttermost" (Gk *panteles*), that is, fully, completely, and for all times. *those who draw near to God through Him.* In v. 19, the author said we draw near through a "better hope." Similarly here, we draw near through Christ, who is our hope. Through trust in Christ, we have access to all the Father's gifts, including the Holy Spirit (Lk 11:11–13). In neither case is this putting our conversion or salvation in our hands. We draw near through our Redeemer and His work. *lives to make intercession.* Jesus' priestly office is not limited to His sacrifice on the cross. Priests also make intercession to God. As a permanent priest, Jesus never stops interceding for His people (Rm 8:34), praying on our behalf so that we may receive the gift of life to the full (cf. Jn 10:10b). Luther writes:

> If here by faith we do not take hold of Christ, who is sitting at the right hand of God, who is our life and our righteousness, and who makes intercession for us miserable sinners before the Father (Heb. 7:25), then we are under the Law and not under grace, and Christ is no longer a Savior. Then He is a lawgiver. Then there can be no salvation left, but sure despair and eternal death will follow. . . . [But] I am baptized; and through the Gospel I have been called to a fellowship of righteousness and eternal life, to the kingdom of Christ, in which my conscience is at peace, where there is no Law but only the forgiveness of sins, peace, quiet, happiness, salvation, and eternal life. (LW 26:11)

7:26 *It was fitting.* (Cf. 2:10.) The descriptions that follow are in accord with the divine nature. These are categorical differences between Jesus and all other priests. Jesus is *holy* because He is sinless (Ps 16:10; Rv 15:4–4), while all other priests were sinners in need of redemption. He was tempted, as we are, but was "without sin" (cf. 4:15). He is *innocent* because He never had personal guilt and *unstained* because He was a spotless victim for His pure sacrifice for sins. This made him *separated from sinners,* sharing their temptations but different in that He resisted those temptations and committed no sin (cf. 4:15). Having completed His work, He is *exalted above the heavens,* recognized for who He is and for what He has accomplished (cf. Php 2:9–11). No other priest is like Him. A true human being, He is also truly the Son of God from eternity and so is forever without sin.

7:27 *no need to offer sacrifices daily.* The work of the Levitical priests was never complete. Each day they would have to offer sacrifices for the continual sins of the people, but before they could do this, they would first have to make a sacrifice for their own sins (cf. 5:3). They could not approach God and His holiness until they were forgiven. But Christ, who is sinless (v. 26), needed no sacrifice for Himself. Furthermore, because of His unique status and the unsurpassed value of the sacrifice He offered, He sacrificed *once for all*. The sacrifice of Christ is eternally unique, valid, and effective. No other sacrifice is needed or appropriate. All true sacrifices have seen their fulfillment in the sacrifice of Jesus. Luther writes about Christ's priestly work: "The cross was the altar on which He, consumed by the fire of the boundless love which burned in His heart, presented the living and holy sacrifice of His body and blood to the Father with fervent intercession, loud cries, and hot, anxious tears (Heb. 5:7)" (LW 13:319).

7:28 *law appoints . . . weakness.* The Levitical priesthood could only draw from sinful men to serve as priests. These sinner-priests necessarily sacrificed for their own guilt before serving the people, and their sacrifices had no end. They needed to continually sacrifice throughout their lives. When they died, they were replaced by similarly sinful priests who likewise had to keep conducting sacrifices. *oath . . . appoints a Son.* This changed with God's own promise concerning the unending priestly office of Jesus. His holy priesthood was focused exclusively on the needs of humans and not on Himself. His priesthood remains eternally in effect (cf. 5:5–10; 7:17, 20–21). Hus notes how this all-sufficient work of Christ moved the Early Church to humility: "The apostles did not call themselves most holy popes, heads of the universal church, or universal pontiffs; but, having with them the High Priest even unto the consummation of the age, they called themselves servants of Christ, his companions in tribulation and ministers of the church" (*The Church*, p. 122). *made perfect forever.* As in 2:10 (see note) and 5:9, "perfect" does not indicate that something was lacking in Jesus. Rather, His work was brought to completion. Salvation is perfect in Christ Jesus.

7:11–28 in Devotion and Prayer The Levitical priesthood was a gift of God, but it was a temporary solution. God established those sacrifices as a means of forgiveness, but they were not an end in themselves. They anticipated the one perfect, final sacrifice by the one perfect, final Priest. Without sin and needing no redemption Himself, Jesus serves eternally as the one who brings our needs to the Father. While the Levites sacrificed animals, Jesus offered Himself.

We were redeemed "not with gold or silver, but with His holy, precious blood and with His innocent suffering and death" (SC Second Article). Nothing more is required for your salvation, and nothing more can be offered for it. He sacrificed Himself "once for all" (v. 27). You are washed with the blood of Christ, forgiven, and free. And even now, our Great High Priest is constantly interceding for you. God has truly provided all we need! • "Paschal Lamb, Your off'ring, finished Once for all when You were slain, In its fullness undiminished shall forever more remain, Alleluia, alleluia, alleluia! Cleansing souls from ev'ry stain." Amen. (*LSB* 534:3; *H82* 307:4; *TPH* 154:3)

Superiority of Jesus' Sacrifice (8:1–10:18)

ESV	KJV
8 ¹Now the point in what we are saying is this: we have such a high priest, one who is seated at the right hand of the throne of the Majesty in heaven, ²a minister in the holy places, in the true tent that the Lord set up, not man. ³For every high priest is appointed to offer gifts and sacrifices; thus it is necessary for this priest also to have something to offer. ⁴Now if he were on earth, he would not be a priest at all, since there are priests who offer gifts according to the law. ⁵They serve a copy and shadow of the heavenly things. For when Moses was about to erect the tent, he was instructed by God, saying, "See that you make everything according to the pattern that was shown you on the mountain." ⁶But as it is, Christ has obtained a ministry that is as much more excellent than the old as the covenant he mediates is better, since it is enacted on better promises. ⁷For if that first covenant had been faultless, there would have been no occasion to look for a second.	8 ¹Now of the things which we have spoken this is the sum: We have such an high priest, who is set on the right hand of the throne of the Majesty in the heavens; ²A minister of the sanctuary, and of the true tabernacle, which the Lord pitched, and not man. ³For every high priest is ordained to offer gifts and sacrifices: wherefore it is of necessity that this man have somewhat also to offer. ⁴For if he were on earth, he should not be a priest, seeing that there are priests that offer gifts according to the law: ⁵Who serve unto the example and shadow of heavenly things, as Moses was admonished of God when he was about to make the tabernacle: for, See, saith he, that thou make all things according to the pattern shewed to thee in the mount. ⁶But now hath he obtained a more excellent ministry, by how much also he is the mediator of a better cov-

⁸For he finds fault with them when he says:

"Behold, the days are coming,
    declares the Lord,
    when I will establish a new covenant
with the house of Israel
    and with the house of Judah,
⁹not like the covenant that
    I made with their fathers
on the day when I took them by
    the hand to bring them out of
    the land of Egypt.
For they did not continue in my
    covenant,
    and so I showed no concern for
    them, declares the Lord.
¹⁰For this is the covenant that I will
    make with the house of Israel
    after those days, declares the
    Lord:
I will put my laws into their minds,
    and write them on their hearts,
and I will be their God,
    and they shall be my people.
¹¹And they shall not teach, each
    one his neighbor
    and each one his brother, saying, 'Know the Lord,'
for they shall all know me,
    from the least of them to the
    greatest.
¹²For I will be merciful toward
    their iniquities,
    and I will remember their sins
    no more."

¹³In speaking of a new covenant, he makes the first one obsolete. And what is becoming obsolete and growing old is ready to vanish away.

9 ¹Now even the first covenant had regulations for worship and an earthly place of holiness. ²For a tent

enant, which was established upon better promises.

⁷For if that first covenant had been faultless, then should no place have been sought for the second.

⁸For finding fault with them, he saith, Behold, the days come, saith the Lord, when I will make a new covenant with the house of Israel and with the house of Judah:

⁹Not according to the covenant that I made with their fathers in the day when I took them by the hand to lead them out of the land of Egypt; because they continued not in my covenant, and I regarded them not, saith the Lord.

¹⁰For this is the covenant that I will make with the house of Israel after those days, saith the Lord; I will put my laws into their mind, and write them in their hearts: and I will be to them a God, and they shall be to me a people:

¹¹And they shall not teach every man his neighbour, and every man his brother, saying, Know the Lord: for all shall know me, from the least to the greatest.

¹²For I will be merciful to their unrighteousness, and their sins and their iniquities will I remember no more.

¹³In that he saith, A new covenant, he hath made the first old. Now that which decayeth and waxeth old is ready to vanish away.

9 ¹Then verily the first covenant had also ordinances of divine service, and a worldly sanctuary.

²For there was a tabernacle made; the first, wherein was the candlestick, and the table, and the shewbread; which is called the sanctuary.

was prepared, the first section, in which were the lampstand and the table and the bread of the Presence. It is called the Holy Place. ³Behind the second curtain was a second section called the Most Holy Place, ⁴having the golden altar of incense and the ark of the covenant covered on all sides with gold, in which was a golden urn holding the manna, and Aaron's staff that budded, and the tablets of the covenant. ⁵Above it were the cherubim of glory overshadowing the mercy seat. Of these things we cannot now speak in detail.

⁶These preparations having thus been made, the priests go regularly into the first section, performing their ritual duties, ⁷but into the second only the high priest goes, and he but once a year, and not without taking blood, which he offers for himself and for the unintentional sins of the people. ⁸By this the Holy Spirit indicates that the way into the holy places is not yet opened as long as the first section is still standing ⁹(which is symbolic for the present age). According to this arrangement, gifts and sacrifices are offered that cannot perfect the conscience of the worshiper, ¹⁰but deal only with food and drink and various washings, regulations for the body imposed until the time of reformation.

¹¹But when Christ appeared as a high priest of the good things that have come, then through the greater and more perfect tent (not made with hands, that is, not of this creation) ¹²he entered once for all into the holy places, not by means of the blood of goats and calves but by means of his own blood, thus securing an eter-

³And after the second veil, the tabernacle which is called the Holiest of all;

⁴Which had the golden censer, and the ark of the covenant overlaid round about with gold, wherein was the golden pot that had manna, and Aaron's rod that budded, and the tables of the covenant;

⁵And over it the cherubims of glory shadowing the mercyseat; of which we cannot now speak particularly.

⁶Now when these things were thus ordained, the priests went always into the first tabernacle, accomplishing the service of God.

⁷But into the second went the high priest alone once every year, not without blood, which he offered for himself, and for the errors of the people:

⁸The Holy Ghost this signifying, that the way into the holiest of all was not yet made manifest, while as the first tabernacle was yet standing:

⁹Which was a figure for the time then present, in which were offered both gifts and sacrifices, that could not make him that did the service perfect, as pertaining to the conscience;

¹⁰Which stood only in meats and drinks, and divers washings, and carnal ordinances, imposed on them until the time of reformation.

¹¹But Christ being come an high priest of good things to come, by a greater and more perfect tabernacle, not made with hands, that is to say, not of this building;

¹²Neither by the blood of goats and calves, but by his own blood he entered in once into the holy place,

nal redemption. [13]For if the blood of goats and bulls, and the sprinkling of defiled persons with the ashes of a heifer, sanctify for the purification of the flesh, [14]how much more will the blood of Christ, who through the eternal Spirit offered himself without blemish to God, purify our conscience from dead works to serve the living God.

[15]Therefore he is the mediator of a new covenant, so that those who are called may receive the promised eternal inheritance, since a death has occurred that redeems them from the transgressions committed under the first covenant. [16]For where a will is involved, the death of the one who made it must be established. [17]For a will takes effect only at death, since it is not in force as long as the one who made it is alive. [18]Therefore not even the first covenant was inaugurated without blood. [19]For when every commandment of the law had been declared by Moses to all the people, he took the blood of calves and goats, with water and scarlet wool and hyssop, and sprinkled both the book itself and all the people, [20]saying, "This is the blood of the covenant that God commanded for you." [21]And in the same way he sprinkled with the blood both the tent and all the vessels used in worship. [22]Indeed, under the law almost everything is purified with blood, and without the shedding of blood there is no forgiveness of sins.

[23]Thus it was necessary for the copies of the heavenly things to be purified with these rites, but the heavenly things themselves with better sacrifices than these. [24]For Christ has entered, not into holy places

having obtained eternal redemption for us.

[13]For if the blood of bulls and of goats, and the ashes of an heifer sprinkling the unclean, sanctifieth to the purifying of the flesh:

[14]How much more shall the blood of Christ, who through the eternal Spirit offered himself without spot to God, purge your conscience from dead works to serve the living God?

[15]And for this cause he is the mediator of the new testament, that by means of death, for the redemption of the transgressions that were under the first testament, they which are called might receive the promise of eternal inheritance.

[16]For where a testament is, there must also of necessity be the death of the testator.

[17]For a testament is of force after men are dead: otherwise it is of no strength at all while the testator liveth.

[18]Whereupon neither the first testament was dedicated without blood.

[19]For when Moses had spoken every precept to all the people according to the law, he took the blood of calves and of goats, with water, and scarlet wool, and hyssop, and sprinkled both the book, and all the people,

[20]Saying, This is the blood of the testament which God hath enjoined unto you.

[21]Moreover he sprinkled with blood both the tabernacle, and all the vessels of the ministry.

[22]And almost all things are by the law purged with blood; and without shedding of blood is no remission.

[23]It was therefore necessary that the patterns of things in the heavens

made with hands, which are copies of the true things, but into heaven itself, now to appear in the presence of God on our behalf. ²⁵Nor was it to offer himself repeatedly, as the high priest enters the holy places every year with blood not his own, ²⁶for then he would have had to suffer repeatedly since the foundation of the world. But as it is, he has appeared once for all at the end of the ages to put away sin by the sacrifice of himself. ²⁷And just as it is appointed for man to die once, and after that comes judgment, ²⁸so Christ, having been offered once to bear the sins of many, will appear a second time, not to deal with sin but to save those who are eagerly waiting for him.

10 ¹For since the law has but a shadow of the good things to come instead of the true form of these realities, it can never, by the same sacrifices that are continually offered every year, make perfect those who draw near. ²Otherwise, would they not have ceased to be offered, since the worshipers, having once been cleansed, would no longer have any consciousness of sins? ³But in these sacrifices there is a reminder of sins every year. ⁴For it is impossible for the blood of bulls and goats to take away sins.

⁵Consequently, when Christ came into the world, he said,

"Sacrifices and offerings you have
  not desired,
  but a body have you prepared
  for me;
⁶in burnt offerings and sin offerings
  you have taken no pleasure.

should be purified with these; but the heavenly things themselves with better sacrifices than these.

²⁴For Christ is not entered into the holy places made with hands, which are the figures of the true; but into heaven itself, now to appear in the presence of God for us:

²⁵Nor yet that he should offer himself often, as the high priest entereth into the holy place every year with blood of others;

²⁶For then must he often have suffered since the foundation of the world: but now once in the end of the world hath he appeared to put away sin by the sacrifice of himself.

²⁷And as it is appointed unto men once to die, but after this the judgment:

²⁸So Christ was once offered to bear the sins of many; and unto them that look for him shall he appear the second time without sin unto salvation.

10 ¹For the law having a shadow of good things to come, and not the very image of the things, can never with those sacrifices which they offered year by year continually make the comers thereunto perfect.

²For then would they not have ceased to be offered? because that the worshippers once purged should have had no more conscience of sins.

³But in those sacrifices there is a remembrance again made of sins every year.

⁴For it is not possible that the blood of bulls and of goats should take away sins.

⁵Wherefore when he cometh into the world, he saith, Sacrifice and offering thou wouldest not, but a body hast thou prepared me:

7Then I said, 'Behold, I have come
    to do your will, O God,
  as it is written of me in the scroll of
    the book.' "

8When he said above, "You have
neither desired nor taken pleasure
in sacrifices and offerings and burnt
offerings and sin offerings" (these are
offered according to the law), 9then
he added, "Behold, I have come to
do your will." He does away with the
first in order to establish the second.
10And by that will we have been sanctified through the offering of the body
of Jesus Christ once for all.

11And every priest stands daily at his
service, offering repeatedly the same
sacrifices, which can never take away
sins. 12But when Christ had offered
for all time a single sacrifice for sins,
he sat down at the right hand of God,
13waiting from that time until his enemies should be made a footstool for
his feet. 14For by a single offering he
has perfected for all time those who
are being sanctified.

15And the Holy Spirit also bears witness to us; for after saying,

16"This is the covenant that I will
    make with them
  after those days, declares the
    Lord:
  I will put my laws on their hearts,
    and write them on their minds,"

17then he adds,

"I will remember their sins and
    their lawless deeds no more."

18Where there is forgiveness of
these, there is no longer any offering for sin.

6In burnt offerings and sacrifices for
sin thou hast had no pleasure.

7Then said I, Lo, I come (in the volume of the book it is written of me,)
to do thy will, O God.

8Above when he said, Sacrifice
and offering and burnt offerings and
offering for sin thou wouldest not,
neither hadst pleasure therein; which
are offered by the law;

9Then said he, Lo, I come to do thy
will, O God. He taketh away the first,
that he may establish the second.

10By the which will we are sanctified through the offering of the body
of Jesus Christ once for all.

11And every priest standeth daily
ministering and offering oftentimes
the same sacrifices, which can never
take away sins:

12But this man, after he had offered
one sacrifice for sins for ever, sat
down on the right hand of God;

13From henceforth expecting till his
enemies be made his footstool.

14For by one offering he hath
perfected for ever them that are sanctified.

15Whereof the Holy Ghost also is a
witness to us: for after that he had
said before,

16This is the covenant that I will
make with them after those days,
saith the Lord, I will put my laws into
their hearts, and in their minds will I
write them;

17And their sins and iniquities will I
remember no more.

18Now where remission of these is,
there is no more offering for sin.

Introduction to 8:1–13 This chapter continues to demonstrate the superiority of Jesus' priesthood and of the covenant He enacts over the old covenant. Melanchthon discusses priesthood in light of this passage, saying:

> We teach that the sacrifice of Christ dying on the cross has been enough for the sins of the whole world. There is no need for other sacrifices, as though Christ's sacrifice were not enough for our sins. So people are justified not because of any other sacrifices, but because of this one sacrifice of Christ, if they believe that they have been redeemed by this sacrifice. So they are called priests, not in order to make any sacrifices for the people as in the Law, that by these they may merit forgiveness of sins for the people. Rather, they are called to teach the Gospel and administer the Sacraments to the people. Nor do we have another priesthood like the Levitical, as the Epistle to the Hebrews teaches well enough. (Ap XIII 8–10)

8:1 *the point . . . we have such a high priest.* This has been evident throughout the discussion of the priesthood, but it is of such critical importance that the author says this to give further emphasis to this truth. This is no idle speculation or academic exercise. The priest we need is the very priest that God gives to us. He is greater than all other priests, for Christ is *seated at the right hand.* Having completed His work, Christ ascended to heaven where He reigns and exercises full divine power according to His human nature. He occupies not only a priestly office but a royal one as well, and He graciously exercises both for the sake of His Church. *throne of the Majesty.* A Hebrew idiom for God the Father. The Greek word for majesty (*megalōsynē*) is used only in Hebrews (1:3; 8:1) and in Jude 25. This usage would have been familiar to the Jewish readers of this book. *heaven.* The KJV more literally translates this as "the heavens." The meaning is the same as the focus is not on the place but on the Triune God who dwells there. Heaven is not the sky or space or a mere physical location (cf. Eph 4:10); it is where God is. The presence of God constitutes heaven. Attributing this heavenly status to Jesus, our High Priest, is an affirmation of His deity.

8:2 *minister.* From the Gk *leitourgos*, this identifies an official assistant or minister of a deity. This word is applied to civil authorities who are God's agents (Rm 13:6); to angels who serve God (Heb 1:7); to those who attend to physical needs (Php 2:25); and to ministers of the Gospel (Rm 16:16). All of these services show God working through another being. We use this same word to denote those who serve God's people in worship when we call them "liturgists." In this passage, the word is applied to Christ, who serves us as He performs His priestly ministry. Using the language of the tabernacle and temple, this ministry is carried out *in the holy places* (KJV "sanctuary"). It can also be literally translated as "of the holy things." Jesus Christ serves us with holy things in His priestly work, as the previous priests served in the tabernacle. Christ's work, however, is infinitely greater than theirs. They served in the tabernacle or the temple; He serves in *the true tent*, or "tabernacle" as the KJV translates (this is also reflected in the ESV note). *the Lord set up.* The earthly tabernacle was established by God and built according to His design and directions (cf. v. 5). At His direction, Israel set up the tabernacle. God chose to meet Israel in the tabernacle—they knew they would encounter Him there as He promised. The true tabernacle is the dwelling place of God in heaven. Christ reentered this tabernacle after He rose from the dead. This is where He serves. Human hands did not make or set up this true tabernacle.

8:3 Offering *gifts and sacrifices* is the essential work of a high priest, as they served as mediator between God and the people (cf. Lv 9:6–7, 22). *necessary.* Just as the OT high priests offered animal sacrifices to God, Christ the Great High Priest also must offer a sacrifice. His sacrifice was infinitely greater than what they offered, for He fulfilled His priestly ministry by offering His own body on the cross (9:12–14; Eph 5:2). He now continually distributes the benefits of His sacrifice and intercedes for us.

8:4 *on earth He would not be a priest.* In the earthly tabernacle, a different priesthood offered a different sacrifice. Though established by God, it would be fulfilled and supplanted by the greatest Priest and the final Sacrifice. Jesus visited the temple where the Levitical priests served (e.g., Mk 1:11), cleansed that temple (Mt 21:12), taught in that temple (e.g., Mt:21:23ff., Mk 10:35–37), and healed in that temple (e.g., Mt 21:14), but He did not offer the sacrifice there as a priest. Not being a Levite, He would not have been allowed to do this. There already were priests there who served *according to the law.* Jesus sacrificed Himself on the cross and carries out His priestly work in the true, heavenly temple. Only a Levitical priest could enter the earthly temple and only if they were authorized and properly prepared. Only Jesus can enter the heavenly temple as High Priest and fulfill His priestly work.

8:5 *a copy and shadow.* The real tabernacle—the true dwelling place of God—is heaven, where Jesus reigns with the Father and the Holy Spirit. The earthly tabernacle was God's means of blessing His people before Christ. It reflected heaven, albeit in an imperfect way, and foreshadowed Christ's person and work. Everything associated with the tabernacle and temple, the priesthood, and the sacrificial system pointed forward to God's great fulfillment of a perfect, final sacrifice of His Son. That "once for all" (7:27) sacrifice is the greatest reality (cf. Col 2:17, Heb 10:1 and notes). *heavenly things.* Chrysostom writes:

> What are the heavenly things he speaks of here? The spiritual things. For although they are done on earth, yet nevertheless they are worthy of the Heavens. For when our Lord Jesus Christ lies slain [as a sacrifice (cf. 10:12)], when the Spirit is with us, when He who sits on the right hand of the Father is here, when sons are made by the Washing . . . how can all these be other than "heavenly things"? (*NPNF1* 14:434)

Moses . . . make everything according to the pattern that was shown you. Moses delivered the covenant to Israel, which included the design for the tabernacle and instructions for how to make and use it. But Moses was not the source of these things; they were revealed to him by God. The Lord Himself established and designed the tabernacle and equipped His people with materials, artisans, and craftsmen to make it (cf. Ex 25:40; Ex 31:1–11). "Pattern" (Gk *typos*) is transliterated "type" and is the word used to describe persons, events, and offices that foreshadow a greater fulfillment. *mountain.* Mount Sinai, where God revealed His Law to Moses.

8:6 *more excellent.* This verse highlights two aspects of Christ's ministry that are greater than what foreshadowed them. His *ministry* or service (Gk *leitourgia*, cf. v. 2) surpasses that of the Levitical priests due to its perfection, completion, and finality. Furthermore, the *covenant He mediates* is greater than the covenant mediated by the former priests (9:15; 12:24) because of its *better promises.* Through the work of Christ, God promises forgiveness of sins and eternal life for all who believe in Him. His ultimate sacrifice has secured these promises (cf. 7:22; 9:15; and notes).

105

8:7 *if the first . . . faultless.* The old covenant, though given by God, was limited. It anticipated its perfect fulfillment in the work of Christ. It was, consequently, not a final solution but a foreshadowing of what God would do in Christ. The fact that the work of the first covenant was never done but always required more sacrifice demonstrated that something greater was needed. The *second* covenant—God's work in Christ—is faultless, perfect, and complete.

8:8 *finds fault.* See notes, vv. 7, 13. These words introduce an extended quote from Jer 31:31–34. In them, God points out the failure of His people (or, as some manuscripts render these words, finds fault with the insufficiency of the first covenant to be the final solution). God would have to intervene to save His people. *establish a new covenant.* The promise of the Gospel had been with humanity since Gn 3. In the intervening years, God had made additional covenants with His people in which He would bless them. The fulfillment of all of His covenants occurred at the cross. There, in the sacrifice of the innocent blood of the Son of God, His covenant would be put into effect. See notes, Heb 8:6, 9–13.

8:9 *not like the covenant.* God was faithful to the previous covenant, but Israel was not. This new covenant would be successful because God would do everything to redeem His people. *bring them out of . . . Egypt.* God blessed Israel in the exodus. It was He who delivered them from slavery and into freedom. He overcame their complacency and reluctance, *took them by the hand* as a father leads his children, and provided for all of their needs. The miraculous events that accompanied and followed the exodus testified to the power, greatness, and tender care of God. In the wilderness, God established the details of the covenant, including the priesthood and sacrificial system that are being discussed here in Hebrews. *they did not continue.* This was the flaw in the first covenant: sinful human beings. Though the old covenant anticipated a greater fulfillment in Christ, the fault was not with God or His covenant but in rebellious Israel. They did not continue in the covenant. *I showed no concern.* When Israel broke the covenant, God was no longer bound to keep His portion of it. God did bless them in ways greater than they could ever deserve, but the covenant was no longer in effect. They had broken and nullified it.

8:10 *I will make.* The new covenant comes from God and from His work. He is decreeing what He will do for His people. *put My* *laws . . . into their minds . . . write them on their hearts.* God's commandments were written on stone tablets (Ex 24:12), but God's people did not keep them. In the new covenant of Christ, God's Word would be internalized. His people would know and believe God's Word. Luther said, "To be in the mind means to be understood; to be in the heart means to be loved" (LW 29:198). *I will be their God and they shall be My people.* God's covenant reestablishes a right relationship with Him. He adopts sinful humans to be His redeemed people. This reverses the problem noted in v. 9 that "they did not continue . . . so I showed no concern for them." Luther ponders God's placing the covenant in our minds and hearts, saying,

> This light of understanding in the mind, I say, and this flame in the heart is the law of faith, the new law, the law of Christ, the law of the Spirit, the law of grace. It justifies, fulfills everything, and crucifies the lusts of the flesh. Thus St. Augustine says beautifully on this passage: "In a sense the man who with a love of righteousness lives righteously lives the Law itself." (LW 27:234)

Calvin also wrote about this covenant, saying,

> There are two main parts in this covenant; the first regards the gratuitous remission of sins; and the other, the inward renovation of the heart; there is a third which depends on the second, and that is the illumination of the mind as to the knowledge of God. (Calvin 188)

8:11 *they shall all know Me.* God's truth is revealed to each person. The saving knowledge of God and the Spirit's gifts will become much clearer. Many more people will know God. On the Last Day, all people will see the Lord—some with joy, but others with weeping (cf. 1Co 13:12; Mt 13:41–42).

8:12 *I will be merciful.* The covenant is established by God (v. 8) and is utterly dependent upon Him. God gives people not what they deserve but what He desires to give, and He is merciful. The entire covenant is an act of God's mercy. Here, God's mercy is expressed in how He deals with their *iniquities* and *sins.* Though these might be construed as breaking the covenant, God chooses to show mercy and promises, *I will remember their sins no more.* The covenant is grounded in God's abundant forgiveness for the sake of Christ.

8:13 *He makes the first one obsolete.* The first covenant is a shadow of the second and fades in the brightness of Christ's new work. It passes away before this superior covenant. See note, v. 5. *ready* *to pass away.* Such words likely indicate that Hebrews was written before the Romans destroyed the temple in AD 70. Jews would continue to offer sacrifices in the temple until that day, but Christ had already fulfilled the covenant. Soon the entire sacrificial system would vanish because it had been brought to its completion.

Ch. 8 in Devotion and Prayer It is far too easy for us to externalize verses like these. "Look what Israel did! They broke the covenant!" It is tempting to complete that with smug self-righteousness: "I would never have broken the covenant. I would have seen God's miracles and heard His Word. I would have faithfully believed." But the truth is that we have heard God's Word and seen even greater miracles than Israel saw, and still we sin. We have been adopted into God's family, yet we still act like children of the world. Our only hope is in Him. God, in His mercy, establishes a new covenant, bought with the blood of Jesus. Because of the work of our Savior, He remembers our sins no more. He places His Word in our minds and hearts. He declares Himself to be our God and makes us His people. God has made this new covenant for us. He strengthens us in the faith through the new testament of His body and blood. In Him, we are blessed with a new covenant—a better covenant through Christ Jesus. • God, be merciful to me, a sinner. For the sake of Christ, forgive me my sins. Strengthen my faith and fill me with joy in knowing that I am Your child. Amen.

Introduction to 9:1–10 These verses describe worship in the earthly tabernacle and the service of the priests. This will be contrasted with the perfect work of Christ in the next section.

9:1 *regulations for worship.* These instructions for tabernacle worship are outlined in the Levitical, ceremonial law (cf. Lv 1–7). Some aspects of Jewish worship in the tabernacle and, later, in the synagogues, carry forward, such as the reading of the Scriptures, the singing of Psalms, and prayer. Other aspects of OT worship, however, were fulfilled by Christ and so were no longer practiced by the Early Church. The cessation of animal sacrifices is the most significant change. As this chapter progresses, it details how the ministry of Christ fulfills and surpasses the first covenant. *earthly place of holiness.* The tabernacle and, later, the temple. The KJV's translation "worldly sanctuary" is not pejorative, but means the same thing as the ESV's "earthly." This qualifier is used to help the reader distinguish the heavenly tabernacle from the earthly one.

9:2 *tent.* In English, we normally use the word "tabernacle" to describe this particular tent and distinguish it from others, but the word is the same. *Lampstand . . . table . . . bread of the Presence.* These furnishings from the tabernacle's outer room would have been familiar to Jewish Christians. The lampstand was made of hammered gold and held seven lamps (Ex 25:31–39). The table, overlaid with gold, held the bread of the Presence: one loaf for each of the twelve tribes. The bread of the Presence was renewed every Sabbath (Ex 25:23–29), and the priests would eat the old bread. *the Holy Place.* This section of the tabernacle was set apart from the outside world for worship. This is why it was holy (i.e., "set apart" in Hbr). Here priests carried out the daily liturgy on behalf of Israel. Chrysostom reflects on the difference between the Holy and Most Holy Place, saying, "The holy place then is a symbol of the former [OT] period (for there all things are done by means of sacrifices); but the Holy of Holies [is a symbol] of this [NT period] that is now present. And by the Holy of Holies he means Heaven" (*NPNF*1 14:438). See note, v. 9.

9:3 The *second curtain* was made of blue, purple, and scarlet yarn and fine linen. Images of Cherubim were woven into it (Ex 26:31–33), reminding the priests who saw it that the presence of God was within. Within the Holy Place, it further set apart *the Most Holy Place.* This is sometimes called "the Holy of Holies" (Gk *Hagia Hagiōn*). The KJV translates, "which is called the Holiest of all." Whatever words are used to describe it, the chief point is that this is a sacred place, because here God has promised to dwell. It was the inmost section of the tabernacle into which no one but the high priest could enter (cf. Lv 16:2–3). Its furnishings are described in the next two verses.

9:4 *golden altar of incense.* This was located near the Most Holy Place (Ex 40:26–27). The high priest burned incense to protect himself from the glory of God when he entered the Most Holy Place (Lv 16:12–13), the smoke literally obscuring his view. God was present at the *ark of the covenant*, choosing to meet His people there through the service of the high priest (Ex 25:10). The ark, completely covered in gold, contained signs of God's work among Israel: some *manna* by which God miraculously fed Israel in the wilderness (Ex 16:33); *Aaron's staff that budded* as a sign that God had chosen him (Nu 17:1–10); and *the tablets of the covenant* (Dt 10:2). On the basis of Ex 16:33 and 1Ki 8:9, Bengel argued that only the tables of the Law were stored in the ark; the pot of manna and Aaron's staff were placed in the holy place near the ark. He thought the word "in" was being used in a broader sense to include "in the presence of" the ark.

9:5 *cherubim of glory.* Mentioned over 90 times in the Bible, cherubim are most commonly associated with the presence of God, which they guard. God is enthroned on cherubim (Ps 80:1). They are probably identical with the "living creatures" of Rv 4:6 who stand around the throne of God (cf. Ex 25:18–22). In the temple, even larger images of cherubim were over the ark (1Ki 8:6–7). The *mercy seat* (Gk *hilastērion*, or "place of atonement") was the golden cover on the ark of the covenant and was flanked by the outstretched wings of the cherubim. God spoke to Moses from this place (Nu 7:89). The mercy seat was the focus of the ritual on the OT Day of Atonement (Lv 16). The parallel description of the ark of the covenant with the golden mercy seat and cherubim is found in Ex 25:18–22. *cannot now speak.* While descriptions of the tabernacle and ark of the covenant are interesting, they are not the main point of this passage. Hebrews is not interested in merely describing furnishings; it is focusing on the priestly work that took place there and its fulfillment in the work of Christ.

9:6 *first section.* Each day, priests served in the Holy Place (v. 2) according to God's institution. They would tend to the lamps, burn incense on the altar before the curtain, and weekly change the bread of the Presence. This brief description is given so that the unique role of the high priest (v. 7) stands out clearly.

9:7 *the second.* This refers to the Most Holy Place. Since God's glory dwelled here, it was particularly sacred. The only person who could enter was *the high priest.* Any other person entering risked death (Lv 16:2). Even the high priest could only enter *once a year.* This took place exclusively on the Day of Atonement (Lv 16:34). Even on that singular day, he could not enter on his own *without taking blood.* Since he himself, and the people he represented, were both sinful, sacrifice needed to be offered for both (Lv 16:15; Ex 30:10). *unintentional sins.* Though the Day of Atonement was for all sins (cf. Lv 16:16, 30), the sinful ignorance of priests and people is stressed here (cf. Rm 10:3). All sin is serious and needs atonement— not only voluntary sins, but those that are committed unintentionally and ignorantly. Even an unintentional or unknown sin rendered a person defiled and unworthy of the presence of God. Access to the Most Holy Place was guarded by these extreme limitations: only the high priest, only on one day, and only after offering blood for atonement. This demonstrates the seriousness of sin in contrast to the consuming holiness of God. Sinners cannot stand on their own in the presence of a holy, almighty God.

9:8 *the Holy Spirit indicates.* Moses did not create this sacrificial system; it was decreed by God. Likewise, the words of the OT were not the invention of the human writers, but are divinely inspired. The Holy Spirit spoke through Moses and gave all the OT rituals a divinely intended meaning. *not yet opened.* The way to heaven, symbolized by the temple's Most Holy Place, was not fully revealed until Christ appeared (cf. 10:20; Mk 15:38; Lk 23:45). The old sacrificial system remained intact until Christ's work was complete.

9:9 *symbolic for the present age.* The ESV note has a helpful alternative translation, saying, "symbolic for the age then present." The earthly temple likely was still standing when this was written, and so the divisions discussed here continued to be in use. So the author is saying that the first section of the temple represented the OT sacrificial system and earth. "Symbolic" translates the Greek word *parabolē* and is more commonly transliterated as "parable." He is saying that the existence of the Holy Place and the extreme measures needed before the high priest could approach the presence of God are recounted to teach us something important. They serve as an illustration. Sin is no small matter; it is serious business and needs a serious solution. But those who fixated on the old covenant without seeing that it pointed forward to God's ultimate solution made a critical error. *Gifts and sacrifices are offered* for sin, it is true. This system was established by God for the benefit of His people. But such things do not give lasting relief from our spiritual malady and were never intended to do so. Indeed, these things *cannot perfect the conscience.* The sacrifices could not provide lasting atonement for the people. They were not an end in themselves, but were effective only as they pointed to Christ's sacrifice. They would ultimately be fulfilled and replaced by His work.

9:10 *deal only with . . . the body.* OT Ceremonial laws concerning food, drink, ritual washings and the like were familiar to the readers. Such burdensome regulations were necessary for a while, but they were temporary, in effect *until the time of reformation.* This is the only usage of the word "reformation" or "rectification" (Gk

111

diorthōrsis) in the NT. These regulations were in place for a time, but only until God's better plan was revealed. This was the institution of Christ's new covenant. The OT ceremonies were fulfilled by His work. Now He comes to us in the gracious gifts of His Gospel and sacraments.

9:1–10 in Devotion and Prayer Everything about the tabernacle emphasized the great divide that sin created between God and His people. For our wellbeing, God kept Himself away from direct contact with humanity. Only the priests could go into the Holy Place. Only the high priest could go into the Most Holy Place, and even then only one day a year and only if he brought the sacrifice of blood. Sin is serious business. A sinner in the presence of this utterly holy God will die. God established the sacrificial system to provide atonement and reconciliation. But it was not His final solution. That old covenant pointed forward to God's perfect, ultimate, new covenant in Christ. The OT services pointed ahead to Christ. In the new covenant, worshipers receive the work that Christ has completed. The gifts that He has earned are distributed to them in Gospel and Sacrament. As they worship, Christians recognize their Lord's gracious presence among them and joyfully anticipate His return. Christ, our Great High Priest, has entered the Holy Place of heaven for us, by the blood of His sacrifice. Through Him, we have been reconciled to the Father. • "Almighty God, our heavenly Father, has had mercy upon us and has given His only Son to die for us and for His sake forgives us all our sins. To those who believe on His name He gives power to become the children of God and has promised them His Holy Spirit. He that believes and is baptized shall be saved. Grant this, Lord, unto us all. Amen" (*LSB*, p. 185).

Introduction to 9:11–28 The time of "reformation" (v. 10), which God had planned from the beginning, was the fulfillment of the covenant of Christ. Having briefly described the service of the priests and the high priest in the earthly tabernacle, Hebrews now describes the perfect fulfillment that is found in the person and work of Christ. His ministry exceeds the former priests in every way. We are truly purified by His perfect work.

9:11 *the good things that have come.* While God blessed His people through the OT priesthood, the gifts that they gave pointed forward to a greater fulfillment in Christ. Through His ultimate priesthood, our Lord brings greater gifts than any other priest, as His gifts of redemption, salvation, and forgiveness are the fulfillment of God's promises. They come to believers now in Word and Sacrament and will be fully bestowed in the future resurrection (cf. 2Co 1:10). *greater and more perfect tent.* Christ's high priestly service takes place in heaven, the true dwelling place of God. *not made with hands.* The earthly tabernacle was designed by God but constructed by men. The perfect, heavenly temple is superior in every way, being made by God and outside of our ordinary human existence (cf. 8:2).

9:12 *He entered once for all.* The earthly high priest had to enter the earthly tabernacle's Most Holy Place every year to atone for repeated sin. Christ entered the true tabernacle of heaven once, and that was enough. His work was complete for all times and every person (cf. 7:27; 10:20). *by means of His own blood.* The Levitical high priest offered the blood of *goats and calves* both for his own sin and for the sins of the people. Jesus offered a sacrifice of infinitely greater value: His own blood. Christ entered heaven to present His sacrificed blood to the Father on our behalf. *securing an eternal redemption.* Jesus' once for all sacrifice and His presentation of that sacrifice in the perfect heavenly temple has truly met all of our needs. Because His sacrifice is of supreme value and eternal, it needs no repetition. These are critical differences between His perfect work and the OT sacrifices. He secured our salvation through His death and resurrection and now distributes it to us each day through His gifts, as Luther writes: "With His own blood, to be sure, He redeemed and sanctified all men just once. But because we are not yet perfectly pure but remnants of sin still cling to our flesh and the flesh wars against the spirit, therefore He comes spiritually every day; day by day He completes the time set by the Father more and more, abrogating and abolishing the Law" (LW 26:360). Calvin also comments on this text:

> He had said that the high priest alone entered the sanctuary once a year with blood to expiate sins. Christ is in this life the ancient high priest, for he alone possesses the dignity and the office of a high priest; but he differs from him in this respect, that he brings with him eternal blessings which secure a perpetuity to his priesthood. Secondly, there is this likeness between the ancient high priest and ours, that both entered the holy of holies through the sanctuary; but they differ in this, that Christ alone entered into heaven through the temple of his own body. That the holy of holies was once every year opened to the high priest to make the

appointed expiation—this obscurely prefigured the one true sacrifice of Christ. To enter once then was common to both, but to the earthly it was every year, while it was to the heavenly for ever, even to the end of the world. The offering of blood was common to both; but there was a great difference as to the blood; for Christ offered, not the blood of beasts, but his own blood. Expiation was common to both; but that according to the Law, as it was inefficacious, was repeated every year; but the expiation made by Christ is always effectual and is the cause of eternal salvation to us. (Calvin 200–201)

9:13 *sprinkling of defiled persons . . . ashes.* These two examples of sacrifices show that cleansing was necessary in God's sight. The blood mentioned was sprinkled in front of the mercy seat on the Day of Atonement (Lv 16:14–16). The ashes of a heifer were part of an elaborate purification ritual for those who had come in contact with unclean things (cf. Nu 19). Such actions were established by God to deal with outward impurity, that is, for *the purification of the flesh.*

9:14 *how much more.* Those sacrificial acts were not an end in themselves; they pointed forward to God's fulfillment. Christ's work is infinitely more valuable, because Christ is not only man but also the infinite God. His perfect sacrifice, presented in the heavenly temple, is of greater worth. *blood . . . purify.* Christ's human blood does a divine work, purifying us from sin; this results in a conscience that is truly free from guilt (cf. v. 12; 1Jn 1:7; Rv 7:14). *through the eternal Spirit offered Himself.* The entire Trinity is involved in our redemption. Christ sacrificed Himself in the power of the Holy Spirit (Jn 3:34; Ac 10:38) to reconcile humanity to the Father, who sent Him. *without blemish.* Sacrificial victims were required to be perfect and without blemish (Lv 1:3). This foreshadowed the sacrifice of the Lamb of God, who was not blemished by sin. Because He was without blemish—that is, without sin—He did not need a sacrifice for Himself, as other priests did, but offered everything for sinful humanity (cf. 7:27; 8:3). *purify our conscience.* The purification rites referenced in v. 13 were for external impurity; the work of Christ cleanses us of all our guilt. We are declared holy because of what He has done (cf. 1:3; 10:22). *dead works.* See note, 6:1. *to serve the living God.* God restores us to life and holiness, and now we gladly and joyfully serve Him. This is the natural response of those who have been freed from sin, guilt, and death.

9:15 *He is the mediator.* Mediation between God and mankind is the essential work of a priest who represents the people to God and God to the people. Chrysostom writes, "The Son became Mediator between the Father and us. The Father willed not to leave us this inheritance, but was enraged against us . . . ; [the Son] accordingly became Mediator between us and Him, and prevailed with Him" (*NPNF*1 14:443). 1Tm 2:5 says "there is one mediator between God and men, the man Christ Jesus." This verse specifically notes that Jesus mediates *a new covenant*—the completion of God's plan of salvation through His work. *called.* Those who are summoned to salvation by the preaching of the Gospel. God is the one who calls (see SC, Third Article). *receive.* God's calling is concrete, not hypothetical. He calls persons, and they will receive His gifts because He gives them. These gifts end with *an eternal inheritance,* which belongs to Christ, the only-begotten Son of God, but which He shares with all those who are adopted into God's family. *a death . . . redeems them.* God does not overlook sin; He deals with it and punishes it in Christ. "The wages of sin is death" (Rm 6:23), and that debt was paid on the cross. Christ's death was the just punishment for our sins, which He took upon Himself to buy back the whole human race and save us from God's righteous wrath. *transgressions committed under the first covenant.* Sins against God's Law, which was enacted as part of the old covenant.

9:16–17 "Covenant" (v. 15) can also be translated as "testament" or "will" (Gk *diathēkē*). These verses show that Christ's death put His "last will and testament" into effect. We are the beneficiaries of this, as we receive an "eternal inheritance" (v. 15). *will.* A will, or testament, is a specific kind of covenant that promises an inheritance to others. The terms of the will are conditioned upon the testator's death. No inheritance is distributed from a will while the testator still lives, therefore death must be *established* before an inheritance is given.

9:18 *not . . . without blood.* Arguing from the lesser to the greater, death was needed for both covenants. In the first covenant, the blood of sacrificed animals was required to make atonement. The new covenant would require Christ's death and the shedding of His precious blood to go into effect. The sacrifice had to be made.

9:19 *Moses . . . took the blood.* The old covenant was communicated with words, but it was confirmed and put into effect with blood. The elements listed, *blood . . . water . . . scarlet wool . . . hyssop,* were used in purification rites (cf. Nu 19; Lv 14:4, 7; Heb 9:13), so it is significant that the *people* were sprinkled as well as the *book*. The entire covenant was confirmed through blood, as were the people who would receive its benefits.

9:20 In sprinkling the book and the people, Moses explained, *this is the blood of the covenant* (Ex 24:8). Christ used similar words to give us His blood of the new covenant in the Holy Supper (1Co 11:25). *God commanded.* This was the means that God provided. They were not to look for another covenant nor for its implementation in any other way. God established the covenant and its terms, and He gave what was necessary to enact it.

9:21 *used in worship.* (Gk *leitourgia*, "of the liturgy or service") The holy vestments (Ex 29:21) and all the appointments necessary to conduct worship in the tabernacle are encompassed by these words. Everything in the OT tabernacle assisted with blood sacrifice and received its holiness from God through that sacrifice. Through blood they were set apart—consecrated and sanctified— for holy service. Even the tabernacle itself (the *tent*) was sprinkled with blood.

9:22 *under the law almost everything is purified with blood.* There was no doubt that the tabernacle was a place of sacrificial death. Even where blood was not applied to the objects being purified, sacrifice often was part of the purification (cf. Nu 19:4). *without the shedding of blood there is no forgiveness of sins.* (Cf. Lv 17:11; Heb 9:7, 18.) This is a particularly critical point. Forgiveness has a bloody, deadly price. Without the shedding of blood, the debt of sin remains unpaid and forgiveness does not exist. Yet all the bloodshed and death of the tabernacle pointed forward to the bloodshed and death of Christ. His blood is what purifies and brings about reconciliation with God. Christ "was crucified, died, and was buried. He did this to reconcile the Father to us" (AC III 2–3).

9:23 *copies of the heavenly things.* The heavenly tabernacle seen by Moses was the original; the tabernacle made by the Israelites was a copy (cf. 8:5). The copies made by human hands (cf. v. 11) were purified with the blood of sacrificed animals. But as the original—the heavenly temple—is superior to the copy, so it was purified with a superior sacrifice. The *better sacrifices* refers to the completed work of Christ. Moses saw the *heavenly things* (Ex 25:40); Christ opens these heavenly realms to us with His own blood.

9:24 *entered, not . . . made with hands.* A clear distinction is made here. Christ did not fulfill His priestly office in the earthly temple, but in *heaven itself* and *in the presence of God.* The earthly temple and its furnishing are *copies* (Gk *antitypos*, "antitypes, counterparts,"), things patterned off an original (Gk *typos*). The copies have their purpose, but they are surpassed by the original, perfect pattern. Christ carried out the ultimate work of sacrifice in the true, perfect, heavenly temple. *into heaven itself.* Christ ascended, but neither God nor the Christ, according to His humanity, is spatially limited to "heaven," for God is omnipresent (cf. Eph 4:10; see FC SD VIII 27–28). *in the presence of God.* Christ has reconciled us to the Father through His blood and continues to be our mediator to the Father (1Tm 2:5). As 1Jn 2:1 reminds us, "we have an advocate with the Father." God sees believers through Christ, our redeemer, mediator, and advocate. *on our behalf.* This gracious work was done for us.

9:25 *nor . . . offer Himself repeatedly.* This is another important difference between the priestly ministry of Jesus and all other priests. Repeated sin required repeated sacrifice. The *high priest* was only allowed to enter the Most Holy Place once a year on the Day of Atonement, but it was essential that he did so. Every year this sacrificial work needed to be repeated. It was never done because sin was never done. He had to enter with the blood of sacrificed animals, *blood not his own,* but it was never the final solution. What a contrast! Christ's perfect sacrifice was and is sufficient. It was not repeated and has no need of repetition. Christ did not enter heaven to sacrifice for us daily, but daily He still intercedes for us.

9:26 *suffer repeatedly.* Each sprinkling of blood in the earthly temple was accompanied by death. Christ was not this type of sacrifice—not a sacrifice that needed to be endlessly repeated when sin inevitably recurred. God has not established a cycle of perpetual suffering and sacrifice; He has provided the final solution. *once for all.* Christ's sacrifice is perfect and finished (cf. Jn 19:30). At the cross, He paid for the sin of all. No further sacrifice or suffering contributes to our salvation in any way. The sacrifice of Christ is not repeated anywhere—not on the cross and not in the Holy Supper. Instead, in the Lord's Supper we eat and drink His body and blood, already sacrificed once for all, and we receive the benefits of His sacrifice (forgiveness, life, and salvation). Nor is the sacrifice of Christ repeated or enhanced in the suffering of believers. Though we may, at times, suffer in this sinful world, the work of Christ is complete. He empowers and blesses us by His grace that we might endure. The Holy Spirit conforms our lives to His life so that we offer to Him sacrifices of praise and thanksgiving. See note, Heb 13:15. Luther says:

> That, I say, is our gospel, that Christ has made us righteous and holy through that sacrifice and has redeemed us from sin, death, and the devil and has brought us into his heavenly kingdom. We have to grasp this and hold it fast through faith alone. . . . All our own works undertaken to expiate sin and escape from death are necessarily blasphemous. They deny God and insult the sacrifice that Christ has made and disgrace his blood, because they try thereby to do what only Christ's blood can do. (LW 36:313)

end of the ages. Christ's sacrifice was the fulfillment of all past ages, and it ushered in the last age of the world, in which we now live. Because of Christ's work, these are the last days. See note, 1:2.

9:27 *die once . . . after that comes judgment.* Because of sin, we are mortal. We do not get a second chance at life on this earth; we live and we will die. Left to ourselves, we would die without hope of salvation and eternal life. We would have received the just wages for our sin (Rm 6:23) and, in facing judgment, would be condemned. We cannot hope for a second life by which we might appease God through our own actions. Such a thing has not been granted to us. We have no hope on our own! Thanks be to God that we are not on our own.

9:28 *offered once.* God's solution perfectly addresses our problem. We die once and then face judgment (v. 27). Christ was offered once, giving Himself to a sacrificial death for us. Now, we anticipate that He *will appear a second time.* When He returns, the last judgment will occur (cf. 2Tm 4:1; Ti 2:13). There are no second chances when He returns. This reality does not, however, fill the child of God with dread. Knowing Christ and what He has accomplished, we look forward to His return with gladness and joy. He comes *not to deal with sin.* He does not need to do this since He has already paid for them. He comes without our sins (Is 53:6), which He bore as a heavy load (Jn 1:29) when the Father made Him to be sin for us (2Co 5:21). He comes not in the likeness of sinful flesh (Rm 8:3) but in the majesty of His transfigured body (Mt 24:30; Php 3:21). He comes *to save those who are eagerly waiting for Him.* He comes for His own people, bringing them the victory that He has won. Judgment Day is good news for the child of God. We are declared righteous for the sake of Christ our Savior. Cranmer wrote:

> The only oblation of Christ (wherewith he offered himself to God the Father once to death upon the altar of the cross for our redemption) was of such efficacy, that there is no more need of any sacrifice for the redemption of the whole world, but all the sacrifices of the old law he took away, performing that in very deed which they did signify and promise. Whosoever therefore shall fix the hope of his salvation in any other sacrifice, he falleth from the grace of Christ, and is contumelious against the blood of Christ. (Cranmer 4:19)

9:11–28 in Devotion and Prayer Worship in the tabernacle and temple was bloody, violent, and perhaps even disturbing. One could not escape the presence and smell of death as sacrifice after sacrifice was offered up for sin. Blood was poured out. Carcasses were burned. Each sacrifice was a reminder: this is what sin costs! Sin is serious stuff. It merits death. In the presence of such a place, there was no avoiding the painful truth: you deserve to die. In our modern world, we try to blunt that reality. Perhaps we do not see death as regularly as the ancients did. We prefer our lives to be more sanitary, our religion more cerebral, our lives more happy. But our wishes do not change the truth. "Without the shedding of blood there is no forgiveness of sins" (v. 22). Thanks be to God, our Savior has come. He comes as both priest and victim to sacrifice Himself for the sin of the world. He shed His blood on the cross, presented Himself as the sacrifice for the sin of the world, and now is our advocate before the Father. He has covered us with His blood, clothed us in His righteousness, and declares us righteous. Now we are the heirs of His last will and testament. Adopted into God's family by the work of Christ, we now live in forgiveness, life, and salvation. We eagerly look forward to the glorious return of our Savior Jesus who brings the fullness of salvation to us. • "Not all the blood of beasts On Jewish altars slain Could give the guilty conscience peace or Wash away the stain. But Christ, the heav'nly Lamb, Takes all our sins away; A sacrifice of nobler name And richer blood than they." (*LSB* 431:1–2)

Introduction to 10:1–18 Melanchthon confessed:

> There are two kinds of sacrifice and no more. One is the *atoning sacrifice*, that is, a work that makes satisfaction for guilt and

punishment. It reconciles God, or reconciles His wrath and merits the forgiveness of sins for others. The other kind is the *eucharistic* [thankful] *sacrifice*, which does not merit the forgiveness of sins or reconciliation. It is practiced by those who have been reconciled, so that we may give thanks or return gratitude for the forgiveness of sins. (Ap XXIV 19, emphasis added)

Verses 1–18 consider the atoning sacrifice that Christ offers for the sin of the world—once for all.

10:1 *shadow . . . true form.* Similar language is found in 8:5, where the tabernacle and priesthood are seen as shadows of greater heavenly realities. Here the argument reaches its culmination. Something can be partially seen or understood by its shadow, but that is not as clear as seeing the thing itself. The true form (Gk *eikōn*, "icon" or "image," as the KJV translates) is the thing itself. In this instance, the earlier sacrifices foreshadowed Christ's person and work. Truth could be seen in the sacrifices but they were not the "true form." They were but a shadow of what God was doing in Christ. (Cf. Col 2:17, where regulations for food and drink, festivals, new moons and Sabbaths are called shadows. Paul responds that "the substance belongs to Christ.") The *realities*, or fulfilment of God's plan, are the *good things to come*, the true and lasting forgiveness, life, and salvation that are given to us by Christ (cf. 9:11 and notes). *make perfect.* Not being God's ultimate solution, the shadows cannot by themselves truly purify from sins and sanctify sinners (see note, Heb 2:10). Though sacrifices are repeated *continually*, sin keeps recurring and is only truly dealt with by Christ's work. *draw near.* Those who draw near through the sacrifice of animals will never find perfection, the complete solution that God offers. Instead, God calls His people to "draw near to the throne of grace" (4:16), where we receive mercy for the sake of Christ. We "draw near to God through Him" (7:25).

10:2 *would they not have ceased?* This functions as a rhetorical question, the Greek grammar implying an affirmative answer. "Of course, they would have ceased!" If those sacrifices were completely effective, there would be no more *consciousness of sins.* No one would see a need for further sacrifice or action if they had fully accomplished their work.

10:3 *reminder of sin.* The ongoing sacrifices did not have the effect of truly and completely removing sin from the sinner. Sins continued to be committed. Guilt remained. Indeed, the fact that the

Day of Atonement kept occurring each year served to remind Israel that they needed cleansing from sin. Each sacrifice brought that fact back to mind: you are a sinner.

10:4 *it is impossible for the blood of bulls . . . to take away sin.* This does not mean these sacrifices were unimportant. God gave this sacrificial system to His people (Lv 17:11). But the fact that they needed repetition demonstrated that they were not the ultimate solution. Sin and guilt returned and needed further acts of atonement. This demonstrates that these things were shadows of the true realities (v. 1). They point forward to Christ. "In fact there has been only one atoning sacrifice in the world, namely, Christ's death" (Ap XXIV 22). Through the OT sacrifices, God forgave sins on the basis of Christ's sacrifice.

10:5–18 Using the OT, the writer displays the testimony of the Son (v. 5) and the Spirit (v. 15) about the institution of the new covenant prepared by the heavenly Father ("You," vv. 5–6). Note that in vv. 15–17, the Holy Spirit is equated with "the Lord" (Hbr *Yahweh*). These verses thus affirm the full deity of each person of the Holy Trinity.

10:5–7 This is a quotation from LXX version of Ps 40:6–8.

10:5–6 *Christ . . . said.* The Spirit of Christ inspired the psalmist. If Jesus also spoke these words during His earthly ministry, the Gospels have not recorded it (cf. Jn 20:30–31; 21:25), but the words of the psalm certainly anticipate the work of Christ. *Sacrifices . . . not desired . . . taken no pleasure.* While God established the system of sacrifice, these sacrifices where only pleasing to God when offered through faith. Mere outward participation was not sufficient. Moreover, the sacrifices themselves would not have been effective were it not for their fulfillment in the sacrifice of Christ. *a body have You prepared.* This is the wording from the LXX, which appears to be seeking to clarify the more difficult Hebrew expression "ears You have dug out [prepared] for me." The Hebrew emphasizes that God helps a person hear His Word. It is possible that the LXX manuscripts that say "body" were reading the word "ears" as a synecdoche, so as to represent the whole person. In that case, a person would commit himself to obeying God after hearing and believing His Word. However, the similarity of the Greek letters for "ears" and "body" when tightly written may also have caused the variant. Since Hebrews cites the LXX text, we see a greater depth. God was not pleased with faithless sacrifices and their endless repetition. His acceptance would come in the sacrifice of the body of Christ, once, for all.

10:7 *to do Your will.* Christ came to fulfill the Law, to satisfy God's justice, and to accomplish the redemption of the human race. Even when the divine will entailed suffering that a human being would naturally seek to avoid, Christ was obedient to the holy will of His Father (Mt 26:39). He comes, in flesh, and fulfills and ends the old sacrifices that He Himself established for a time. This shows they were temporary and that, with His own sacrifice, Christ would establish the new covenant. This was not a random happenstance, but the eternal plan of God, foretold in the prophetic Word, *written of Me in the scroll of the book.* This is God's planned and promised fulfillment. Bengel wrote:

> The Messiah places Himself as surety by both expressions; and hence the presence, in the highest degree, of the Spirit of prophecy is perceived. David had before his eyes, and in his hand, the book in which the psalm was written, and shows this very book as the written contract of the Messiah; comp. Neh. x. 1. (Bengel 4:432)

10:8 *sacrifices and offerings and burnt offerings and sin offerings.* Grouping all of these words from Ps 40 together emphasizes again the magnitude of sin and the need for atonement. While these are offered *according to the law*, they are not a final solution.

10:9 *then He added, "Behold I have come."* The sequence is important. The coming of the Messiah is a direct response to the insufficiency of the sacrifices. God did not desire those things in themselves, therefore the Christ comes *to do* God's *will.* This marks a change of covenants as *He does away with the first in order to establish the second.* The sacrificial system is set aside with God's lack of desire and pleasure (vv. 5, 6). The covenant was not forgotten; it was replaced by the establishment of the new covenant through the sacrifice of the body of Christ.

10:10 *will.* Gk *thelēma*, God's perfect desire or intention that was fulfilled in the sending of Christ. This is not to be confused with "testament" or "covenant" as described in 9:16 (see note there). This is God's intent—what He chooses to do. God's gracious will is expressed in the new testament as a "will," or covenant. *sanctified.* It is the will of God that we be sanctified, that is, that we are declared holy because our sins have been taken away. (This is the wider meaning of sanctification and should not be confused with the more narrow meaning of sanctification which is the fruit of faith, worked by the Holy Spirit in the lives of believers.) Note that this word is passive. God does this for us—He declares us holy for the sake of Christ. God acts upon His will by *offering . . . the body of Jesus Christ.* Christ is the sacrifice of the new covenant. "Christ's passion was an offering and satisfaction, not only for original guilt, but also for all other sins" (AC XXV 25). Because of the incomparable worth of the Son of God, that perfect sacrifice is offered *once for all* (cf. 7:27; 9:2). God's perfect, gracious will results in this final and perfect sacrifice for all mankind. Knox wrote, "The scripture witnesses that God the Father gave his Son unto the world, that the world might be saved by him; and that Jesus Christ offered himself once unto God, for the destruction of sin, and to take away the sins of many" (397).

10:11 *every priest stands.* The work of the Levitical priests was never really done. They stood ready to carry out their office whenever needed. This meant they were *offering repeatedly the same sacrifices.* Nu 28:3 speaks of *daily* sacrifices. Sin was a constant reality, so sacrifices kept being offered. While God used the sacrifices as His means of forgiveness until the time of Christ, it wasn't these repeated offerings that did what was needed. In fact, they *never* truly *take away sin.* That only happens through the perfect sacrifice of Christ. Each repeated sin became the occasion for further sacrifice.

10:12 This verse again contrasts Christ with the Levites. They offered the same sacrifices repeatedly because their sacrifices never really take away sin (v. 11), but He offers *for all time a single sacrifice.* Here is the culmination and fulfillment of all sacrifice. Nothing further is needed once Christ, the Lamb of God, has sacrificed Himself. This already demonstrates His supremacy, but Hebrews has another piece of evidence: after He offered Himself as sacrifice, *He sat down at the right hand of God.* The earthly priests could never sit while their work was incomplete, so they always stood. Christ sits, showing that His atoning sacrifice is finished. He *sat at the right hand of God.* This is not a physical location, but describes His position of power and authority (see note, 8:1). While His sacrificial work is complete, He continues His priestly ministry by interceding for us as our own High Priest. See 8:1 and note.

10:13 *waiting.* Christ has finished His work. There is nothing remaining for Him to do before this final demonstration of His victory is manifest. *His enemies . . . made a footstool.* This is an allusion to

Ps 110, which was also quoted in 1:13. In biblical times, a conqueror placed his foot on his defeated enemies to indicate triumph. Christ's victory is total. St. Paul uses this same imagery, saying, "He must reign until He has put all His enemies under His feet. The last enemy to be destroyed is death. For 'God has put all things in subjection under His feet'" (1Co 15:25–27). Everything in this image stresses that Christ's work is complete and that He is victorious.

10:14 *single offering.* The sacrifice of Himself, once for all (cf. 7:27; 9:12; 10:10), was sufficient. *Perfected . . . sanctified.* All of this is the result of Christ's work, which is graciously given to believers. As in v. 10, "sanctified" is used in the broad sense of "being made or declared holy." We have been declared righteous and holy because of the one-time sacrifice of Christ. Through this, we are "perfected" (Gk *teleiō*), brought to completion, finished, or made what God intended us to be (see 2:10; 7:9, 19 and notes). *for all time.* This Gk word (*diēnekēs*) denotes time without interruption, eternal or endless time. By His perfect, singular offering, Christ has sanctified His people permanently. His work is complete. Martin Luther wrote about how this is worked out in the life of the believer, saying:

> Everything is forgiven through grace, but not everything is yet healed through the gift. The gift is poured in, the leaven is added, and it works to remove the sin which has already been forgiven to the person, and to drive out the evil guest, whom it has permission to drive out. Meanwhile, as this is happening, it is called sin and in its nature truly is sin, but now it is sin without wrath. (StL 18:1165)

Elsewhere, Luther wrote to show the connection of this sacrifice to the Eucharist, saying: "Of this sacrifice and offering he has instituted a perpetual remembrance in that he intends to have it proclaimed in the sacrament of the altar and thereby have faith in it strengthened" (LW 40:14).

10:15 *Holy Spirit also bears witness.* As in 3:7 and 9:8, these words affirm the inspiration and authority of Scripture. Though a human writer put the words on the page, the words of Scripture are inspired by God and therefore are the Word of God. In Sacred Scripture we hear God's voice (cf. 2:4; 2Pt 1:21; 2Tm 3:15–17).

10:16 Jer 31:33 is quoted once again (as in 8:10; see note there), reinforcing God's establishment of the new covenant in Christ.

10:17 Quoting Jer 31:34 (as in 8:12; see note there), this passage shows how we are "for all time . . . being sanctified" (v. 14). This has occurred because God has chosen to forgive us for the sake of Christ. This is the testimony of the Holy Spirit (v. 15).

10:18 *where there is forgiveness there is no longer any offering.* This wraps up the whole argument. There is no offering that remains because there is no further need for sacrifice. God has fulfilled His promise and kept the covenant. He has brought life and forgiveness through the work of Christ, our ascended Lord. Christ's perfect sacrifice brings perfect forgiveness.

10:1–18 in Devotion and Prayer It is hard for us to contemplate the magnitude of human sin. We are so accustomed to ignoring or excusing sin that we often fail to recognize its pervasive and destructive character. God provided a system of sacrifice, but the work of the earthly priests was never done. Whenever there was more sin, more sacrifices needed to be offered. When human beings today become aware of sin (even though they are only partially aware of it, not realizing how bad the problem truly is), we are often tempted to try to fix it ourselves. We try to bargain with God: "I'll do better" or "if you forgive me, I promise I will do this other good thing." But there is nothing we can offer, no bargain we can strike. When we consider God's Word honestly, we realize that we don't just commit sins; we are sinners. But Christ is not. He took our sins on Himself and became the one perfect, final offering for sin. He sacrificed Himself for the sin of the whole world—even for my sin, even for yours. He "perfects" (completes) us and "sanctifies" us (makes us holy). He does this when He applies the benefits of His sacrifice to us in Holy Baptism, in His Holy Supper, in the Absolution declared over us at His command. Though we struggle to comprehend the depths of His mercy and grace, He has done it all. He has sat down at the right hand of God because His work is done. He has done it for you. • "God's own child, I gladly say it: I am baptized into Christ! He, because I could not pay it, Gave my full redemption price. Do I need earth's treasures many? I have one worth more than any That brought me salvation free Lasting to eternity! Amen." (*LSB* 594:1)

PART 3

EXHORTATION TO FAITHFULNESS (10:19–12:29)

Invitation to Faithfulness (10:19–39)

ESV	KJV
[19]Therefore, brothers, since we have confidence to enter the holy places by the blood of Jesus, [20]by the new and living way that he opened for us through the curtain, that is, through his flesh, [21]and since we have a great priest over the house of God, [22]let us draw near with a true heart in full assurance of faith, with our hearts sprinkled clean from an evil conscience and our bodies washed with pure water. [23]Let us hold fast the confession of our hope without wavering, for he who promised is faithful. [24]And let us consider how to stir up one another to love and good works, [25]not neglecting to meet together, as is the habit of some, but encouraging one another, and all the more as you see the Day drawing near. [26]For if we go on sinning deliberately after receiving the knowledge of the truth, there no longer remains a sacrifice for sins, [27]but a fearful expectation of judgment, and a fury of fire that will consume the adversaries. [28]Anyone who has set aside the law of Moses dies without mercy on the evidence of two or	[19]Having therefore, brethren, boldness to enter into the holiest by the blood of Jesus, [20]By a new and living way, which he hath consecrated for us, through the veil, that is to say, his flesh; [21]And having an high priest over the house of God; [22]Let us draw near with a true heart in full assurance of faith, having our hearts sprinkled from an evil conscience, and our bodies washed with pure water. [23]Let us hold fast the profession of our faith without wavering; (for he is faithful that promised;) [24]And let us consider one another to provoke unto love and to good works: [25]Not forsaking the assembling of ourselves together, as the manner of some is; but exhorting one another: and so much the more, as ye see the day approaching. [26]For if we sin wilfully after that we have received the knowledge of the truth, there remaineth no more sacrifice for sins, [27]But a certain fearful looking for of judgment and fiery indignation, which shall devour the adversaries. [28]He that despised Moses' law died

three witnesses. [29]How much worse punishment, do you think, will be deserved by the one who has spurned the Son of God, and has profaned the blood of the covenant by which he was sanctified, and has outraged the Spirit of grace? [30]For we know him who said, "Vengeance is mine; I will repay." And again, "The Lord will judge his people." [31]It is a fearful thing to fall into the hands of the living God.

[32]But recall the former days when, after you were enlightened, you endured a hard struggle with sufferings, [33]sometimes being publicly exposed to reproach and affliction, and sometimes being partners with those so treated. [34]For you had compassion on those in prison, and you joyfully accepted the plundering of your property, since you knew that you yourselves had a better possession and an abiding one. [35]Therefore do not throw away your confidence, which has a great reward. [36]For you have need of endurance, so that when you have done the will of God you may receive what is promised. [37]For,

"Yet a little while,

and the coming one will come and
will not delay;

[38]but my righteous one shall live
by faith,

and if he shrinks back,
my soul has no pleasure in him."

[39]But we are not of those who shrink back and are destroyed, but of those who have faith and preserve their souls.

without mercy under two or three witnesses:

[29]Of how much sorer punishment, suppose ye, shall he be thought worthy, who hath trodden under foot the Son of God, and hath counted the blood of the covenant, wherewith he was sanctified, an unholy thing, and hath done despite unto the Spirit of grace?

[30]For we know him that hath said, Vengeance belongeth unto me, I will recompense, saith the Lord. And again, The Lord shall judge his people.

[31]It is a fearful thing to fall into the hands of the living God.

[32]But call to remembrance the former days, in which, after ye were illuminated, ye endured a great fight of afflictions;

[33]Partly, whilst ye were made a gazingstock both by reproaches and afflictions; and partly, whilst ye became companions of them that were so used.

[34]For ye had compassion of me in my bonds, and took joyfully the spoiling of your goods, knowing in yourselves that ye have in heaven a better and an enduring substance.

[35]Cast not away therefore your confidence, which hath great recompence of reward.

[36]For ye have need of patience, that, after ye have done the will of God, ye might receive the promise.

[37]For yet a little while, and he that shall come will come, and will not tarry.

[38]Now the just shall live by faith: but if any man draw back, my soul shall have no pleasure in him.

[39]But we are not of them who draw back unto perdition; but of them that believe to the saving of the soul.

Introduction 10:19–12:29 In these verses, Hebrews begins another section of urgent exhortation, warning against the dangers of apostasy. Having been declared holy by the work of Christ and baptized in His Name (10:19–22), believers are to hold to their confession (10:23), encourage each other in a lively faith (10:24), and worship together (10:25). God's free forgiveness is never to be a license to sin, for such a thankless, immature attitude demeans Christ and His work. Without faith, we fall under judgment. (10:26–31). Believers are reminded of ways God previously worked through them so that, knowing His faithfulness, they can endure (10:32–39). The Christian does all things by faith in Christ, and we have many helpful examples of faith and God's faithfulness in the saints who have gone before us (ch. 11). Like those saints, we therefore run our race, focused on Jesus, who endured much for us (12:1–3). In contrast, our struggles are seen in their proper perspective. In fact, we see that God disciplines us in love, as a father disciplines his beloved children (12:4–11). Christians are therefore encouraged to carry on in faith (12:12–17). We can do this because we have come into God's presence and are receiving a place in God's unshakable kingdom (12:18–29).

10:19 *brothers*. In these words of exhortation, the writer is speaking to fellow Christians who are joined in a bond of love. "Brothers" is inclusive of Christian men and women. *confidence*. (Gk *parrēsia*) This means boldness or courage to say or do appropriate things even in the face of difficulty or danger. In 4:16, Christians were told to draw near God's throne of grace with confidence. Here we are called to confidently *enter the holy places*. Given the previous discussion about the priesthood and tabernacle, these are striking words. The high priest entered the Most Holy Place only once a year after offering the proper sacrifices, and he had to take a sacrifice of blood with him (9:25). Inappropriate entry into the presence of God could be fatal! (Cf. Lv 16:1.) Now, however, because of the work of Christ, we have confidence to enter boldly into the holy places—to go where God is. That is, we have confidence to go before our heavenly Father, trusting that we will be accepted. We are able to do this by the sacrifice of the *blood of Jesus* (cf. 9:12), the perfect and final sacrifice for sin.

10:20 *new and living way*. The old way into the earthly tabernacle was through the blood of sacrificed animals, which was offered over and over again. *new*. This is the only biblical use of this Greek word (*prosphatos*). It means "recently come about or discovered."

129

God provided a completely different way of access to Himself in the work of Christ. Moreover, this is a *living* way, since Christ rose from the dead after sacrificing Himself. Our Redeemer Lives, and Christ is the way (cf. Jn 14:6; see also Heb 9:8 and note). *through the curtain, that is, through His flesh.* As the high priest passed through the curtain with the blood of the sacrifice to enter the Most Holy Place, we enter heaven only through Christ's flesh, which was sacrificed for all. When Christ's body and soul were divided in death, the curtain of the temple was torn from top to bottom, revealing what was formerly hidden from view (Mt 27:51). Just as the curtain was torn open, our way into heaven, through Christ, is now open. Luther writes of the way in which Christ opens the way to heaven for His people, saying:

> He first sets forth the example of Christ, our Leader, who fights in the forefront. Although under no compulsion, yet for the purpose of buoying up our confidence He crossed over first of all, and He smooths the exceedingly rough road. Then the apostle points out that Christ not only gave an example by crossing over, but that He also holds out His hand to those who follow. (LW 29:226)

10:21 *over the house of God.* The house of God is, of course, where God dwells. In the OT, He promised to dwell in the tabernacle/temple (though He was not restricted to its confines; cf. 1Ki 8:27). In the NT, God dwells in His Church, which is now His house (cf. 1Co 3:16). Christ, our *great priest*, serves His Church (cf. 3:6).

10:22–24 The response of faith is found in these verses. Since Christ is our priest who has opened heaven to us (vv. 20–21), we receive God's gifts of faith (v. 22), hope (v. 23), and love (v. 24). Cf. 1Co 13:13.

10:22 *draw near.* This is not a meritorious work that we do, but a response to the faith and other gifts that God gives (cf. 4:16; 7:19, 25; 10:1 and notes). *a true heart.* An honest, believing heart does not presume to think that we can conceal anything from God. We are completely open to our God. Apart from faith, this is a terrifying thought, but in faith, we have *full assurance*, complete confidence in God's grace (cf. Mk 9:24). *sprinkled clean from an evil conscience.* The Levitical high priest sprinkled sacrificial blood to make atonement. In Christ's perfect fulfillment of atonement, His own cleansing sacrifice is put on us. Our consciences are relieved and strengthened so that we see ourselves and the certainty of God's mercy clearly (cf. 1Pt 1: 18–19; Ezk 36:25–26). We confess that "where the heart is not in a right relationship with God, or cannot take such confidence, it will not dare to pray anymore. Such a confident and joyful heart can spring from nothing else than the certain knowledge of the forgiveness of sin" (LC III 92). *our bodies washed with pure water.* The priests' consecration included ritual washings (cf. Nu 8: 6–7; Lv 8:6). In a much greater way, Christ blesses us when He institutes the Sacrament of Baptism, in which we are washed and His grace is given to us (Eph 5:26; Ti 3:5; 1Co 6:11). In Baptism we are given a true heart and receive God's myriad blessings. Luther writes of the new life God gives in Baptism:

> This old man consists of error, concupiscence, wrath, fear, apprehension, despair, evil conscience, horror of death, etc. Those are characteristics of the old, carnal man. They diminish, however, in the new man, but they are not extinguished until he himself is extinguished by death. . . . Rather the process of removal has begun, and as a person increases in spiritual health these evils are removed. This spiritual health is nothing more than faith in or love in Christ. (LW 31:124)

10:23 *the confession of our hope.* Confession (Gk *homologia*) means "same words." We say the same thing as what God says. We agree with Him and proclaim our faith with our fellow believers (cf. 4:14 and notes). Christ is the "apostle and high priest of our confession" (3:1). We confess the certain hope we have in Christ. The author admonishes his readers to *hold fast* to this confession and to do so *without wavering.* God gives amazing blessings to the baptized. We have received the benefits of Christ's work and now enter into God's presence through Him. Hold on to this great gift! *He who promised is faithful.* The exhortation to hold the confession does not mean that we are alone. God, who promised these gifts to us, is faithful to His promises. He will fulfill everything He promised (cf. 1Co 1:9).

10:24–25 God calls each person to faith, yet the Christian faith is not a solitary religion. He places us in the communion of His Church, the Body of Christ. He gives us our brothers and sisters that we might be blessed by them and be a blessing to them. God's gift of the Church is a tremendous help in light of the many challenges and temptations that Christians face in the world. We confess in the Large Catechism:

> It is not enough to teach and instruct alone. There is also need for daily encouragement. . . . So here also there is need for us to

continue to preach so that people may not become weary and disgusted. For we know and feel how the devil always opposes this and every Christian exercise. He drives and deters people from them as much as he can. (LC V 44)

Heb 3:13 gave similar encouragement to Christians to exhort each other. Our responsibility to care for our fellow believers is an important one and a gift from God. Their care and exhortation towards us is, likewise, a blessed gift.

10:24 *stir up.* This word can have either a negative sense (as in stirring up trouble) or positive one (as it is used here). It means agitating or provoking a response. In this instance, of course, it means encouraging one another to do things that are pleasing to God and are a blessing to others. In particular, we are to stir one another up to *love* (Gk *agapē*) and *good works*. These are highlighted as the fruit of faith, the true heart that is given in our Baptism (v. 22), and an application of our confession and trust in God's faithfulness (v. 23).

10:25 *neglecting to meet together.* Christians who first read this Epistle faced the same temptation as Christians do today. Having received God's blessings, they were tempted to remain by themselves and not gather together to worship. Not only is such a Christian failing to recognize God's faithful promise to bless them in worship, but they are also depriving their fellow believers of the full fellowship of the Church. God calls Christians to gather together to hear His Word preached, receive the Sacraments, pray, sing, and give thanks (cf. Rm 10:14; Lk 22:19–20; Ac 2:38, 42; Rm 15:30; Ps 30:4). Those who despise the Church and neglect to come together more easily fall from the faith. *all the more . . . see the Day drawing near.* "The Day" is the final return of Christ for judgment (cf. Heb 10:37; Mt 25:31–32). We live in the last days (1:2) and need our fellow Christians for support and encouragement. Worship together is not a burden but a blessing. John Calvin reflected on this, saying:

> It is an evil which prevails everywhere among mankind, that every one sets himself above others, and especially that those who seem in anything to excel cannot well endure their inferiors to be on an equality with themselves. And then there is so much morosity almost in all, that individuals would gladly make churches for themselves if they could; for they find it so difficult to accommodate themselves to the ways and habits of others. The rich envy one another; and hardly one in a hundred can be found among

the rich, who allows to the poor the name and rank of brethren. Unless similarity of habits or some allurements or advantages draw us together, it is very difficult even to maintain a continual concord among ourselves. Extremely needed, therefore, by us all is the admonition to be stimulated to love and not to envy, and not to separate from those whom God has joined to us, but to embrace with brotherly kindness all those who are united to us in faith. And surely it behoves us the more earnestly to cultivate unity, as the more eagerly watchful Satan is, either to tear us by any means from the Church, or stealthily to seduce us from it. And such would be the happy effect, were no one to please himself too much, and were all of us to preserve this one object, mutually to provoke one another to love, and to allow no emulation among ourselves, but that of doing good works. For doubtless the contempt of the brethren, moroseness, envy, immoderate estimate of ourselves, and other sinful impulses, clearly shew that our love is either very cold, or does not at all exist. (Calvin 240–41)

10:26–27 These warning verses describe the sin against the Holy Spirit, a challenging issue requiring careful interpretation. Such passages call for self-reflection and a faithful application of God's Law and Gospel. Words of warning like these are spoken to secure sinners and to those who have no regard for the will of God. They are misapplied when they are used to drive the already penitent and sorrowful further into despair and away from Christ. For more on this challenging topic, see 6:4–6; 12:17 and notes; cf. Mk 3:29–30; Mt 12:31–32. Also refer to the contrasting examples of Saul and David, both of whom fell into manifest sin and would face God's rebuke and wrath. Saul did not repent but turned away from the Lord (1Sm 15:10–11). David repented when confronted with his sin (2Sm 12:13).

10:26 *go on sinning deliberately.* This is persistently and willfully doing what we know is wrong without sorrow, repentance, or regard for God's will. *no longer remains a sacrifice for sins.* There is only one sacrifice for sins: the once-for-all sacrifice of Christ for the sins of the world. If a person refuses this gift, there is no hope remaining (see also notes, 6:4–6). Salvation is found in no one else than Jesus Christ (Ac 4:12). God has already given His perfect and final solution. Nothing else will be given. Chrysostom said, "He did not say, no more is there repentance, or no more is there remission, but 'no more' is there a 'sacrifice,' that is, there is no more a second Cross" (*NPNF*1 14:457).

There is no salvation apart from Christ's sacrifice. Therefore, the one who sins is called to repent and believe the Gospel.

10:27 *fearful expectation of judgment.* The child of God has nothing to fear on Judgment Day, for they are declared righteous for Christ's sake. But those who reject His saving work should rightly be afraid of judgment. Standing alone, they will surely be condemned (cf. 2:3; 12:25). They will face a *fury of fire*, that is, hell. If they have rejected Christ, their only hope of salvation, this is the only remaining outcome.

10:28 Arguing from the lesser to the greater, this verse shows the consequence of ignoring God's Law. *Anyone who has set aside the law.* That is, they have set it aside for themselves, violating the Law, treating it as invalid or spurning it. *dies without mercy.* Such a person has no hope for pardon since their guilt is obvious. *two or three witnesses.* Under the Law, this was the testimony required to establish the truth of an accusation (cf. Dt 17:6; Mt 18:16).

10:29 *how much worse?* If violating the first covenant had such dire consequences, how much more will there be consequences for violating the new and final covenant? *trampled . . . profaned the blood of the covenant.* These shocking words demonstrate the seriousness of rejecting Christ. Acting like sin does not matter ignores the terrible cost that Christ paid for the sin of the world. Looking for salvation apart from Christ despises the greatest gift that God has given. The sacrifice of Christ is thus profaned, made to be nothing and despised. The blood of Jesus, poured out for the forgiveness of sins (Mt 26:28), is treated with contempt. These words are directed against believers who, knowing the truth, act in faithless ways. These are people who have received the blessings of Christ's work. They were *sanctified*, that is, forgiven and declared holy for Christ's sake (cf. 9:13,14). Having received such blessings, how can they act in such a faithless manner? This *outraged the Spirit of grace.* This verse is the only time that "outraged" is used in the NT. This word can also be translated "insulted." Despising God's gifts, particularly the sacrifice of Christ on our behalf, is insulting to God. As there is no hope apart from Christ, this is of utmost seriousness. The Lutheran reformers wrote, "God will receive into grace all who repent and believe in Christ, . . . [but] He also will punish those who willfully . . . despise God's Spirit. . . . They will be hardened, blinded, and eternally condemned if they persist in such things" (FC SD XI 83).

10:30–31 Two OT quotations are given, reinforcing the teaching that all will face judgment on the Last Day. God will have *vengeance* (Dt 32:35), and He will *judge His people* (Dt 32:36). Such passages warn the reader about despising God's Word, since judgment can be *fearful.* While these words are here used as a warning, we should also note that not all will be condemned. The one who receives God's gifts in faith has been redeemed and will stand with Christ, vindicated by His righteousness, which has been imputed to them.

10:32 *recall the former days.* Following the fearsome warning, the author now takes a gentler approach, asking his readers to remember a time when their faith was strong. Though he warns them about falling away, he also lovingly calls them back to sincere faith. *after you were enlightened.* When they were new to the faith, having received the Holy Spirit in their conversion and Baptism, they demonstrated the fruits of faith in their lives (see note, 6:4; see also FC Ep II 13). *Endured a hard struggle with sufferings.* We do not know the details of this struggle. Evidently these Christians had endured challenges and persecution of some type because of their faith. During such times, their faith was strong and active.

10:33 *publicly exposed.* The afflictions they faced were visible to all. We see many examples of this in the NT era (cf. Ac 4; 8:1–3; 12:1–5; 14:19; 16:16–24; 19:21–41; 21:27–28:31). *reproach.* They received verbal abuse and insults. *affliction.* This was probably physical abuse. Their status as Christians meant they faced a variety of difficult situations. They evidently did not shrink from these, but remained strong in their confession, even being *partners* with those who received such treatment. They did not hide their faith when some were persecuted but continued to acknowledge their Savior.

10:34 *compassion on those in prison.* Supporting those imprisoned for their faith could draw attention to one's own status as a Christian and thus invite persecution. Even with this risk, these Christians cared for their fellow believers who were in prison (cf. 13:3; Mt 25:36; 2Tm 1:16). *joyfully accepted the plundering.* When they were deprived of their property because of their faith, they did not respond with anger but in joy. They counted such treatment as an honor. This, too, is a response of faith. Following Jesus, they were able to "rejoice and be glad," knowing that their reward was in heaven (Mt 5:10–12). In fact, they knew they had *a better possession,* namely, the kingdom of heaven. They knew that God was preparing far greater blessings for them (cf. 12:28; 1Pt 1:4). Unlike earthly possessions that do not last, they looked forward to *an abiding one* (cf. Mt 6:19–21), the treasure of heaven.

10:35 *confidence*. As in v. 19, confidence is boldness and courage to say and do the right thing in the face of difficulty. They have confidence but here are exhorted to remain confident, knowing that God is faithful. Though they face persecution, by faith they can trust God and look forward to His great blessings. They know that by God's grace they will receive a *great reward*. Luther says, "They already have the kingdom of heaven, and yet . . . they will have it even more gloriously when it is revealed" (LW 21:292).

10:36 *you have need of endurance*. Here is the application. The author has reminded them of the quality of their faith and their trust in God's promise. They have already demonstrated that, with God's blessing, they are able to bear up under persecution. Now as they again face challenges, they once more need to be strong in the faith. God was faithful in the past; He will always be faithful. Therefore they are called to be strong. They are thus able to live in the faith until they have *done the will of God*, that is, confessing the Gospel through a godly life and a steadfast faith. There is no doubt about the outcome. Living in the faith, they will *receive what is promised*. God will fulfill all of His promises to them not only in heaven but also while they live in the faith. God's faithfulness always exceeds our need.

10:37–38 These verses combine and interpret the LXX versions of Is 26:20 and Hab 2:3.

10:37 *little while*. While they may face persecution, it is temporary and short lived. *the coming one will come*. Christ is their Savior, who promises, "Surely I am coming soon" (Rv 22:20).

10:38 *righteous one*. This righteousness is a gift of God, declared for the sake of Christ Jesus. *shall live by faith*. This is a call to Christians to live in the faith to which they have been called (cf. Hab 2:4; Rm 1:17). But to those who still think that this is unimportant, it also holds a warning: do not shrink back away from the faith that God gives. God would have us live in the faith He gives.

10:19–39 in Devotion and Prayer God calls us to a confident faith. Since He has accomplished everything for us, since He is faithful, and since He has prepared a place for us, we can trust His Word and promises. We have been baptized into Christ and draw near to God with a true heart. We know that we inherit the kingdom of heaven and receive many blessings for the sake of Christ. We boldly and joyfully confess these truths. The problem occurs when we are tempted to forget that all of this is a gift of God's grace. Do we think that our sin does not matter or that we are strong enough not to need the nourishment of Word and Sacrament or the fellowship of Christ's Church? Do we have so little regard for our fellow Christians that we do not want to spend time with them to support and bless them? Do we act as if we do not need a Savior, that we are just fine on our own? Watch out! This is the response not of faith but of the flesh. Do not treat Christ and His work with contempt. Do not forget that our only hope is in Him. Remember it well: we are utterly reliant upon God's grace. Remember it well, and know that God remembers it too. He is gracious and merciful. He will strengthen us in the faith and draw us to Him. In the fellowship of His Church, He blesses us and equips us to live in this challenging world. Thank God! He is always faithful. • Heavenly Father, forgive me for acting as if I do not need You and Your gifts. Forgive me for acting as if I alone matter. Take my sin and give me Jesus' righteousness. Help me to rejoice that You are my strength and my salvation. Bless me and equip me to be a blessing to my fellow Christians that together we may worship You and serve others. In Jesus' name. Amen.

OT Examples of Faith: Following in the Faith of Our Fathers (ch. 11)

ESV	KJV
11 ¹Now faith is the assurance of things hoped for, the conviction of things not seen. ²For by it the people of old received their commendation. ³By faith we understand that the universe was created by the word of God, so that what is seen was not made out of things that are visible. ⁴By faith Abel offered to God a more acceptable sacrifice than Cain, through which he was commended as righteous, God commending him by accepting his gifts. And through his faith, though he died, he still speaks.	*11* ¹Now faith is the substance of things hoped for, the evidence of things not seen. ²For by it the elders obtained a good report. ³Through faith we understand that the worlds were framed by the word of God, so that things which are seen were not made of things which do appear. ⁴By faith Abel offered unto God a more excellent sacrifice than Cain, by which he obtained witness that he was righteous, God testifying of

HEBREWS

⁵By faith Enoch was taken up so that he should not see death, and he was not found, because God had taken him. Now before he was taken he was commended as having pleased God. ⁶And without faith it is impossible to please him, for whoever would draw near to God must believe that he exists and that he rewards those who seek him. ⁷By faith Noah, being warned by God concerning events as yet unseen, in reverent fear constructed an ark for the saving of his household. By this he condemned the world and became an heir of the righteousness that comes by faith.

⁸By faith Abraham obeyed when he was called to go out to a place that he was to receive as an inheritance. And he went out, not knowing where he was going. ⁹By faith he went to live in the land of promise, as in a foreign land, living in tents with Isaac and Jacob, heirs with him of the same promise. ¹⁰For he was looking forward to the city that has foundations, whose designer and builder is God. ¹¹By faith Sarah herself received power to conceive, even when she was past the age, since she considered him faithful who had promised. ¹²Therefore from one man, and him as good as dead, were born descendants as many as the stars of heaven and as many as the innumerable grains of sand by the seashore.

¹³These all died in faith, not having received the things promised, but having seen them and greeted them from afar, and having acknowledged that they were strangers and exiles on the earth. ¹⁴For people who speak thus make it clear that they are seeking a homeland. ¹⁵If they had been

his gifts: and by it he being dead yet speaketh.

⁵By faith Enoch was translated that he should not see death; and was not found, because God had translated him: for before his translation he had this testimony, that he pleased God.

⁶But without faith it is impossible to please him: for he that cometh to God must believe that he is, and that he is a rewarder of them that diligently seek him.

⁷By faith Noah, being warned of God of things not seen as yet, moved with fear, prepared an ark to the saving of his house; by the which he condemned the world, and became heir of the righteousness which is by faith.

⁸By faith Abraham, when he was called to go out into a place which he should after receive for an inheritance, obeyed; and he went out, not knowing whither he went.

⁹By faith he sojourned in the land of promise, as in a strange country, dwelling in tabernacles with Isaac and Jacob, the heirs with him of the same promise:

¹⁰For he looked for a city which hath foundations, whose builder and maker is God.

¹¹Through faith also Sara herself received strength to conceive seed, and was delivered of a child when she was past age, because she judged him faithful who had promised.

¹²Therefore sprang there even of one, and him as good as dead, so many as the stars of the sky in multitude, and as the sand which is by the sea shore innumerable.

¹³These all died in faith, not having received the promises, but having

thinking of that land from which they had gone out, they would have had opportunity to return. [16]But as it is, they desire a better country, that is, a heavenly one. Therefore God is not ashamed to be called their God, for he has prepared for them a city.

[17]By faith Abraham, when he was tested, offered up Isaac, and he who had received the promises was in the act of offering up his only son, [18]of whom it was said, "Through Isaac shall your offspring be named." [19]He considered that God was able even to raise him from the dead, from which, figuratively speaking, he did receive him back. [20]By faith Isaac invoked future blessings on Jacob and Esau. [21]By faith Jacob, when dying, blessed each of the sons of Joseph, bowing in worship over the head of his staff. [22]By faith Joseph, at the end of his life, made mention of the exodus of the Israelites and gave directions concerning his bones.

[23]By faith Moses, when he was born, was hidden for three months by his parents, because they saw that the child was beautiful, and they were not afraid of the king's edict. [24]By faith Moses, when he was grown up, refused to be called the son of Pharaoh's daughter, [25]choosing rather to be mistreated with the people of God than to enjoy the fleeting pleasures of sin. [26]He considered the reproach of Christ greater wealth than the treasures of Egypt, for he was looking to the reward. [27]By faith he left Egypt, not being afraid of the anger of the king, for he endured as seeing him who is invisible. [28]By faith he kept the Passover and sprinkled the blood, so

seen them afar off, and were persuaded of them, and embraced them, and confessed that they were strangers and pilgrims on the earth.

[14]For they that say such things declare plainly that they seek a country.

[15]And truly, if they had been mindful of that country from whence they came out, they might have had opportunity to have returned.

[16]But now they desire a better country, that is, an heavenly: wherefore God is not ashamed to be called their God: for he hath prepared for them a city.

[17]By faith Abraham, when he was tried, offered up Isaac: and he that had received the promises offered up his only begotten son,

[18]Of whom it was said, That in Isaac shall thy seed be called:

[19]Accounting that God was able to raise him up, even from the dead; from whence also he received him in a figure.

[20]By faith Isaac blessed Jacob and Esau concerning things to come.

[21]By faith Jacob, when he was a dying, blessed both the sons of Joseph; and worshipped, leaning upon the top of his staff.

[22]By faith Joseph, when he died, made mention of the departing of the children of Israel; and gave commandment concerning his bones.

[23]By faith Moses, when he was born, was hid three months of his parents, because they saw he was a proper child; and they were not afraid of the king's commandment.

[24]By faith Moses, when he was come to years, refused to be called the son of Pharaoh's daughter;

that the Destroyer of the firstborn might not touch them.

²⁹By faith the people crossed the Red Sea as on dry land, but the Egyptians, when they attempted to do the same, were drowned. ³⁰By faith the walls of Jericho fell down after they had been encircled for seven days. ³¹By faith Rahab the prostitute did not perish with those who were disobedient, because she had given a friendly welcome to the spies.

³²And what more shall I say? For time would fail me to tell of Gideon, Barak, Samson, Jephthah, of David and Samuel and the prophets—³³who through faith conquered kingdoms, enforced justice, obtained promises, stopped the mouths of lions, ³⁴quenched the power of fire, escaped the edge of the sword, were made strong out of weakness, became mighty in war, put foreign armies to flight. ³⁵Women received back their dead by resurrection. Some were tortured, refusing to accept release, so that they might rise again to a better life. ³⁶Others suffered mocking and flogging, and even chains and imprisonment. ³⁷They were stoned, they were sawn in two, they were killed with the sword. They went about in skins of sheep and goats, destitute, afflicted, mistreated—³⁸of whom the world was not worthy—wandering about in deserts and mountains, and in dens and caves of the earth.

³⁹And all these, though commended through their faith, did not receive what was promised, ⁴⁰since God had provided something better for us, that apart from us they should not be made perfect.

²⁵Choosing rather to suffer affliction with the people of God, than to enjoy the pleasures of sin for a season;

²⁶Esteeming the reproach of Christ greater riches than the treasures in Egypt: for he had respect unto the recompence of the reward.

²⁷By faith he forsook Egypt, not fearing the wrath of the king: for he endured, as seeing him who is invisible.

²⁸Through faith he kept the passover, and the sprinkling of blood, lest he that destroyed the firstborn should touch them.

²⁹By faith they passed through the Red sea as by dry land: which the Egyptians assaying to do were drowned.

³⁰By faith the walls of Jericho fell down, after they were compassed about seven days.

³¹By faith the harlot Rahab perished not with them that believed not, when she had received the spies with peace.

³²And what shall I more say? for the time would fail me to tell of Gedeon, and of Barak, and of Samson, and of Jephthae; of David also, and Samuel, and of the prophets:

³³Who through faith subdued kingdoms, wrought righteousness, obtained promises, stopped the mouths of lions.

³⁴Quenched the violence of fire, escaped the edge of the sword, out of weakness were made strong, waxed valiant in fight, turned to flight the armies of the aliens.

³⁵Women received their dead raised to life again: and others were tortured, not accepting deliverance;

that they might obtain a better resurrection:

³⁶And others had trial of cruel mockings and scourgings, yea, moreover of bonds and imprisonment:

³⁷They were stoned, they were sawn asunder, were tempted, were slain with the sword: they wandered about in sheepskins and goatskins; being destitute, afflicted, tormented;

³⁸(Of whom the world was not worthy:) they wandered in deserts, and in mountains, and in dens and caves of the earth.

³⁹And these all, having obtained a good report through faith, received not the promise:

⁴⁰God having provided some better thing for us, that they without us should not be made perfect.

Introduction to 11:1–40 Because the benefits of Christ's work are given to us in our Baptism, we draw near to God with the full assurance of faith (10:22) and we hold fast to our confession, knowing that God is faithful (10:23). God's righteous ones live by faith (10:38). Now the author digs deeply into our spiritual heritage, demonstrating with numerous examples that the saints of the OT likewise lived by faith. Trusting in the Messiah who was to come, they endured many challenges, believing that God would fulfill His promises, and God commended them from their faith. These examples from our spiritual ancestors demonstrate God's faithfulness and provide encouragement for believers of all ages as we, too, trust in God's faithfulness.

The Nature of Faith

Alistar McGrath, in *Reformation Thought: An Introduction* (3rd ed., Malden, MA: Blackwell Publishing, 1999), describes Luther laying the foundation for the reformers' understanding of justifying faith (pp. 111–31). Luther noted that faith was in a person—the Lord—in whose promises one would trust. This faith unites a believer to the Lord. It is above all things *trust* in the Lord, who is the Savior. In other words, faith is not something we offer to God in order to save ourselves. Rather, when the Lord declares us righteous in Christ, justified by His grace without our works, that declaration creates faith in us so that we trust Him for salvation. Luther writes about this with vibrant warmth. For example, Luther wrote in his preface to Romans:

> Faith is not the human notion and dream that some people call faith. . . . [Faith] is a divine work in us which changes us and makes us to be born anew of God, John 1[:12–13]. It kills the old Adam and makes us altogether different men, in heart and spirit and mind and powers; and it brings with it the Holy Spirit. O it is a living, busy, active, mighty thing, this faith. It is impossible for it not to be doing good works incessantly. (LW 35:370)

Charles Partee, author of *The Theology of John Calvin*, (Louisville: Westminister John Knox Press, 2008) chafes a little at the view that Luther's descriptions of faith and justification brought warmth to Calvin's doctrine at those points. Yet Partee notes Calvin's indebtedness to Luther and that Calvin used courtroom language (forensic justification) to present his views, an emphasis that naturally resulted in a cooler presentation (223). What is more, Calvin favored the term *knowledge* when describing faith, as his Institutes open with the topic of knowing God. For example, Calvin wrote:

> The true knowledge of Christ consists in receiving him as he is offered by the Father, namely, as invested with his Gospel. For, as he is appointed as the end of our faith, so we cannot directly tend toward him except under the guidance of the Gospel. . . . For faith includes not merely the knowledge that God is, but also, no chiefly, a perception of his will toward us. It concerns us to know not only what he is in himself, but also in what character he is pleased to manifest himself to us. We now see, therefore, that faith is the knowledge of the divine will in regard to us, as ascertained from his word. (*Institutes of the Christian Religion*, Henry Beveridge, trans. [Edinburgh, 1945–46], 3.2.6)

Although Luther's understanding of faith prevailed among the reformers, Ernst Ziegler also points out that the eastern Swiss humanists, such as Ulrich Zwingli, were focused especially on reform of life. As a consequence, their writings say very little about justifying faith. They likewise tend to focus on the community of faith rather than the personal justification through faith so important to Luther and those in his sphere of influence. As a consequence, Zwingli tends to write about Jesus as a moral example rather than as a gracious, justifying Savior who is personally present in the life of a believer (McGrath, 122–23). ❧

11:1 *faith*. "Faith is not only knowledge in the intellect, but also confidence in the will" (Ap V 183). Faith is trust in someone or something. It is not self-referential, but always has an object. Everyone has faith in something just as everyone has a god (whatever they "fear, love, and trust above all things," SC, First Commandment). Hebrews calls us to true faith—the only faith that can save: faith in Christ Jesus. *assurance*. Or "confidence." The Greek word (*hypostasis*) is used to describe something substantive—what something truly is. It is the word used to describe the nature of God in 1:3. Heb 3:14 uses it in the same way as this verse, meaning "confidence." Concerning this verse, Bernard of Clairvaux writes:

> The substance, he says, of things hoped for, not a fantasy of empty conjectures. You hear, that is a substance; and therefore it is not allowed you in our faith, to suppose or oppose at your pleasure, nor to wander hither and thither amongst empty opinions, through devious errors. Under the name of substance something certain and fixed is put before you. You are enclosed in known bounds, shut in within fixed limits. For faith is not an opinion but a certitude. (*SLSB*, pp. 272–73)

hoped for. The Greek word for hope (*elpizō*, here as a participle, "being hoped for") does not describe wishful thinking or fanciful dreams of what might be if all circumstances turn out perfectly. It denotes confident and reasonable expectation that something will happen in the future. Although faith and hope are related, Melanchthon notes a distinction:

> If anyone wants a distinction between faith and hope, we say that the object of hope is properly a future event, but that faith is concerned with future and present things. Faith receives the forgiveness of sins offered in the promise in the present. (Ap V 191)

conviction. The only instance of this Greek word in the NT, it means evidence or proof. *not seen*. Faith trusts in God's promises with the conviction that they will certainly come to pass, even when the fulfillment of those promises has not yet been witnessed. Luther reflects on such faith, saying:

> One of the noblest and most precious virtues of faith is to close one's eyes to this, ingenuously to desist from exploring the why and the wherefore, and cheerfully to leave everything to God. Faith does not insist on knowing the reason for God's actions, but it still regards God as the greatest goodness and mercy. Faith

holds to that against and beyond all reason, sense, and experience, when everything appears to be wrath and injustice. (LW 43:52)

Wesley thought that this chapter uses faith in a broad sense. He explains:

The definition of faith given in this verse, and exemplified in the various instances following, undoubtedly includes justifying faith, but not directly as justifying. For faith justifies only as it refers to, and depends on, Christ. But here is no mention of him as the object of faith; and in several of the instances that follow, no notice is taken of him or his salvation, but only of temporal blessings obtained by faith. And yet they may all be considered as evidences of the power of justifying faith in Christ, and of its extensive exercise in a course of steady obedience amidst difficulties and dangers of every kind. (Wesley 586)

Calvin sees this chapter flowing directly from the previous passage and thinks that the chapter division (these were later editorial additions to the text) is misplaced and unhelpful. He writes:

Whoever made this the beginning of the eleventh chapter, has unwisely disjointed the context; for the object of the Apostle was to prove what he had already said—that there is need of patience. He had quoted the testimony of Habakkuk, who says that the just lives by faith; he now shews what remained to be proved—that faith can be no more separated from patience than from itself. (Calvin 260)

Cranmer considers the similarities and differences between these OT saints and those who lived after Christ:

All these fathers, martyrs, and other holy men, whom St. Paul spake of, had their faith surely fixed in God, when all the world was against them. They did not only know God to be lord, maker, and governor of all men in the world; but also they had a special confidence and trust, that he was and would be their God, their comforter, aider, helper, maintainer, and defender. This is the Christian faith, which these holy men had, and we also ought to have. And although they were not named Christian men, yet was it a Christian faith that they had; for they looked for all benefits of God the father, through the merits of his son Jesu Christ, as we now do. This difference is between them and us, for they

145

looked when Christ should come, and we be in the time when he is come. (Cranmer 2:156–57)

11:2 *people of old.* Our forebears in the faith. The KJV renders this literally, "the elders." Some of these will be specifically mentioned in this chapter, but these words apply to all the faithful of old. *were commended.* (KJV "received a good report.") Scripture testifies that the OT saints are righteous and pleasing to God. As this chapter demonstrates, they were commended for and *by* their faith.

11:3 *by faith we understand the universe was created.* "Understand" means that we know (Gk *noeō*) that this is true. This does not mean that we necessarily understand everything about the universe or details of creation that are not revealed in God's Word. We know about the origin of God's creation by *faith*; it is revealed to us and we believe. This chapter's gallery of faith is presented in roughly chronological order, so the first topic described involves creation. Yet it is noteworthy that the first example of faith is not about our ancestors but believers of all generations—including us. We have faith in what God has said. By faith we understand. *created by the word of God.* This "word" (Gk *rhēma*) is not the same as the "Word" (Gk *logos*) in Jn 1, the Word that became flesh (Jn 1:14). Using this term emphasizes the way in which God created: He spoke creation into existence, declaring it to be (Gn 1:3). Of course, Scripture teaches that Christ is God and that "all things were made through Him" (Jn 1:1–4). This is what we believe by faith. God said, "Let there be . . . and there was." *what is seen was not made out of things that are visible.* God's creation was *ex nihilo*—from nothing (cf. Rm 4:17). The universe itself and all matter came into existence when God spoke His powerful word. Just as God's word created real, visible things from nothing, so our faith is certain, although it does not yet see all of the realities it believes and confesses.

11:4 *by faith Abel offered . . . a more acceptable sacrifice.* Gn 4 says that Cain brought "an offering of the fruit of the ground" (Gn 4:3) and that Abel brought "the firstborn of his flock" (Gn 4:4). Genesis says "the Lord had regard for Abel and his offering," but not for Cain and his offering (Gn 4:4–5). Hebrews clearly identifies the difference: Abel's offering was given in faith (see note, v. 6). The Lutheran reformers reflect on the difference between the works offered by faith and works that are not pleasing to God:

146

In this life the good works of believers are imperfect and impure because of sin in the flesh, nevertheless they are acceptable and well pleasing to God. However, the Law does not teach how and why the good works of believers are acceptable. It demands a completely perfect, pure obedience if it is to please God. But the Gospel teaches that our spiritual offerings are acceptable to God through faith for Christ's sake. (FC SD VII 22)

commended as righteous. God accepts both the sacrifice and the one who offered it not on the basis of the work but because of faith. *he still speaks.* Human experience might suggest that Abel's martyrdom silenced his voice forever, but his example, recorded in Scripture, still speaks to us about the crucial importance of faith. Abel thus speaks to all generations (see note, 12:1). Yet an even greater sacrifice and word is found in Jesus (cf. 12:24). Luther says:

It is evident that in theology the work does not amount to anything without faith, but that faith must precede before you can do works. . . . The sacrifice of Abel was better because he believed. But because Cain was an ungodly man and a hypocrite, he performed a work that was moral, or rather one that was reasonable, by which he sought to please God. Therefore the work of Cain was hypocritical and faithless; in it there was no faith in grace but only a presumption about his own righteousness. (LW 26:264)

11:5 *by faith Enoch was taken up.* Like Elijah (2Ki 2:11), Enoch did not die but was taken into heaven (KJV "translated") while he was still alive. *pleased God.* While Enoch is generally remembered for the way in which he was taken to heaven, the point here is that he had faith in the true God. Gn 5:22–24 says that "Enoch walked with God." This is a figure of speech that the LXX clarifies when it says Enoch "pleased God." As a result of his faith, after living a long life on earth, Enoch "was not [LXX adds "found"] for God took him." Enoch's earthly days ended miraculously as God took him to heaven. See note, v. 6. Hebrews properly notes the order of events: *before he was taken he was commended.* Enoch walked with God in faith, and consequently God took him to Himself.

11:6 *without faith it is impossible to please Him.* These words apply to every person listed in this chapter. In the immediate context, Enoch (v. 5) "walked with" or "pleased" (LXX) God. This cannot be done without faith. No human work, effort, or intention is sufficient. Faith in Christ makes one pleasing to God. So Melanchthon declares,

"Only justified people, who are led by the Spirit of Christ, can do good works. Without faith and Christ as Mediator, good works do not please" (Ap V 251). *whoever . . . must believe that He exists . . . He rewards.* Saving faith trusts both in God's existence and in His mercy for Christ's sake. One cannot *draw near* to someone that does not exist, nor would they even consider the possibility. Neither will a person look to someone for aid if they do not think there is hope of a positive answer. *rewards.* While rewards can mean "compensation" or other financial payment, grammatically, the emphasis of this sentence is on "He." The focus is not on the gift but on the giver. The rewards God gives are undeserved, gracious gifts (cf. Mt 5:12). "We confess that eternal life is a reward; it is something due because of the promise, not because of our merits" (Ap V 242). Calvin wrote:

> The Apostle shews how faith obtains favour for us, even because faith is our teacher as to the true worship of God, and makes us certain as to his goodwill, so that we may not think that we seek him in vain. These two clauses ought not to be slightly passed over—that we must believe that God is, and that we ought to feel assured that he is not sought in vain. (Calvin 270)

11:7 *events . . . yet unseen.* Noah began the long work of building the ark, believing God's warning about the coming flood. His trust, despite an initial inability to see evidence of an impending disaster, illustrates "the conviction of things not seen" described in v. 1. *in reverent fear.* This phrase translates a single word in Greek, meaning to show God proper, reverent respect. Noah was concerned with what God said, not with pleasing other people. *for the saving of his household.* Eight members of Noah's family were saved on the ark and not merely them but the animals of the world as well. *condemned the world.* Through the ark, he showed that God's threat of judgment and destruction was genuine. All who did not receive God's deliverance on the ark were destroyed. In 1Pt 3:20, it says that God waited patiently in the days of Noah, but those who did not go on the ark were disobedient and rejected God. *heir of the righteousness that comes by faith.* An heir receives an inheritance. One might be tempted to think that Noah's salvation consisted in his obedience and ark building. These words make it clear that Noah was righteous by faith. He believed God and was given the blessings of faith. His obedience in following God's command was not the basis of his deliverance and commendation, but was the fruit of faith (cf. Gn 6:9; Rm 4:13).

11:8 *Abraham*, father of the Jewish people, is likewise an example of faith, with several faithful incidents referenced here. Rm 4 demonstrates that he was not saved by his works but by his faith. "Abraham believed God and it was counted to him as righteousness" (Rm 4:4). *called to go out.* God called Abram to leave his homeland and journey to a new land that would be given to him (Gn 12:1–4). He went in faith, *not knowing where he was going* but only that God had called, trusting that He would guide him and provide everything needed.

11:9 *land of promise as in a foreign land.* It was the land of promise because God promised it to him and his descendants (cf. Gn 12:1–9; Ac 7:5). Though the land would belong to his descendants, Abraham and his family lived as aliens and nomads, *in tents*, as if the land was not theirs (cf. Gn 12:8; 13:3, 18; 18:1, 9). They did not yet build permanent homes. Still, Abraham trusted God's promise as did his son *Isaac* and grandson *Jacob*.

11:10 *the city.* This is a contrast to the tents in which they lived. The heavenly Jerusalem is their true and permanent home (cf. 12:22; 13:14; Gal 4:26). The promise to Abraham and his offspring was greater than an earthly home; God promised an eternal inheritance in the true promised land. The heavenly city, like the heavenly temple (cf. 9:11), is not made by human hands. God is the *designer and builder.*

11:11 The great patriarch Abraham was not alone in having faith, nor in being commended for it. As Isaac and Jacob are remembered (v. 10), so is his wife, *Sarah*. Both Abraham (Gn 12:18) and Sarah (Gn 18:12) initially laughed at God's announcement that she herself would conceive and bear a son. By human understanding, she was too old to bear a child. By ordinary human reasoning, she gave her servant Hagar to her husband to conceive a child to be his heir (Gn 15), but God's plan was greater than this. Despite her age, Sarah *herself* would *conceive* (cf. Gn 17:15–21). It took faith to trust God, but *Sarah . . . considered Him faithful.* God overcame her doubt and she felt her child growing within her. She came to believe God's promise and trusted His faithfulness and was not disappointed. Chrysostom wrote, "While her laughter indeed was from unbelief, her fear [was] from Faith. . . . When unbelief had been cleared out, Faith came in its place" (*NPNF*1 14:471).

11:12 *one man . . . as good as dead.* Abraham's advanced age made God's promise even more incredible. He believed God's promise that he would have *descendants as many as the . . . sand.* God promised Abraham innumerable descendants (Gn 22:17). Humanly speaking, this was a ridiculous promise as evidenced by the initial reaction of both Abraham and Sarah. God gave them the gift of faith; they trusted His promise, and it was fulfilled.

11:13 *these all died in faith, not having received the things promised.* Not all of the promises were completely fulfilled in their lifetimes. Abraham and Sarah would have innumerable offspring, though they only saw Isaac. See also the note at vv. 39–40. The was promised to them, but they lived in it as sojourners. Still, they believed, having *seen and greeted.* In faith, they trusted God's promises as if they had been fulfilled already. *Acknowledged . . . exiles.* In light of their eternal, heavenly home, they were able, by faith, to accept the current circumstances of this life while considering them from the perspective of God's promises and faithfulness (cf. Gn 23:4; Ps 39:12; 1Pt 1:1).

11:14 *homeland.* Literally, "fatherland." In the context of faith, this suggests the even greater fatherland—the country of our heavenly Father. Acknowledging the impermanence of their earthly lot was itself a confession of their belief in the life to come.

11:15 *opportunity to return.* Their status as exiles and strangers did not cause them to pine for the past or to return to the lives they once lived. It drew them to long for the future that God was preparing for them.

11:16 *a better country . . . a heavenly one.* As in v. 14, in faith they were drawn not merely to God's earthly promises but to His heavenly dwelling. They were drawn to God Himself. *God is not ashamed.* This is a tender phrase, reflecting God's fatherly love. He acknowledges His people (cf. Mt 10:32) and names Himself the God of Abraham, Isaac, and Jacob (Ex 3:6). Similarly, Jesus is not ashamed to call us brothers (2:11). *He has prepared a city.* As He promised, God prepares a place for His people to dwell with Him eternally (cf. Mt 25:34; Jn 14:2). Their hope for a heavenly country and for the presence of God is not disappointed.

11:17 *Abraham was tested . . . who had received.* This test must have been particularly difficult for Abraham. Isaac was key to the fulfillment of the promise of descendants. That a child would be born to Abraham and Sarah at their advanced age was miraculous. Yet God, who fulfilled His promise and gave this boy, called for his sacrifice, seemingly destroying the fulfillment of the promise (cf. Gn 22:1–10). *in the act of offering.* This phrase emphasizes the immediacy of the action. Abraham was going to obey God even though it seemed counter to the promise. But this was a test, and God stayed Abraham when he had the knife in hand to slay his son (Gn 22:10). Abraham clearly trusted God; he had faith and put it into action!

11:18 *through Isaac shall your offspring be named.* This quotation from Gn 21:12 marked a distinction between Abraham's children. Ishmael, the son of Sarah's servant Hagar, was not the line of the promise. God's promise would be fulfilled through Sarah herself (v. 11). Thus killing Isaac would seem to derail the promise.

11:19 *raise the dead.* Had God allowed Abraham to follow through with the sacrifice, He surely would have needed to return him to life in order to keep His promise of descendants. Hebrews is saying Abraham had such faith, and it was not disappointed. Though God stayed Abraham's hand, *figuratively . . . he did receive him back.* God allowed Isaac to live and the promise was fulfilled. Having been willing to sacrifice his son, Abraham received his living son back again. This occurred when God offered a substitute for Isaac. A ram, provided by God, would die as a sacrifice in Isaac's place (Gn 22:13). Chrysostom speaks of this story, noting that it foreshadowed the substitutionary sacrifice of Christ: "By means of the ram [Abraham] received him again, having slain it in his stead. But these things were types: for here it is the Son of God who is slain" (*NPNF*1 14:478).

11:20–21 *Isaac . . . Jacob . . . Joseph.* Abraham's pivotal story receives more attention than the others in this chapter of faith. Now, with quick examples, we see that God's promise carried forward through the generations, each of which continued to believe. *Isaac invoked future blessings.* In Gn 25:29–34, Esau trades his birthright as the firstborn of twin sons for a bowl of stew. When Isaac was old, he blessed Jacob, thinking that it was Esau before him (Gn 27). The messianic line passed from Isaac to Jacob with this blessing. The story of human scheming may trouble us, but faith in God's promise was still manifest. Isaac believed that God would keep his promise, and so he blessed his son Jacob. The one receiving the blessing did, in fact, help fulfill the promise. These blessings were not immediately seen but were fulfilled in the future. *Jacob* carried forth the promise. Though the sinful plans of some of his sons caused Joseph to be sold into Egyptian slavery, that act was used by God to preserve Jacob's family and the promise. At the end of his life, Jacob blessed his sons (cf. Gn 49:1–27), but first he blessed Ephraim and Manasseh (cf. Gn 48:16, 20) as if they were his own sons and brought them in the covenant. He did this while bowing in worship *over the head of his staff*, as the LXX says (cf. Gn 47:31; the Hebrew reads "upon the head of his bed"). In the weakness of old age, Jacob continued to believe the promise and to worship God (cf. Gn 47:31). *Joseph . . . exodus . . . directions concerning his bones.* Though God had prospered Joseph and his family in Egypt, he knew that it was not the land of promise. Thus he foretold Israel's return to the land that God had promised to Abraham and asked that his bones be buried there in his fatherland (Gn 50:24–25; Ex 13:19).

11:23 *by faith Moses, when he was born, was hidden.* One might read this as saying that Moses' parents did this by faith since it was their action that caused Moses to be hidden. Yet this is also Moses' story. Moses passively received the benefits of faith, even as we passively receive the gifts that God gives us. God's servants in this were Moses' *parents*, who were *not afraid of the king's edict.* They feared God more than the wicked pharaoh and so acted to preserve the life of their son (cf. Ex 1:17, 21; 2:2–3; Ac 7:20).

11:24 *Moses, when he was grown up.* Moses was raised by Pharaoh's daughter who found him in the reeds by a river (cf. Ex 2:3). Eventually Moses demonstrates faith when he rejected identification with the Egyptians and flees to Midian (cf. Ex 2:11–22). While Moses was in Midian, God called him to deliver His people, Israel, from slavery (cf. Ex 3ff.).

11:25 *choosing to be mistreated . . . pleasures.* Moses' faith was naturally accompanied by action. It would have been easier to remain with the Egyptians, and in worldly terms, this seemed more advantageous. Certainly there were more worldly pleasures to be enjoyed in Pharaoh's court. But they were sinful pleasures and, furthermore, they were *fleeting*. Like many temptations, they were enticing for a little while but would not last (cf. 1Jn 2:17). Faith looked to the lasting gifts that God promised.

11:26 *reproach of Christ.* Not reproach received from Christ, but the reproach that the world often directs against Christ and His followers. Jesus says, "Blessed are you when others revile you and persecute you and utter all kinds of evil against you falsely on My account" (Mt 5:11). This reproach came upon Moses because he followed the true God in faith. Note that the object of his, and Israel's, faith is Christ. The Israelites suffered in Egypt because they hoped in the Messiah. (Cf. Php 3:7–8; 1Pt 4:14.) *greater wealth.* God's promises, though unseen, surpassed the treasures of Egypt. *reward.* The fulfillment of God's promises, which is a gracious gift (cf. 10:35 and the note at 11:6).

11:27 *by faith he left Egypt, not being afraid.* Though at first afraid (Ex 2:14), Moses fled in faith from Egypt, intending to return when the time was right. After God called him and he returned, Moses led all Israel out of Egypt, taking silver, gold, and livestock with them (Ex 12:33–37). Called and empowered by God, he was no longer afraid but acted in faith. *anger of the king.* This anger was seen in the way Pharaoh treated the Israelites, in the threats he made against Moses (cf. Ex 10:28), and in how he pursued them to his peril (cf. Ex 14). *as seeing . . . invisible.* They did not see God directly when this happened, but their faith was so strong, it was as if they were seeing Him (cf. 1Tm 1:17).

11:28 *Passover.* Ex 12 tells the story of the first Passover, a meal that has repeated each year. Telling the story of God's deliverance is a central part of the Passover remembrance. Here the emphasis is on the sprinkling of blood and the deliverance from death that was part of the first Passover. The blood of the Passover lambs was *sprinkled* or "poured," as the word can also be translated. The angel of death passed over the homes marked with the blood of the lambs (cf. Ex 12:21–30). Trusting God's word, they applied the blood and lived. We, too, are spared from eternal death when we are covered with the blood of Christ, our Passover Lamb. The Greek word for Passover is *pascha.* In 1Co 5:7, Christ is called "our Passover Lamb (*pascha*)." *Destroyer of the firstborn.* The angel that administered God's judgment through pestilence (Ex 12:23; cf. 2Sm 24:15–16; 1Co 10:10). In faith, Israel kept the Passover and followed God's instructions. They were preserved from death that night and were kept safe in God's protection.

11:29 *by faith the people crossed the Red Sea.* The commendation now extends to the whole nation. In the miracle at the Red Sea (cf. Ex 14:21–30), the people walked between the waters that were miraculously parted by God's power. This took trust in God, even though that power was being manifested before them. The same water that killed the Egyptians was the water of salvation to the Israelites. This is a type of Baptism, in which our old nature dies with Christ and God's new creation rises with Him (cf. 1Co 10:2).

11:30 *by faith the walls of Jericho fell.* The mighty walls of Jericho fell when, at God's direction, the Israelites marched around the city, blew trumpets, and shouted (Jsh 6:15, 16, 20). Their actions were not sufficient to cause such destruction; it happened by the hand of God. The Israelites believed God, did what He told them to do, and saw His mighty power.

11:31 *Rahab the prostitute.* A further detail of the Jericho story. The walls of this mighty city fell when Israel had faith, but this resident of Jericho was spared because of her faith. Scripture says that God will judge the sexually immoral (13:4), yet God transformed Rahab through repentance and faith. She acted on her faith and was delivered when her city was destroyed. *friendly welcome.* Rahab welcomed the Israelite spies and sheltered them, saying, "I know that the LORD has given you the land" (Jsh 2:9; cf. Jsh 2:1, 8–13). Her recognition that this was the Lord's work is an indication of her faith.

11:32 *what more shall I say? . . . time would fail me.* These words may support the notion that Hebrews was preached as a sermon. See "Anonymous," pp. 11–12. The many other examples of faithful believers who could be mentioned demonstrates that those already listed are particularly important. *Gideon* was a judge who was used by God to delivered Israel from the Midianites. He destroyed altars to Baal and defeated the mighty Midianite army with only 300 soldiers (cf. Jgs 6:11–8:35). *Barak* responded to Deborah's call to action to raise an army to fight Sisera and the Canaanites (cf. Jgs 4:6–5:31). The story of *Samson* is the longest among the judges (cf. Jgs 13:2–16:31). Though he was a complicated man with struggles and weaknesses, God used him in the resistance fight against the Philistines. *Jephthah* was one of the later judges who commanded an army against the Ammonites (cf. Jgs 11:1–12:7). If there was not room enough to speak of these other names, then there certainly is not room to fully speak of King *David* (cf. 1Sm 16–30; 2Sm). God calls David "a man after

My heart, who will do all My will" (Ac 13:22). Numerous examples of faith and of God's grace are found in David's life. *Samuel*. The great prophet who lived during the days of Saul and David (cf. 1Sm 16–30). Samuel served as Israel was transforming from a theocracy to a monarchy. The remarkable thing about this list of names is that many of them are rightly open to criticism. Gideon seemed overly timid. Barak would not go into battle without Deborah with him. Samson acted shamefully. Jephthah made a rash vow and sacrificed his daughter as a result. David committed adultery and caused Uriah to die. These individuals are not highlighted here as examples of human perfection or exemplary virtue. They are examples of faith. These sinner-saints, despite their many failings, trusted in God, were forgiven, and are commended for their faith.

11:33 *conquered kingdoms*. As the list of the faithful was long and open ended, so are their accomplishments that the author highlights collectively. Some, such as the judges and kings, *conquered kingdoms* and *enforced justice* in Israel. In other words, they protected the nation from enemies and governed fairly. These are common things in governmental service, but what is commended is the faith in which this was done. *stopped the mouths of lions*. This may be referring to Samson (Jgs 14:6), David (1Sm 17:34–35), or Daniel (Dn 6:22).

11:34 *quenched the power of fire*. Shadrach, Meshach and Abednego (Dn 3:13–30) were thrown into a fiery furnace but were safely preserved by God's power. *escaped the edge of the sword*. This could apply to various individuals, including Elijah (1Ki 19:1–8) or Jeremiah (Jer 26:23–24). Others, like Gideon, were made *strong out of weakness*. Small groups of people were emboldened to become *mighty in war* and to route *foreign armies*. Again and again, the story of God's people shows how He cared for Israel and provided all that was needed. The individuals noted here are remembered not for their valor but for their faith. Wesley wrote: "Faith animates to the most heroic enterprises, both civil and military. Faith overcomes all impediments effects the greatest things; attains to the very best; and inverts, by its miraculous power the very course of nature" (589).

11:35 The examples of faith and God's faithfulness continue. *Women received by their dead by resurrection*. Elijah raised a woman's son (1Ki 17:17–24), as did Elisha (2Ki 4:25–37). The widow of Nain saw her son rise (Lk 7:11–15), and Mary and Martha received the resurrected Lazarus (Jn 11:17–44). *Some were tortured.* The Greek word *tympanidzō* is the source of our English word "timpani," which is a drum. This graphically violent word means to be tortured to death, perhaps by being stretched on a wheel while being beaten. This is likely an allusion to 2Macc 6:18–31, where Eleazar was beaten to death while being stretched on a rack rather than eating pork or even pretending to eat pork. The following story in 2Macc 7 shows seven brothers and their mother tortured to death for refusing to take part in the pagan sacrifices and eat pork. *refusing to accept release.* Their opponents offered them escape from prison and torture if they would deny the faith. They did not. *So that they might rise again.* They retained their faith and eternal life despite the pains of torture. Calvin wrote, "The nature of faith is the same now as in the days of the holy fathers whom the Apostle mentions. If, then, we imitate their faith, we shall never basely break down through sloth or listlessness" (305).

11:37 *they were stoned.* Naboth was stoned on the evidence of false testimony when Jezebel conspired to sieze his property (1Ki 21:1–14), and Stephen, the first Christian martyr, was stoned for his testimony of Jesus (Ac 7). *they were sawn in two.* The pseudepigraphical book *The Martyrdom and Ascension of Isaiah* says that Isaiah was sawn in half with a wood saw but that he did not cry out or weep while it happened (5:11–15; see also *ANF* 1:259; 3:716.) *killed with the sword.* Elijah reports that the people of Israel had "killed your prophets with the sword" (1Ki 19:10), and King Johoiakim killed the prophet Uriah, the son of Shemaiah, with a sword (Jer 26:23). *Went about in skins . . . mistreated.* This is seen in a variety of people, including Elijah (2Ki 1:8).

11:38 *the world was not worthy.* What an ironic situation! The world despised God's saints and treated them with contempt, but God judges things differently. These faithful people are worthy of remembrance and praise. Through faith, God considers them worthy to receive His promises. *wandering about . . . dens and caves.* Like the other descriptions in these verses, this could apply to many of God's people. This includes prophets like those Obadiah hid from Jezebel (1Ki 18:4). Mattathias and his followers likewise hid in caves when they refused to deny their faith and fled for safety (1Macc 2:29–41).

11:39–40 *commended through their faith.* This, again, is the reason why these examples are being recounted. All of these saints were sinners. None is remembered in this list because of his or her own merit. They are remembered for their faith and for God's faithfulness. *did not receive what was promised.* They looked forward to God's promises but did not see all of His promises fully fulfilled in their own lifetimes. Most notably, they themselves did not see and hear the promised Messiah. They died, trusting that God would keep His promises in His perfect time. *made perfect.* The full resurrection, which will come for the OT saints and for us on the Last Day. They did not receive this blessing *apart from* later believers. We, who are united in Christ Jesus, will all receive these blessings together.

Ch. 11 in Devotion and Prayer Faith, the gift of God, causes the believer to hear His voice. Trusting our Lord's promises, we cling to them even when we do not always see them fulfilled when we would like. At times, faith is tested. We are tempted to abandon faith, to give in to the ways of the world, to enjoy its fleeting, sinful pleasures. We are not the first to face such temptations. The saints who have gone before us were able, by God's grace, to endure. They continued to trust God and looked forward to His promises. We, who live in the last days, have seen more than many of these saints saw. We have seen the Lord's promised Messiah come. We have seen Him bear our burdens, suffer unspeakable tortures, and die on our behalf. And we have seen the Lord's promise of resurrection fulfilled as He rose from the grave. In times of trial, God will strengthen us. Take heart. Look to Jesus. Believe that God will keep all of His promises. He will. He will keep the promises He has made to us and to all His saints. We will see them all fulfilled, and we will live with Him eternally. • "Lord, be our light when worldly darkness veils us; Lord, be our shield when earthly armor fails us; And in the day when hell itself assails us, Grant us Your peace, Lord." Amen. (*LSB* 659:3)

Jesus as the Ultimate Example of Faithfulness (12:1–13)

ESV	KJV
12 ¹Therefore, since we are surrounded by so great a cloud of witnesses, let us also lay aside every weight, and sin which clings so closely, and let us run with endurance the race that is set before us, ²looking to Jesus, the founder and perfecter of our faith, who for the joy that was set before him endured the cross, despising the shame, and is seated at the right hand of the throne of God.	*12* ¹Wherefore seeing we also are compassed about with so great a cloud of witnesses, let us lay aside every weight, and the sin which doth so easily beset us, and let us run with patience the race that is set before us,
³Consider him who endured from sinners such hostility against himself, so that you may not grow weary or fainthearted. ⁴In your struggle against sin you have not yet resisted to the point of shedding your blood. ⁵And have you forgotten the exhortation that addresses you as sons?	²Looking unto Jesus the author and finisher of our faith; who for the joy that was set before him endured the cross, despising the shame, and is set down at the right hand of the throne of God.
"My son, do not regard lightly the discipline of the Lord,	³For consider him that endured such contradiction of sinners against himself, lest ye be wearied and faint in your minds.
nor be weary when reproved by him.	⁴Ye have not yet resisted unto blood, striving against sin.
⁶For the Lord disciplines the one he loves,	⁵And ye have forgotten the exhortation which speaketh unto you as unto children, My son, despise not thou the chastening of the Lord, nor faint when thou art rebuked of him:
and chastises every son whom he receives."	⁶For whom the Lord loveth he chasteneth, and scourgeth every son whom he receiveth.
⁷It is for discipline that you have to endure. God is treating you as sons. For what son is there whom his father does not discipline? ⁸If you are left without discipline, in which all have participated, then you are illegitimate children and not sons. ⁹Besides this, we have had earthly fathers who disciplined us and we respected them. Shall we not much more be subject to the Father of spirits and live? ¹⁰For they disciplined us for a short time as it seemed best to them, but he disci-	⁷If ye endure chastening, God dealeth with you as with sons; for what son is he whom the father chasteneth not?
	⁸But if ye be without chastisement, whereof all are partakers, then are ye bastards, and not sons.
	⁹Furthermore we have had fathers of our flesh which corrected us, and we gave them reverence: shall we not much rather be in subjection unto the Father of spirits, and live?
	¹⁰For they verily for a few days chastened us after their own pleasure; but

plines us for our good, that we may share his holiness. ¹¹For the moment all discipline seems painful rather than pleasant, but later it yields the peaceful fruit of righteousness to those who have been trained by it.

¹²Therefore lift your drooping hands and strengthen your weak knees, ¹³and make straight paths for your feet, so that what is lame may not be put out of joint but rather be healed.

he for our profit, that we might be partakers of his holiness.

¹¹Now no chastening for the present seemeth to be joyous, but grievous: nevertheless afterward it yieldeth the peaceable fruit of righteousness unto them which are exercised thereby.

¹²Wherefore lift up the hands which hang down, and the feeble knees;

¹³And make straight paths for your feet, lest that which is lame be turned out of the way; but let it rather be healed.

Introduction to Chapter 12 The helpful examples of faith, seen in the lives of the saints that were detailed in the previous chapter, pale in comparison to our Lord Jesus. He is the founder and perfecter of faith (vv. 1–2). His work helps us endure trials, which we receive as discipline for our own benefit (vv. 3–11). This encourages us to endure (vv. 12–17) until we receive God's unshakable kingdom (vv. 18–29).

12:1 *cloud of witnesses.* The many saints just discussed (ch. 11) show that we are not alone in the struggle to live faithfully in the world as we confess Christ. Like a cloud that is seen in the sky, the saints' examples are visible, though we cannot touch those who went before us (cf. Mt 17:1–5). *witnesses.* Gk *martys*, from which "martyr" comes. The OT saints are not presented as those who are watching over us as guards to see what we are doing, but as those who testify to God's faithfulness. Their lives are examples of faith and demonstrations of God's trustworthiness. God commended those who bore witness to their faith, and they are examples of right faith and good works. *lay aside every weight . . . clings.* This begins a metaphor of a runner in a race. A distance runner cannot carry extra burdens or wear constricting clothing if he or she means to run effectively. In this life, believers still have sin clinging closely to them. Though justified, we are also sinners until we reach heaven. In repentance and faith, we confess that sin and hear God's liberating absolution. Luther says:

Therefore sin remains in the spiritual man for the exercise of grace, for the humbling of pride, for the repression of presumptuousness. . . . Only to those who manfully struggle and fight against their faults, invoking the grace of God, does God not impute sin. Therefore he who comes to confession should not think that he is laying down his burden so that he may lead a quiet life, but he should know that by putting down his burden he fights as a soldier of God and thus takes on another burden for God in opposition to the devil and to his own personal faults (LW 25:339).

let us run with endurance. The Christian life, as a long-distance race, calls us to stay on the path until the goal is reached. "Endurance" (the KJV renders this "patience") means being committed to the race even though it is difficult. A runner may be tempted to give up when he or she gets tired; but a successful runner keeps going with the goal in mind (cf. 10:36). *race.* The Greek word (*agōn*) is the source of our English word "agony." It can also mean a struggle, fight, or competition. While "race" is clearly the sense in mind here, the specific word used reminds us that it can be a difficult race (cf. 2Tm 4:7; 1Co 9:24). *that is set before us.* We choose neither God nor our path; God chose us and has established our way. Likewise, Jesus had a goal set before Him: us. (cf. v. 2).

12:2 *looking to Jesus.* The great cloud of witnesses encourages us, but faith's object is not the saints but Christ alone. We are called to run the race focused on Him and His work, not distracted by sin or worldly concerns. He is described as *the founder and perfecter of our faith.* "Founder" (Gk *archēgos*) is one who establishes something from the beginning, a trailblazer who goes before others to establish a safe and reliable way. It is also the word for an "author," as the KJV translates. Our faith originates with Him; He is its source. He is also its perfecter (Gk *teleiōtēs*), the one who brings it to its completion. (The KJV translates it as "finisher.") Jesus opened the way to salvation, and His new covenant will never be superseded. He creates our faith through the Gospel and Sacraments, and His Spirit brings us to the consummation of our salvation. (See note, 2:10; cf. Eph 2:8–9.) *for the joy set before Him.* Jesus was motivated to fulfill His work because of the joy of bringing others to heavenly glory by way of the cross. Though it cost Him dearly, He *endured the cross,* suffering and dying a shameful death that He did not deserve. He did this for us. *despising the shame.* Christ was not afraid to redeem humanity, despite the shame of such a death. Any difficulties we experience in this life pale in comparison to what Christ suffered on our behalf. *is seated at the right hand.* Once again, these words emphasize Christ's completed work and His position of eternal, divine power and authority. See 1:3; 8:1; 10:12 and notes.

12:1–2 in Devotion and Prayer The life of the child of God is like an endurance race. At times, it may be difficult and many distractions and pitfalls threaten to dissuade us and cause us to fail. But it is God who has called us to this race, and He equips us with everything needed. We run with the knowledge that the saints who have gone before us have faced similar and even greater challenges. In faith, they endured and finished the race. But most of all, we run with our eyes fixed on Jesus and His cross. He is the one who established our faith and has gone before us. He is the one who perfects and finishes it. In Him, our race is already won. The victory belongs to Jesus and, in grace, He will share His victory with us. •

Unto Jerusalem, Like flint He set His face,
Fulfilling all the Father's will To suffer in our place.

Despising all its shame, He bore the heavy cross.
The Sinless in the sinner's stead, He counted all as loss.

O Christ our living Lord, Who sits at God's right hand,
O strengthen us to bear the cross Amid life's shifting sand.

So let us fix our eyes on Christ, the Lamb of God
Who authored and perfected faith by walking Calv'ry's road.

Amen. (Steven P. Mueller, 2010)

12:3 *endured from sinners.* The *hostility* and suffering came from the hands of the leaders and crowds in Jerusalem who opposed Jesus, but all mankind was responsible for His suffering. They deserved the suffering and hostility that they poured out on our innocent Lord. *not grow weary or fainthearted.* Jesus did not come merely to set an example for us. Nonetheless, we do learn from His example and can take encouragement from Him. The way in which He endured gives us strength and courage.

12:4 *not yet resisted to . . . shedding your blood.* These words put the trials experienced by the readers in perspective. They had suffered (10:33), but they had not faced the most extreme sufferings. They had not "resisted unto blood," as the KJV more literally renders this verse. Christ was faithful even in shedding His blood. These words "not yet" may also anticipate a coming persecution, perhaps that faced under Emperor Nero (see "Anonymous," pp. 11–12).

12:5–6 *discipline . . . loves.* This quote from Pr 3:11–12 reminds readers that the trials and challenges that Christians face may have a greater purpose. Through punishment and correction, parents discipline their children with the goal of teaching them. This is evidence of love and distinguishes discipline from simple punishment, which may only have the goal of curbing or preventing bad behavior. As with earthly parents, not all of God's training seems pleasant at the time. Yet sometimes, in retrospect, God's love is most clearly evident in times of severe reproof and discipline. Indeed, the "love" here is *agapē*—self-giving love. God truly disciplines for our own well-being. Luther ponders the difference between God's discipline and punishment, saying, "If so many judgments, pains, deaths, martyrdoms, crosses, swords, fires, and beasts, with which the saints are chastised, are fatherly rods and loving chastisements, what will be the wrath of the Judge over the ungodly? . . . And if His judgment begins at the house of God, what will be the end of those who do not believe the Gospel?" (LW 11:467–68). Cranmer writes of the significance of God's loving discipline and His enduring care: "If we sin, he correcteth us, but he never withdraweth his mercy from us and though he punish us with adversity, yet doth he never forsake his people" (Cranmer 4:161).

12:7 *It is for discipline.* Some afflictions and challenges that Christians experience may be punishment. Some may be the external consequence for specific sins. Knowing his readers, the author is specific to their circumstances: whatever they were experiencing was to be received as discipline. This is a sign of love, for *God is treating you as sons.* The fact that God disciplines His people is a sign that He cares for them. Thus the suffering they are experiencing actually demonstrates that they are disciples. See note, 2:10.

12:8 *without discipline . . . you are illegitimate children.* These words are meant to shock people who consider themselves God's children. You don't want to be disciplined? What would that make you? That's how a person treats a child they do not love or a child that does not belong to them. If you seek to avoid discipline, you are actually asking to be treated like a child born out of wedlock or a slave, instead of like a beloved child (cf. Gal 4:21–31). God loves you too much to let you live without guidance and correction!

12:9 *we have had earthly fathers who disciplined.* Once again, the author is arguing from the lesser to the greater. If our imperfect, earthly parents disciplined us for our good, should we not expect our perfect heavenly Father to likewise discipline His beloved children? But what would it imply if we were never disciplined? This would indicate a different relationship (cf. v. 8). *we respected them.* Despite not enjoying being disciplined, children respect their parents who discipline them in love. How much more do we respect our perfect, heavenly Father, whose love is perfect and not tainted by sin. *be subject.* We recognize our status as God's children and His role in disciplining us for our good. *Father of spirits.* This wording draws a contrast between "earthly fathers" (lit. "fathers of the flesh") and God, our Creator and Redeemer. God is Father to the baptized; they belong to Him in both body and soul (Rm 8:15; 1Co 12:13; see also Jn 3:5; cf. Nu 27:16; Jn 3:6; Rv 22:6). We *live* because of His grace.

12:10 *They disciplined . . . as seemed best to them.* Because they are sinful, the discipline of our earthly parents is imperfect. Parents can, and do, make mistakes. Our heavenly Father, being perfect, *disciplines us for our good.* He truly knows what is in our best interest and unfailingly acts accordingly. With our limited knowledge, this is not always evident to us. So Luther writes, drawing a parallel to Christ: "It seems to us as though we were forsaken by God on the cross, but precisely then we are loved and cared for most" (LW 12:296). (Cf. Rm 8:28.) *share His holiness.* God covers us in holiness for the sake of Christ. As He continues to bless us, He disciplines us through hardship, in which the Holy Spirit quenches lust and kills the flesh, to prepare us for eternal life (Rm 8:18–27). Cf. Heb 12:14; 1Pt 4:1–2; see SC, Baptism, Part 4.

12:11 *discipline seems painful.* Though it is exactly what we need, the discipline itself is not enjoyable. No one wants to face hardship and affliction, even if they know that good may come of it. In the case of God's discipline, good will certainly come of it, but it remains painful and unpleasant when it is experienced. Yet it results in *the peaceful fruit of righteousness.* God gives His children a peaceful conscience and righteous heart before Him (Jas 3:17–18).

12:12–13 *lift . . . strengthen.* Returning to the metaphor of the race (vv. 1–2), the author tells his readers how to respond to difficulties and afflictions: Be strong and keep going! *make straight paths.* As a runner watches his or her step to avoid injury, Christians should watch where they are going so that they do not put themselves in danger. Avoid putting yourself in the way of temptation. *not be put out of joint.* Just as a sprained ankle must be protected lest the injury become even worse, discouraged Christians must be cared for and protected by their fellow believers. Calvin wrote, "Indiscreet ardour is no less an evil than inactivity and softness" (322–23).

Warning against Disobedience, Using OT Examples (12:14–29)

ESV	KJV
[14]Strive for peace with everyone, and for the holiness without which no one will see the Lord. [15]See to it that no one fails to obtain the grace of God; that no "root of bitterness" springs up and causes trouble, and by it many become defiled; [16]that no one is sexually immoral or unholy like Esau, who sold his birthright for a single meal. [17]For you know that afterward, when he desired to inherit the blessing, he was rejected, for he found no chance to repent, though he sought it with tears. [18]For you have not come to what may be touched, a blazing fire and darkness and gloom and a tempest [19]and the sound of a trumpet and a voice whose words made the hearers beg that no further messages be spoken to them. [20]For they could not endure the order that was given, "If even a beast touches the mountain, it shall be stoned." [21]Indeed, so terrifying was the sight that Moses said, "I tremble with fear." [22]But you have come to Mount Zion and to the city of the living God, the heavenly Jerusalem, and to innumerable angels in festal gathering, [23]and to the assembly of the firstborn who are enrolled	[14]Follow peace with all men, and holiness, without which no man shall see the Lord: [15]Looking diligently lest any man fail of the grace of God; lest any root of bitterness springing up trouble you, and thereby many be defiled; [16]Lest there be any fornicator, or profane person, as Esau, who for one morsel of meat sold his birthright. [17]For ye know how that afterward, when he would have inherited the blessing, he was rejected: for he found no place of repentance, though he sought it carefully with tears. [18]For ye are not come unto the mount that might be touched, and that burned with fire, nor unto blackness, and darkness, and tempest, [19]And the sound of a trumpet, and the voice of words; which voice they that heard intreated that the word should not be spoken to them any more: [20](For they could not endure that which was commanded, And if so much as a beast touch the mountain, it shall be stoned, or thrust through with a dart: [21]And so terrible was the sight, that Moses said, I exceedingly fear and quake:)

in heaven, and to God, the judge of all, and to the spirits of the righteous made perfect, ²⁴and to Jesus, the mediator of a new covenant, and to the sprinkled blood that speaks a better word than the blood of Abel.

²⁵See that you do not refuse him who is speaking. For if they did not escape when they refused him who warned them on earth, much less will we escape if we reject him who warns from heaven. ²⁶At that time his voice shook the earth, but now he has promised, "Yet once more I will shake not only the earth but also the heavens." ²⁷This phrase, "Yet once more," indicates the removal of things that are shaken—that is, things that have been made—in order that the things that cannot be shaken may remain. ²⁸Therefore let us be grateful for receiving a kingdom that cannot be shaken, and thus let us offer to God acceptable worship, with reverence and awe, ²⁹for our God is a consuming fire.

²²But ye are come unto mount Sion, and unto the city of the living God, the heavenly Jerusalem, and to an innumerable company of angels,

²³To the general assembly and church of the firstborn, which are written in heaven, and to God the Judge of all, and to the spirits of just men made perfect,

²⁴And to Jesus the mediator of the new covenant, and to the blood of sprinkling, that speaketh better things than that of Abel.

²⁵See that ye refuse not him that speaketh. For if they escaped not who refused him that spake on earth, much more shall not we escape, if we turn away from him that speaketh from heaven:

²⁶Whose voice then shook the earth: but now he hath promised, saying, Yet once more I shake not the earth only, but also heaven.

²⁷And this word, Yet once more, signifieth the removing of those things that are shaken, as of things that are made, that those things which cannot be shaken may remain.

²⁸Wherefore we receiving a kingdom which cannot be moved, let us have grace, whereby we may serve God acceptably with reverence and godly fear:

²⁹For our God is a consuming fire.

12:14 Finished with the metaphor of the race, the author once again exhorts his readers. Here are some of the blessed things we are called to do as we run the race with our eyes fixed on Jesus. *Strive for peace with everyone*. Do not wait for peace to come upon you. Pursue it. Actively seek peace, without compromising confession of the truth (cf. Zec 8:16–19; Rm 12:18; 14:19). *holiness*. Through Christ's sacrifice, Christians are already considered holy in God's sight (Heb 3:1).

Just as Christians will be completely holy in heaven, they should strive to be holy on earth. Strive to live as the person God has declared you to be. *Without which no one will see the Lord.* Seeing God face-to-face and enjoying His gracious presence is a description of heaven (1Co 13:12; 1Jn 3:2–3; cf. 1Co 6:9–11). Of course, seeing the Lord is dependent on the holiness that Christ gives to us, not on our response to that declaration.

12:15 *fails to obtain the grace of God.* This is more literally translated as "that no one lacks the grace of God." These words are another call for us to care for others (cf. 10:24–25). We lack the grace of God when we have not heard the Gospel or when we do not believe. We fail to obtain its benefits when we do not repent and receive God's free absolution. In loving care, watch out for those who are missing God's wonderful blessings. Care for each other by bringing His grace where it is needed! (Cf. 4:1.) *no root of bitterness.* This is an allusion to Dt. 29:18 where someone's heart is turning away from God. Such a person will bring forth the evil fruit of false doctrine or of godless living. This is particularly serious since the danger is not only to the person who is turning but to others who may be led astray by them and become *defiled,* the opposite of holy (v. 14).

12:16 *sexually immoral.* Or "a fornicator," this refers to any sexual expression that is outside of God's will (cf. 1Co 6:9–10). *unholy.* This can also be translated "profane." To be holy is to be set apart for God; to be profane is the opposite—not set apart for God. We might say "worldly." *like Esau, who sold his birthright.* Esau is likely referenced in the context of immorality because he went away from his parents' wishes and married Hittite women, rather than women from God's covenant people (cf. Gn 26:35; 27:46). Further evidence of his lack of concern for the things of God was the fact that he traded his birthright to his brother for a meal (Gn 25:29–34). This showed that he "despised his birthright" (Gn 25:34). He gave up great blessings for passing pleasures.

12:17 *blessing.* The promise that formerly belonged to him, which he abandoned. *rejected.* Isaac had already given the blessing; it therefore remained with Jacob (Gn 27:34–40). Esau spoke as if this was a separate issue from selling his birthright (Gn 27:36), but the two are connected. Esau abandoned the blessing for a temporary benefit. *no chance to repent.* His actions had consequences and could not be taken back. This does not mean that he could not repent from his sin but means that he could not take back his word to Jacob. Luther applies this to speak of a more important repentance:

> It is clear how the passage in Heb. 12:16–17 is to be understood. . . . God, who does not deceive or lie, has offered His mercy to all men who truly repent; and repentance for sin always finds room before God. . . . But there is another repentance that is . . . false . . . namely, when I repent in such a way that I am not ashamed of having offended God but am ashamed because I have done harm to myself. (LW 5:151–52)

12:3–17 in Devotion and Prayer Because you have been Baptized into Christ, you have put on Christ (Gal 3:27). Clothed in the righteousness of the Son of God, God now sees you as holy for Jesus' sake. But while we remain in this fallen world, we experience a paradox of two things: we are simultaneously saint and sinner. God sees us as holy, but we know the sin we continue to struggle with. This is a reality that will always be part of our earthly life, but it does not mean that we give up. God calls us to struggle against sin. He calls us to a life that is pleasing to Him—and that is also a blessing to us. So for our own good, He disciplines us to correct us, train us, and make us stronger. He has a variety of tools at His disposal: struggles, challenges, and afflictions can all help us grow. This is discipline—something every faithful, loving parent does for his or her children. We do not like discipline, but it is what we need, and it shows that God truly cares. He loves you as His own true child. When times of discipline come, remember that they are signs of His perfect love. Respond by trusting in Jesus and putting your faith into practice by encouraging others and by doing works of service. The Lord is ever serving you, granting repentance, taking away your sins, and equipping you for a godly life. • Heavenly Father, You know what is best for me. Help me to trust You and to receive Your discipline as a sign of Your love. Conform me into the image of Your Son, Jesus Christ. Amen.

Introduction to 12:18–24 This section presents a contrast between two covenants. Verses 18–21 describe the institution of old covenant on Mount Sinai. This is contrasted with the institution of new covenant, described as Mount Zion, God's heavenly kingdom (vv. 22–24).

12:18 *what may be touched.* The earthly Mount Sinai was a physical place on the earth, but when God was revealing the Law, it was a fearsome place. *fire . . . tempest.* God's presence on Sinai was accompanied by awesome, frightening signs of His glory (cf. Ex 19:18; 20:18; Dt 4:11; 5:22).

12:19 *trumpet.* This loud sound announced God's presence but terrified the people (Ex 19:16). *voice.* The voice of God proclaimed His Law (cf. Ex 19:5). We might think of this as a welcome experience. Wouldn't we want to hear God's voice? But God's glory overwhelms sinful people. Israel begged that *no further messages be spoken to them.* Unable to bear God's messages directly, they wanted and needed Moses to be their mediator to God (Ex 20:19; Dt 18:16).

12:20 *stoned.* Since God was present, Sinai was a holy place, unfit for sinners and for the profane things of this world. The penalty for profaning God's holiness was death (Ex 19:12–13). Death is the rightful penalty for one who disobeys God's Law (Rm 6:23), but it is unbearable. Since all have sinned, all deserve death. This is the just, but terrible, verdict of Sinai's covenant.

12:21 *I tremble with fear.* This is not a direct quote from the books of Moses, but the thought can be deduced from Dt 9:19. Though Moses was the divinely appointed mediator of the covenant, he also was a sinner. He therefore trembled in the presence of God's holiness.

12:22–24 Contrasting with vv. 18–21 where God's terrifying might is seen in the revelation of the Law, these verses describe the unseen riches in Christ viewed by faith.

12:22 *to Mount Zion and to the city of the living God, the heavenly Jerusalem.* God's unmediated glory at Sinai terrified sinners as He revealed the Law. But now we have come to the place where God is graciously and lovingly present. God is present in His Church as He blesses His people through Gospel and Sacraments (cf. Gal 4:21–31; Ps 48; Rv 14:1). He is present for all of His people, both the Church Militant on earth and the Church Triumphant in heaven. We are called, with the faithful of all times and places, into the presence of God. As at Sinai, God is present in His holiness, but here He comes to us in His grace through Christ. *innumerable angels.* Angels are associated with God's presence, and they were specifically mentioned in reference to Mt. Sinai (Dt. 33:2). Myriads of angels, who worship around God's throne (Rv 5:11; 7:11), are depicted here as being part of a *festal gathering.* This term was used occasionally for Israel's festivals. Together these words indicate a large event: all heaven gathers together, with all the saints, in praise of God.

12:23 *assembly.* Or "congregation," this is the Church. *firstborn . . . enrolled in heaven.* Together, these words are a description of the Christian Church. Christ is the firstborn from the dead (Col 1:18; Rm 8:29). We who have been adopted into God's family rise with Him and are identified with Him. Our names are "written in heaven" (Lk 10:20) or in "the book of life" (Rv 3:5; 20:12; 21:27). *to God.* Neither the Church nor heaven is anything of itself. What makes them special is that God is graciously present. *spirits of the righteous made perfect.* See note, 10:14. The souls of departed Christians are with Christ in heaven. Although believers here do not communicate with the blessed dead (cf. Is 63:16), the Church Militant on earth is bound together with the Church Triumphant in heaven as one Body of Christ (Rm 12:5). We are part of this one Church—united in Christ Jesus.

12:24 *Jesus, the mediator of a new covenant.* Moses was the mediator of Sinai's covenant, yet he trembled in fear at God's presence (v. 21). Jesus, the mediator of the new covenant, is Himself God. As our Great High Priest (4:14ff.), Jesus sacrifices Himself and pours out His blood for us (9:11ff.). In the Church, Jesus is present for us especially through His body and blood (cf. Lk 22:20). *the sprinkled blood.* The two other NT passages that speak of blood and the new covenant refer clearly to the Lord's Supper (Lk 22:20; 1Co 11:25). Heb 10:22 reminds us that our hearts are "sprinkled clean from an evil conscience." This is the blood of Christ. *a better word than the blood of Abel.* Abel, the first martyr, was commended for His faith (11:4). His innocent blood cried out to God from the ground (Gn 4:10), leading to Cain's judgment. Our sin caused Jesus' blood to be shed, but His blood is shed for our forgiveness. "Abel's blood for vengeance Pleaded to the skies; But the blood of Jesus For our pardon cries" (*LSB* 433:4).

While reflecting on the blood of the Old Testament offerings and on the nature of the Lord's Supper, Bengel included a long excursus on the sprinkled/shed blood of Jesus, which poured out on the ground at the cross. He noted that the blood is listed as a separate item—distinct from the resurrected body of Jesus. He wrote, "The blood is looked upon . . . as it is in heaven" in the same way that Jesus, God, the angels, and the saints are in heaven. He includes the following points: (1) The blood of Jesus Christ was most abundantly shed in His suffering and after His death. (2) The state of the shed blood followed the actual shedding of that blood. (3) That blood, even in its state of being shed, was free from all corruption. (4) It cannot be affirmed that the blood that was shed was again put into the veins of our Lord's body. (5) At the time of the ascension, the blood separated from the body was carried into heaven (cf. Heb 9:12). (6) The blood of Jesus Christ always remains blood shed. (7) This same fact was acknowledged by the ancient Doctors of the Church. (8) The personal union [of the divine and human natures in Christ] and the state of the shed blood well agree (are quite compatible with one another). (9) The resurrection and the glorious life of Jesus Christ does not set aside the state of the shed blood. (10) The state of the shed blood very strongly confirms communion in both kinds. (11) The same cause [reason] admirably supports our faith [in communion]. (12) This circumstance demands more ample consideration from the lovers of Christ.

12:25 *do not refuse Him who is speaking.* Having been brought to Mt. Zion—the Church—we should recognize God's gifts and not despise them. Christ is the one who speaks through the Gospel and through the preaching of His servants. Listen to Him. *they did not escape Him who warned them on earth.* God revealed the Law on Mount Sinai and spoke to Israel through Moses. Since they did not listen to Moses but repeatedly broke the Law, as all people do, they fell under judgment. There is no escape from God. *Him who warns from heaven.* Christ, the Word, who revealed the Gospel on Mount Zion and still speaks through the apostles and prophets (Lk 10:16). We have received great blessings in the Church. Do not neglect the gift you have been graciously given, for your only hope is in Christ. For "how shall we escape if we neglect such a great salvation?" (2:3). Christ is our only hope.

12:26 *At that time.* When the Law was first given at Mt. Sinai. *His voice shook the earth.* Ex 19 says that Sinai trembled greatly when the Lord descended on it. *Yet once more.* Quoting Hg 2:6, the shaking of Mt. Sinai is seen as foreshadowing the upheavals in nature that accompany the last days (Mt 24:29). At the giving of the first covenant, only the mountain shook and the people were terrified. How much more fearsome when the whole earth and even the heavens are shaken at the Lord's return!

12:27 *things that are shaken . . . made.* The created world, which is set to pass away. Subjected to futility due to sin, the natural world must pass away. This happens so that *the things that cannot be shaken may remain.* God Himself, His heavenly kingdom, His gifts, and the people He has joined to Himself by grace are safe and secure, even at the Last Day.

12:28 *grateful . . . a kingdom that cannot be shaken.* While signs of the end may seem frightening, the child of God has nothing to fear. What remains is the kingdom of heaven, which God graciously gives to His people. His kingdom will never pass away and He prepares a place for us. In grateful response, Christians are called to *offer to God acceptable worship.* Along with being *grateful,* this is the proper response of faith. "Offer" and "worship" are a single word in Greek. Responding to the gifts that He gives, we worship the triune God in faith. This is possible only through grace in Christ. *with reverence and awe.* Not frivolous, nonchalant, or trivial. God's presence calls for serious hearing, genuine repentance, and extraordinary joy. Such a response recognizes His presence and what He has done for us (cf. Ps 2:12).

12:29 *our God is a consuming fire.* This verse returns us to the context of judgment that surrounds us. This world and all that is in it will pass away at God's judgment. He destroys whatever is useless and contrary to Himself (cf. 10:27). But while all around us may be perishing, we are protected in the mercy of God our Father.

12:18–29 in Devotion and Prayer The Son of God's presence and speaking are the center of worship. He comes to us in ways that He determines. When the Son of God spoke the Law, His people were terrified. Who can bear such glory? But the Incarnate Son of God comes gently among us. He gives Himself for us, and His sprinkled blood speaks better things to us: forgiveness, life, and salvation. Gently He comes in human words, in water, in bread, in wine. Faithfully He gives us His holiness. In love, He calls us to worship where we receive these gifts and are blessed to be able to respond to Him. He calls us to receive them with our brothers and sisters. He has written our names in His book of Life. How blessed we are to be part of His Church! • Lord Jesus Christ, sprinkle us with Your blood and fill us with Your Spirit, that through You we may offer acceptable worship to the Father. Amen.

PART 4

FINAL EXHORTATIONS (13:1–19)

ESV	KJV
13 ¹Let brotherly love continue. ²Do not neglect to show hospitality to strangers, for thereby some have entertained angels unawares. ³Remember those who are in prison, as though in prison with them, and those who are mistreated, since you also are in the body. ⁴Let marriage be held in honor among all, and let the marriage bed be undefiled, for God will judge the sexually immoral and adulterous. ⁵Keep your life free from love of money, and be content with what you have, for he has said, "I will never leave you nor forsake you." ⁶So we can confidently say, "The Lord is my helper; I will not fear; what can man do to me?" ⁷Remember your leaders, those who spoke to you the word of God. Consider the outcome of their way of life, and imitate their faith. ⁸Jesus Christ is the same yesterday and today and forever. ⁹Do not be led away by diverse and strange teachings, for it is good for the heart to be strengthened by grace, not by foods, which have not benefited those devoted to them. ¹⁰We have an altar from which those who serve the tent have no right to eat. ¹¹For the bodies of those animals whose blood is brought into the holy	*13* ¹Let brotherly love continue. ²Be not forgetful to entertain strangers: for thereby some have entertained angels unawares. ³Remember them that are in bonds, as bound with them; and them which suffer adversity, as being yourselves also in the body. ⁴Marriage is honourable in all, and the bed undefiled: but whoremongers and adulterers God will judge. ⁵Let your conversation be without covetousness; and be content with such things as ye have: for he hath said, I will never leave thee, nor forsake thee. ⁶So that we may boldly say, The Lord is my helper, and I will not fear what man shall do unto me. ⁷Remember them which have the rule over you, who have spoken unto you the word of God: whose faith follow, considering the end of their conversation. ⁸Jesus Christ the same yesterday, and to day, and for ever. ⁹Be not carried about with divers and strange doctrines. For it is a good thing that the heart be established with grace; not with meats, which have not profited them that have been occupied therein. ¹⁰We have an altar, whereof they

places by the high priest as a sacrifice for sin are burned outside the camp. ¹²So Jesus also suffered outside the gate in order to sanctify the people through his own blood. ¹³Therefore let us go to him outside the camp and bear the reproach he endured. ¹⁴For here we have no lasting city, but we seek the city that is to come. ¹⁵Through him then let us continually offer up a sacrifice of praise to God, that is, the fruit of lips that acknowledge his name. ¹⁶Do not neglect to do good and to share what you have, for such sacrifices are pleasing to God.

¹⁷Obey your leaders and submit to them, for they are keeping watch over your souls, as those who will have to give an account. Let them do this with joy and not with groaning, for that would be of no advantage to you.

¹⁸Pray for us, for we are sure that we have a clear conscience, desiring to act honorably in all things. ¹⁹I urge you the more earnestly to do this in order that I may be restored to you the sooner.

have no right to eat which serve the tabernacle.

¹¹For the bodies of those beasts, whose blood is brought into the sanctuary by the high priest for sin, are burned without the camp. ¹²Wherefore Jesus also, that he might sanctify the people with his own blood, suffered without the gate. ¹³Let us go forth therefore unto him without the camp, bearing his reproach. ¹⁴For here have we no continuing city, but we seek one to come. ¹⁵By him therefore let us offer the sacrifice of praise to God continually, that is, the fruit of our lips giving thanks to his name. ¹⁶But to do good and to communicate forget not: for with such sacrifices God is well pleased. ¹⁷Obey them that have the rule over you, and submit yourselves: for they watch for your souls, as they that must give account, that they may do it with joy, and not with grief: for that is unprofitable for you. ¹⁸Pray for us: for we trust we have a good conscience, in all things willing to live honestly. ¹⁹But I beseech you the rather to do this, that I may be restored to you the sooner.

13:1 *Let brotherly love continue.* The Greek word for brotherly love is *philadelphia*. Originally used in regard to love for biological siblings, the NT particularly uses this word to describe love of, or affection towards, a fellow Christian (e.g., Rm 12:10; 1Th 4:9; 2Pt 1:7). Such love already exists among those joined in God's family. Here they are encouraged to continue to love one another in both heart and action.

13:2 *Do not neglect . . . hospitality.* The word for hospitality (Gk *philoxenia*) literally means "love of the stranger." It denotes the generous welcome shown to strangers and guests. With few inns available to travelers, the ancient world placed a high importance on such hospitality. Hospitality was a virtue for both Jews and Christians (cf. Rm 12:13). St. Ambrose wrote:

> A man ought therefore to be hospitable. . . . Such is the favor in which hospitality stands with God, that not even the draught of cold water shall fail of getting a reward. You see that Abraham, in looking for guests, received God Himself to entertain. (*NPNF2* 10:59–60; cf. Gn 18:1–21)

some have entertained angels unawares. This is likely an allusion to Lot's hospitality (Gn 19:1–3) when he welcomed angels into his home and defended them against his wicked neighbors. However, since "angel" literally means "messenger," this may alternatively be speaking of human beings who bring the message of the Gospel to others as the apostles did. In either case, the point is that we are encouraged to demonstrate hospitality. This applies not merely to entertaining family and friends; it extends to strangers. We, who have received much from God, are called to be generous.

13:3 *remember those who are in prison.* As the end of the verse shows, this refers to believers suffering persecution, possibly under Emperor Nero (see "Anonymous," pp. 11–12). Christians are called to support their fellow believers, particularly in the most challenging of times (cf. 10:34; Mt 25:36). They do this *as though in prison with them*, sympathizing with their challenging situation and recognizing that any Christian might share their fate. Likewise, they are to care for those who are *mistreated*, those who face affliction, torture or martyrdom because of their faith (cf. 11:35–38). *since you also are in the body.* Christians are bound to one another in the holy body of Christ. Thus, "if one member suffers, all suffer together" (1Co 12:26).

13:4 *Let marriage be held in honor.* This instruction about marriage first addresses the overall response to marriage: it is to be held in honor. Marriage is one of God's good gifts to the world, and Christians in particular should honor and uphold this precious gift. As a specific concern, the author writes, *let the marriage bed be undefiled*, that is, not contaminated by sexual immorality. Husband and wife belong to each other as one flesh (cf. Mt 19:4–6) and are not to violate that sacred gift by being in sexual relationships with other people (cf. Lv 18). *God will judge.* God's Law threatens those who violate it with various punishments. The precise nature of the judgment is not specified here, but it may be bodily afflictions, heart-break, and (apart from repentance and faith) condemnation. The blessings of God's gift of marriage should be sufficient cause for His people to hold it in honor, but if they are so hard hearted that they do not recognize these gifts, perhaps the threat of punishment will curb the impulse to sin. *sexually immoral.* Any sexual activity that is outside of God's will (see note, 12:16).

13:5 *free from the love of money.* Money itself is not the problem; the love of money is what's warned against here—putting money before other more important things. Covetous hearts can easily turn money into a god that a person fears, loves, and trusts more than the true, living God. "The love of money is a root of all kinds of evils. It is through this craving that some have wandered away from the faith and pierced themselves with many pangs" (1Tm 6:10). Instead, be *content with what you have.* Contentment is the opposite of covet-ousness. Christians can be truly content with our circumstance when we know that God provides for all of our needs (cf. 1Tm 6:8; Php 4:11; Mt 6:25). Furthermore, our divine provider *will never leave you nor forsake you.* This quote from Jsh 1:5 makes us even more confi-dent. The God who provides will never leave us. What could we ever lack if He is with us!

13:6 This quote from Ps 118:6 further reminds readers that our gracious Father will provide for all of our needs.

13:7 *leaders.* This is a general description that can apply to vari-ous types of leaders, but their description here makes their identity clear. These leaders *spoke . . . the word of God* to the people, and they themselves were good examples of faith. They are distinct from the rest of "the saints" (v. 24). Leaders, thus, appear to be elders or pas-tors. Some of these leaders may have already been put to death for their Christian confession (since "spoke" is past tense, and their lives already had an outcome). *the outcome.* Confessing Christ to the end, they died trusting in Him and, by God's grace, received their eternal, heavenly reward. *imitate.* These leaders spoke God's Word faithfully and their lives had a holy outcome. They are thus worthy examples to follow. But what is to be imitated? Their *faith*! The most important thing to say about these leaders is that they had faith. Their teaching, good works, and their very lives are commendable because these things were the fruit of their faith (cf. 6:12; 1Th 1:6).

13:8 *Jesus Christ is the same.* Jesus is the object of the leaders' faith, and He is the object of our faith. This Jesus, who has redeemed us and who promises great blessings to us, is completely reliable. We know we can trust Him. According to His eternal divinity, He is unchangeable (Mal 3:6). His covenant of grace likewise does not change (cf. Jn 1:1; Jn 8:58; Rv 1:4, 8).

13:9 *Do not be led astray by diverse and strange teachings.* Because God does not change, neither does His Word. What He decrees is true. Those who teach contrary to Holy Scripture endanger people with their falsehood. Sadly, there are many false teachings and teachers. They are *diverse*, that is, they are at variance with God's Word, and they are *strange.* In other words, they do not belong among God's people because they are not from God. Then as now, false teachings that are not in accord with Scripture arose to lead Christians astray. The example given, *not by foods*, may indicate the particular false teaching that this Letter's recipients were hearing. This might have been dietary rules that were wrongly imposed upon Christians (cf. Col 2:16) or sacrificial meals that troubled consciences and caused doubting (cf. 1Co 10:25–29a). OT sacrificial meals strengthened faith in the coming Messiah. But with Christ's coming, these meals are no longer needed. Whatever the details of the false teachings they were facing, they obviously were replacing the Gospel with works of the Law. The solution is to remember what has been faithfully taught from God's Word and *for the heart to be strengthened by grace.* Christians are called to a confident faith in the Gospel—God's free salvation in Christ Jesus. Calvin wrote:

> He concludes that we ought not to fluctuate, since the truth of Christ, in which we ought to stand firm, remains fixed and unchangeable. And doubtless, variety of opinions, every kind of superstition, all monstrous errors, in a word, all corruptions in religion, arise from this—that men abide not in Christ alone; for it is not in vain that Paul teaches us, that Christ is given to us by God to be our wisdom. (Calvin 345–46)

13:10 Instead of being ensnared by these false teaching, Christians are to be strengthened by the grace of Christ (v. 9), which is freely given to us. God gives us this gift at the *altar*, the Table of the Lord (1Co 10:21), from which the faithful receive the Lord's body and blood. Here we receive food from God; food that heals and re-stores (see note, 9:26). *serve the tent.* The priests of the old covenant or, more generally, those who still seek cleansing and forgiveness through the OT rituals performed at the temple. "Tent" is used to describe the impermanent nature of their devotion. The old covenant was passing away and could not last. Those who continued to follow the old covenant after it had been fulfilled in Christ were not serving God but were only serving the tent itself and acting as if the fulfill-ment had not occurred. *no right to eat.* In the old covenant, there were specific laws for what could and could not be eaten and who was eligible to eat various things. Only those who were authorized and properly prepared were allowed to eat of certain portions of the sacrifices. Some things belonged only to God and were not eaten by priests or other worshipers. Likewise in the new covenant, those who eat must have God's authorization. God gives the true body and blood of Jesus under the bread and wine in the Sacrament of the Altar. Consequently, those who commune must come in faith and be properly prepared in faith (1Co 11:28). Not all are to eat from this altar, "lest they eat and drink judgment" on themselves (1Co 11:29). "The priest stands daily at the altar, inviting some to the Communion and keeping back others" (AC XXIV 36).

13:11 *bodies . . . are burned outside.* This is an example from the old covenant. On the Day of Atonement, the bodies of the sacri-ficed animals were not eaten but were taken outside the camp of the people to be burned (cf. Ex 29:14; Lv 16:27).

13:12 *Jesus also suffered outside the gate.* Again showing how the OT sacrifices pointed forward to Jesus, who completed and ful-filled them in His perfect sacrifice. On the Day of Atonement, the animals were sacrificed, their blood was sprinkled in the Most Holy Place, and their bodies were burned outside of the camp. Jesus sac-rificed Himself as the perfect, final sacrifice. He died outside of the city of Jerusalem (Jn 19:17). When He died, the curtain that hid the Most Holy Place was torn in two from top to bottom (Mt 27:51). He has sprinkled us with His blood and given us full atonement. He did this to *sanctify the people*—to make them holy—*through his own blood* (cf. 9:12).

13:13 *let us go to him outside.* In response to what Christ has done for us, Christians follow Him in faith. This may lead to being rejected by unbelievers. Following Jesus can, quite literally, make us "outsiders" in the world, but we belong to God. *outside the camp.* This phrase is used in Exodus, Leviticus, and Numbers to describe where unholy things, such as refuse, should be discarded. Here it is used ironically to describe the abuse and rejection of Jesus by the Jerusalem authorities. They condemned their God to die outside of the city as if He were unholy or garbage, yet He died for them and for all. Likewise, Christians are called to be faithful when they *bear the reproach He endured* (cf. 11:26; 1Pt 4:14). The first readers of this Letter would face persecution for their faith, but they did not forsake their Savior.

13:14 *here we have no lasting city.* This is an acknowledgment of the impermanence of life in this fallen world. This world is not our true or lasting home. Rather, we trust God's promises and look forward to *the city that is to come.* This is the new Jerusalem, the kingdom of heaven (cf. 11:10, 16; 12:28; Gal 4:26; Rv 21:2). Luther writes of our life in this temporary place, saying:

> God permits [a Christian] to remain alive in the flesh and lets his body walk the earth in order that he may help others and bring them to heaven too. Therefore we must use everything on earth in no other way than as a guest who travels across country. . . . Thus we must also deal with temporal goods as if they did not belong to us. We must limit our enjoyment of them to what is necessary for the preservation of the body. With the rest we must help our neighbor. (LW 30:35)

13:15–16 These verses give exhortation and encouragement for Christians in difficult times. The Lutheran reformers say,

> In these last times it is certainly no less needful to encourage people to Christian discipline ‹to the way of right and godly living› and to do good works. We need to remind them of how necessary it is that they exercise themselves in good works as a declaration of their faith [Matthew 5:16] and gratitude to God. (FC Ep IV 18)

13:15 *through Him.* We are only able to respond to God because of what He has first done for us in Jesus Christ. Even now our response of thanks and praise are offered through the mediation of Jesus. *continually offer a sacrifice of praise to God.* This is the kind of sacrifice that Christians now make. Such sacrifices do not merit grace or forgiveness, but respond to God's grace in faith. Melanchthon teaches:

These sacrifices are not satisfactions. . . . He asks us to offer praises, that is, prayer, thanksgiving, confession, and the like. These benefit not by the outward act, but because of faith. (Ap XXIV 25–26; cf. Ps 107:22; 116:17)

Cranmer wrote about sacrifice in his Answer to Gardyner, Bishop of Winchester:

I call a sacrifice gratificatory, or the sacrifice of the Church, such a sacrifice as doth not reconcile us to God, but is made of them that be reconciled, to testify their duties, and to show themselves thankful unto him. And these sacrifices in Scripture be not called propitiatory, but sacrifices of justice, of laud, praise, and thanksgiving. But you [Gardyner] confound the words, and call one by another's name, calling that propitiatory which the Scripture calleth but of justice, laud, and thanking. And all is nothing else but to defend your propitiatory sacrifice of the priests in their masses, whereby they may remit sin, and redeem souls out of purgatory.

And yet all your wiles and shifts will not serve you; for by extending the name of a propitiatory sacrifice unto so large a signification as you do, you make all manner of sacrifices propitiatory, leaving no place for any other sacrifice. For, say you, all good deeds and good thoughts be sacrifices propitiatory; and then be the good works of the lay people sacrifices propitiatory, as well as those of the priest. And to what purpose then made you, in the beginning of this book, a distinction between sacrifices propitiatory and other? Thus, for desire you have to defend the papistical errors, you have not fallen only into imaginations contrary to the truth of God's word, but also contrary to yourself.

But let pass away these papistical inventions, and let us humbly profess ourselves, with all our sacrifices, not worthy to approach unto God, nor to have any access unto him, but by that only propitiatory sacrifice which Christ only made upon the cross. And yet let us with all devotion, with whole heart and mind, and with all obedience to God's will, come unto the heavenly Supper of Christ, thanking him only for propitiation of our sins. In which holy communion the act of the minister and other be all of one sort, none propitiatory, but all of lauds and thanksgiving. And such sacrifices be pleasant and acceptable to God, as St. Paul, done of them that be good; but they win not his favour and put away his indignation from them that be evil: for such reconciliation can no creature make, but Christ alone. (Cranmer 3:544–45) *the fruit of lips.* God's forgiveness leads us, in response, to confess Him and praise Him (see SC, Second Commandment). Luther says,

> We learn that we do not offer Christ as a sacrifice, but that Christ offers us. . . . That is, we lay ourselves on Christ by a firm faith in his testament and do not otherwise appear before God with our prayer, praise, and sacrifice except through Christ and his mediation. Nor do we doubt that Christ is our priest or minister in heaven before God. Such faith, truly, brings it to pass that Christ takes up our cause, presents us and our prayer and praise, and also offers himself for us in heaven. (LW 35:99)

13:16 *do good.* Here is another fruit of forgiveness. This is the only time this particular Gk word (*eupoiia*) is used in the NT, but its meaning is straightforward. A specific type of doing good is to *share* (Gk *koinonia*) *what you have*, to treat your possessions as if they belong to all. Do good and use what you have for the good for your neighbor. These are important things for life together that are too easy for selfish sinners to forget. Indeed, God considers such service to our neighbor as *sacrifices . . . pleasing to God.* He Himself does not need our sharing, but through it, He blesses our neighbor. He receives such works as if they are done for Him (cf. Mt 25:34–40). However, it is not the works themselves that are pleasing, since they are always tainted by sin; rather, "our spiritual offerings are acceptable to God through faith for Christ's sake" (FC SD VI 22).

13:17 *Obey your leaders and submit.* Previously (v. 7) the readers were to remember their faithful leaders who set a good example of faith. Now they are given instruction regarding their current leaders (which we would more typically call pastors.) The call to obedience and submission is not to their personal whims, but is in reference to their office as ministers of the Gospel. As Melanchthon says, "This passage requires obedience to the Gospel. It does not establish a dominion for the bishops apart from the Gospel" (Ap XXVIII 20). Cf. SC, Table of Duties. *watch over your souls . . . give an account.* The spiritual office of the pastor is indicated here. Pastors are to care for the members of their congregation, to teach them the Word of God, and to protect them from spiritual threats. As a shepherd watches over a flock and protects it from predators, a pastor watches over and cares for his congregation. But the flock does not belong to the pastor; it belongs to the Good Shepherd who calls pastors to "feed my sheep" (Jn 21:15–17). So these spiritual leaders will have to *give* *an account* of their ministry to God. Since pastors are called to be such a blessing to their congregations, the members are to receive their ministry with thanksgiving. They attend to faithful pastors who teach God's Word, obeying and submitting to this biblical teaching. Members are called to follow in a way that gives pastors *joy* and does not cause them to respond in *groaning*. A true, faithful pastor is filled with joy when his hearers believe God's Word and live godly lives according to it. The people are admonished to receive their ministry in such a way that the members are a blessing to their pastors even as the pastors are blessings to their congregations. Particularly in these difficult last days, this is one way that pastors and people, bound together in the grace and love of God, can be a blessing to each other. Luther writes, "I have the commission and charge, as a preacher and a doctor, to see to it that no one is misled, so that I may give account of it at the Last Judgment" (LW 21:44).

13:18 *pray for us.* The author request prayers for himself that he may act with integrity and faith (see the continuance of this prayer request in v. 19). At the same time, the context of v. 17 gives particular reason for prayer. Congregations are to receive the ministry of their faithful pastors. Because pastors, like all members of their congregation, are sinners, they are subject to temptation. The people of God are thus called by God to pray for their pastors that they, too, may be faithful to God's word. Pray that they fulfill their calling in faith and that they have a pure *conscience*. Pray that they are faithful to God's Word, are bold in proclaiming the Gospel, and *act honorably* in all they do so that they do not become a hindrance to people hearing the Gospel.

13:19 *I may be restored.* This is a personal prayer request of the writer. Since we do not know the identity of the author (see "Anonymous," pp. 11–12), we do not specifically know what hinders him. All we know is that he wanted to return quickly to this congregation and asked for their prayer.

13:1–19 in Devotion and Prayer Christians who live in this fallen world, away from their true and permanent home, face many challenges. Temptations abound. We face reproach and ridicule from the world. Some even face open persecution and martyrdom. We may be tempted to wring our hands and complain about the unfairness of it all. God calls us to something greater: live as His people. Whatever the world is doing, love one another. Take care of other people. Be faithful to your spouse. Be content, knowing that God will take care of your needs. Receive the blessings of Word and Sacrament from your faithful pastor. Pray for each other. Such things are a blessing to us, and because they are done in faith, they are sacrifices of praise that please God. Above all, remember that you are redeemed by Jesus, who is the same yesterday, today, and forever. Because He never changes, His promises always endure. • "Give us lips to sing Thy glory, Tongues Thy mercy to proclaim, Throats that shout the hope that fills us, Mouths to speak Thy holy name." Amen. (*LSB* 578:5)

PART 5

BLESSINGS AND GREETINGS (13:20–25)

ESV	KJV
[20]Now may the God of peace who brought again from the dead our Lord Jesus, the great shepherd of the sheep, by the blood of the eternal covenant, [21]equip you with everything good that you may do his will, working in us that which is pleasing in his sight, through Jesus Christ, to whom be glory forever and ever. Amen. [22]I appeal to you, brothers, bear with my word of exhortation, for I have written to you briefly. [23]You should know that our brother Timothy has been released, with whom I shall see you if he comes soon. [24]Greet all your leaders and all the saints. Those who come from Italy send you greetings. [25]Grace be with all of you.	[20]Now the God of peace, that brought again from the dead our Lord Jesus, that great shepherd of the sheep, through the blood of the everlasting covenant, [21]Make you perfect in every good work to do his will, working in you that which is wellpleasing in his sight, through Jesus Christ; to whom be glory for ever and ever. Amen. [22]And I beseech you, brethren, suffer the word of exhortation: for I have written a letter unto you in few words. [23]Know ye that our brother Timothy is set at liberty; with whom, if he come shortly, I will see you. [24]Salute all them that have the rule over you, and all the saints. They of Italy salute you. [25]Grace be with you all. Amen.

13:20–21 This final blessing recalls Christ's roles as Shepherd and Lamb: His perfect leadership and holy sacrifice.

13:20 *the God of peace.* This is an expression favored by Paul (Rm 15:33; 16:20; Php 4:9; 1Th 5:23). God grants us peace with Himself and our fellow believers through the work of Christ. This is demonstrated again in the following words. *brought again from the dead.* All three persons of the Trinity were involved in Christ's resurrection (cf. Ac 2:24; Jn 10:18; Rm 8:11). The once-for-all sacrifice of Jesus on the cross was sufficient for the sins of the world. He was raised in victory. *blood of the eternal covenant.* This phrase is connected to the verb "equip" in the next verse: God will equip Christians by the blood of the covenant. With His blood, Christ empowered the new covenant of grace, a final covenant with eternal blessings. This is an *eternal* covenant both in having eternal benefits and in being God's unchanging promise. Nothing will ever supplant this perfect covenant that God has made.

13:21 *equip you with everything good.* Through Christ's redeeming work we are given everything good, everything needed to *do His will.* God's primary will is that we have faith in Christ, revealed in the Gospel. This renews us to serve Him as His Word directs us. *working in us.* God works in us by His Holy Spirit through the Word and Sacraments (cf. Php 2:13). *pleasing in His sight.* "Without faith it is impossible to please Him" (11:6). God has called us to faith and equips us to do His will. Now, because He has declared us holy, our works are pleasing to Him. This is all a gift of His grace. *to whom be glory forever and ever. Amen.* These words are a final doxology of blessing and, aside from a brief postscript, they serve as the end of this Letter. Since Christ has done all this for us, what better way to respond than by praising Him.

13:20–21 in Devotion and Prayer Truly we have been blessed. Redeemed by Jesus Christ and declared holy, God has freely given us the gifts of heaven. We are also blessed that He chooses to bless the world through us. He equips us for all good works to do His will. He works in us to do His will. Through us, others are blessed and we rejoice in God's goodness. • O God, through the precious blood of Jesus You have made us Your own people. Equip us with everything good to do Your will. Work in us to accomplish Your purposes. Let us give all glory to You, Father, Son, and Holy Spirit. Amen.

13:22–25 While Hebrews may have initially been preached as a sermon (ending at 13:21), it was also sent as a letter. These verses are a typical conclusion to a first-century letter, including both greetings and blessings.

13:22 *brothers.* Once again, "brothers" is a word expressing affection for his fellow Christians that includes both men and women. *word of exhortation.* This is his description of the entire Epistle to the Hebrews itself. Since he has written *briefly,* the author does not want to be misunderstood. Many of the topics in this Letter could have been explored in greater detail. He wants his readers to know his purpose and loving intent.

13:23 *our brother Timothy has been released*. This is encouraging news about a fellow Christian (cf. Php 1:1; Col 1:1; Phm 1).

13:24 *Greet*. This is a polite, but sincere, sign of fellowship. Greetings were often given to specific people by name; here they are addressed to the entire congregation, to *all your leaders . . . all the saints* (see notes, Heb 13:7, 17). No one is left out in this greeting. The Letter and its word of encouragement are for the entire congregation. *Those who come from Italy*. Either those who are with the author in Italy or those who have come from Italy to the author. Since we do not know the specific circumstances of the author (see "Anonymous," pp. 11–12), we are unsure of their identity. It is possible that the recipients of the Letter could be in Rome or near Jerusalem. The Letter hints at no other possible locations.

13:25 *Grace*. What greater blessing is there than the grace of God? The final prayer of the author for his readers—including you—is that people receive and know the grace of God in Christ Jesus the Savior.

13:22–25 in Devotion and Prayer Hebrews, this anonymous Epistle, sets forth God's grace in Christ, earned on the cross, ratified in the new covenant, vindicated in the resurrection, and distributed in Word and Sacrament. God brings us to faith and keeps us in the faith. By holding fast to the teaching of this sermon and by receiving God's grace through faith, we have fellowship with the writer of Hebrews and with all the saints and look forward to our inheritance with them in heaven. Christ has done it all for us. He equips us to bear the cross in this life and brings us, with all the saints, into the heavenly city. • "Now may the God of peace who brought again from the dead our Lord Jesus, the great shepherd of the sheep, by the blood of the eternal covenant, equip you with everything good that you may do His will, working in us that which is pleasing in His sight, through Jesus Christ, to whom be glory forever and ever. Amen" (Heb 13:20–21).

BIOGRAPHICAL SKETCHES

The following brief sketches introduce preachers and commentators cited or referenced in this volume. They appear in chronological order by the date of their death or era of influence. Although some of them are ancient and medieval Church Fathers respected by the reformers, they are primarily writers of the Reformation era and heirs of the Reformation approach to writing biblical commentary. This approach includes

(1) interpreting Scripture in view of Scripture and by faith, so that passages are understood in their literary and in their canonical contexts;

(2) emphasis on the historic and ordinary meaning of the words and literary expressions;

(3) careful review of manuscripts and texts in search of greater accuracy;

(4) faith in the canonical Scripture as divinely inspired, truthful, and authoritative;

(5) respect for the ancient, ecumenical creeds (Apostles', Nicene, and Athanasian) as touchstones of faithful interpretation and application of Scripture; and most importantly

(6) focus on Christ and justification through Him as the chief message of Holy Scripture (e.g., the distinction of Law and Gospel or sin and grace in interpretation and application).

For more information about these figures, see Edward A. Engelbrecht, gen. ed., *The Church from Age to Age: A History from Galilee to Global Christianity* (St. Louis: Concordia, 2011).

Ancient and Medieval Fathers

Ambrose. (c. 339–97) Governor of Milan who was suddenly made bishop, though only a catechumen at the time. He became a great preacher and defender of orthodoxy, influencing the conversion of Augustine.

John Chrysostom. (c. 347–407) Bishop of Constantinople and a key figure in the early Christological controversies. He was called "golden-mouthed" because of his brilliant oratory style. His commentaries on Scripture are sermons, valued by the church from ancient times.

Bernard of Clairvaux. (1090–1153) Cistercian Abbot and Preacher. Bernard's sermons often beautifully proclaim Christ and God's grace, which made him a favorite medieval Father in the eyes of the reformers.

Hus, John. (c. 1372–1415) Priest and martyr. Lecturer and rector at the University of Prague, an enormously popular preacher and writer, greatly influenced by Augustine's theology and John Wycliffe's writings. Hus was falsely accused of heresy and condemned at the Council of Constance when the Medieval Church was sorely divided. His efforts heralded the Reformation.

Reformers

Luther, Martin. (1483–1546) Augustinian friar and preeminent reformer, lecturer on the Bible at the University of Wittenberg. Luther's preaching, teaching, and writing renewed biblically based piety in western Christendom. His translation of the Bible influenced the work of Bible publication throughout Europe, notably William Tyndale and the King James translators.

Cranmer, Thomas. (1489–1556) Archbishop of Canterbury and martyr. Cranmer served as a writer and editor for the Book of Common Prayer, one of the most influential works of the Reformation.

Melanchthon, Philip. (1497–1560) Lecturer on classical literature and languages at the University of Wittenberg. Melanchthon's *Commonplaces* and the Augsburg Confession laid the foundation for all subsequent works of Protestant dogmatic theology. He also wrote significant biblical commentaries.

Calvin, John. (1509–64) Preacher and lecturer on theology, founder of the Academy of Geneva. Calvin organized reformation efforts for Swiss, French, Dutch, and English Protestants. Calvin's *Institutes of the Christian Religion* and his extensive commentaries on Scripture are the most influential works of the second generation reformers.

Knox, John. (c. 1513–72) Scottish preacher and reformer. Knox edited the Book of Common Order used in Scottish churches and wrote a history of the Reformation in Scotland.

Heirs of the Reformation

Gerhard, Johann. (1582–1637) Professor of theology at Jena and devotional writer. Gerhard wrote the most extensive dogmatic of the Protestant age of orthodoxy, the *Theological Commonplaces*, and was widely regarded for his knowledge of biblical Hebrew.

Bengel, Johann Albrecht. (1687–1752) New Testament scholar and professor. Bengel wrote the first scientific study of Greek New Testament manuscripts. His *Gnomon* on the New Testament is an influential, succinct commentary of enduring value.

Wesley, John. (1703–91) Missionary preacher. Wesley preached throughout England, Scotland, Ireland, and the American colonies. His *Explanatory Notes upon the New Testament* is a classic evangelical commentary, which drew upon principles and emphases of the Reformers.